ABOUT JIM HAYNES

Before becoming a professional entertainer in 1988, Jim Haynes taught in schools and universities from outback New South Wales to the UK and back again. He has two masters degrees in literature, from the University of New England and the University of Wales.

He has won the Bush Laureate Book of the Year award three times. Jim has also made many recordings of Australian humour, verse and songs, and appears regularly on television and radio. He lives within walking distance of Randwick Racecourse with his partner Robyn and goes to the races as often as possible.

OTHER BOOKS BY JIM HAYNES

I'll Have Chips

Memories of Weelabarabak

An Australian Heritage of Verse

The Great Australian Book of Limericks

An Australian Treasury of Popular Verse

Great Australian Drinking Stories

All Aboard (co-author)

Cobbers

GREAT
AUSTRALIAN
RACING STORIES

JIM HAYNES

ABC
Books

For my dad, Len Haynes

First published by ABC Books for the
AUSTRALIAN BROADCASTING CORPORATION
GPO Box 9994 Sydney NSW 2001

First published in October 2005

ISBN 0 7333 1600 X.

Photo credits: ABC Archives 4, 107, 173, 211; AJC pages 2 (bottom), 6, 21, 27
(both images), 42, 63, 84, 86 (both images), 88, 89 (both images), 121, 122, 170,
177, 180 (top), 193, 237, 256, 276, 294; AJC/Ern McQuillan 2 (top), 85 (top),
153, 159; Atkins technicolour Adelaide/John Atkins 70, 79; Jim Haynes' collection
11, 49, 99, 104, 112, 228, 232, 233, 239, 243, 296, 313; EMPICS 67, 297, 317;
Ern McQuillan 1, 85 (bottom), 132, 180 (bottom), 190; Newspix 291; Steve Hart 50,
65, 74, 76, 306; VRC 231, 240, 241.

Front cover photographs courtesy of Getty Images;
back cover photograph courtesy of Ern McQuillan
Cover design by Christabella Designs
Typeset by Kirby Jones in 11/15pt Sabon
Printed in Australia by Griffin Press, Adelaide

5 4 3 2 1

CONTENTS

Acknowledgments

My thanks to: Brigitta Doyle for her patience and guidance; Stuart Neal for indulging my passions; Linda Brainwood for organising photographs; Nicole Levett for the typing; Joanne Burgess and John Ryan at the AJC Archive; Kathy Peters, VRC Art and Heritage Curator; Penny Mansley for copy editing; Jennifer Blau for help with the cover; Robyn McMillan for story proofing; Les Carlyon and Deb Callaghan; Ern McQuillan; Steve Hart at Steve Hart Photographics; John Atkins at Atkins Technicolour Adelaide; Laura Hitchcock at Empics UK; Barry Biggs, Secretary Oakbank Racing Club; Peter Jenkins at Wallabadah; The Australian Jockey Club; The Victoria Racing Club; The Oakbank Racing Club; The Wallabadah Racing Club; Sandy at the Book Orphanage; Frank Daniel for finding verse; Harper Collins and A&R; The Mitchell Library, State Library of NSW.

INTRODUCTION

My lifetime love affair with racing began the first day I was dressed in my Sunday best and taken to Randwick by my dad. We probably went into the Leger enclosure, although I don't remember exactly.

If Mum was with us we always went straight into the Paddock. If it was just Dad and me we'd go into the Leger and the rule was that if Dad backed a winner in either of the first two races he paid the extra admission and we went through to the Paddock. Tommy Smith dominated Sydney racing back then and it was a treat to see George Moore ride horses like Tulloch and Sky High.

'Tommy Smith dominated Sydney racing back then ...' T. J. Smith with Tulloch

As a kid I hung around the stables owned by Sid Nicholls at Mascot. Many good training families, like the Piggins, the O'Sullivans and the Nicholls, had stables in the district back then. Prior to World War II there were six racetracks in that area. Apart from Randwick there was Kensington, where the University of New South Wales is now; Rosebery, which became a housing estate in the 1960s; Ascot, which made way for the airport, Victoria Park, which is now another housing estate near Moore Park; and Moorfield out towards Kogarah.

Victoria Park, Ascot, Kensington and Rosebery generally ran mid-week races, but held occasional Saturday meetings. These tracks operated from the late nineteenth century as 'Pony Tracks'. Even into the 1940s each meeting at these tracks included a pony race, known as a 14.2 Handicap – the number was the height limit, 14.2 hands, on the runners.

Pony racing is a forgotten part of our racing history. Many people today assume that thoroughbred racing is the only form of horseracing we've ever had, but 'unregistered' or pony racing was huge in Sydney from the 1890s to the 1930s and I am pleased to say this collection includes a couple of great stories about the little battlers and their owners and trainers.

Moorefield was not a pony track. It was located between Kogarah and Brighton and was sold by the STC in the early 1950s for housing development.

I was fascinated by the stable atmosphere and Sid Nicholls, whose son was a schoolmate of mine, was kind enough to let me go to the races with the horses and even gave me an official finish photo of his good old welter performer, Sea Hound, winning at Hawkesbury. That photo still hangs in my office.

Sea Hound ran second in the Villiers twice and was one of the first horses on which I ever won any real money. Back then the welter was usually the 'lucky last' on any Sydney race programme and I got my dad to put my pocket money on Sea Hound up at the local SP one Saturday. The gallant old gelding beat a horse called Ginnagulla in a photo at twelve to one. It was one of my first small steps along the rocky road of joy and pain that is the life of the punter.

Right: '... it was a treat to see George Moore ...'

Below: '... horses like Tulloch and Sky High.' Sky High wins the 1961 All-aged Stakes

'It was located between Kogarah and Brighton.' Saddling Paddock, Moorefield Racecourse early twentieth century

One birthday I was given a collection of stories by Jim Bendrodt. My mum was very keen to get me reading as a kid and books were always a big part of my life. By about the age of ten she was trying to stop me reading all night so I'd be able to wake up and go to school next morning. I had a torch hidden under my mattress and, after she turned my light out, I would read under the covers until I fell asleep or the batteries went flat. Those Jim Bendrodt stories thrilled me as a kid and I read them over and over. My favourites are in this collection.

Wherever life took me I always made sure to visit the local racetracks. As a schoolteacher in the bush I experienced many picnic and bush race meetings. I later lived in the UK for a few years and I was able to get a taste of racing there as well.

Easter visits to family in Adelaide always meant the Great Eastern Steeplechase and business trips to Melbourne, Brisbane or Adelaide somehow always ended up including a day at Flemington, or Eagle Farm, or Morphettville.

My work with rhymed verse on radio and in collections for books and recorded albums kept bringing me into contact with great racing stories and yarns in the form of poetry and it was always in the back of my mind to produce a volume such as this. Once I started to look it was obvious that an enormous amount of good prose had also been written about racing over the years.

It has been well chronicled that Australians have a particular obsession with racing. It seems to suit our character and embody certain values that are a part of our short European history and national heritage.

The importance of horses in the development of the colonies in the nineteenth century is one obvious reason why Aussies took to racing as they did. But there are other, less obvious, reasons.

Our national character includes ideas such as taking a chance, 'having a go', letting your hair down after a spell of hard work, socialising after living in isolation for a while, the love of a long weekend or a holiday, and the belief that handicapping the more talented performers makes things 'more interesting'.

We also love to have a bet.

Many of our best-loved verse writers were also horsemen or racing men. Adam Lindsay Gordon, Will Ogilvie and Harry Morant were horse-breakers and steeplechase riders. Banjo Paterson rode at Randwick and Rosehill and was a member of the New South Wales polo team. C. J. Dennis wrote dozens of wonderful poems about racing and punting and even sour old Henry Lawson wrote a few.

Some of our best known prose writers, such as Rolf Boldrewood and Lennie Lower, are represented here along with such great non-Australian authors as Mark Twain, and the greatest turf writer of all time, Nat Gould.

Gould more or less 'invented' the racing novel. Born in Manchester in 1857, he came to Australia in 1884 and worked as a reporter in Brisbane and Sydney before spending eighteen months at Bathurst as editor of the *Bathurst Times*. While there he wrote his first novel, *With the Tide*, which was published in England under the title *The Double Event* and was an immediate success. It was dramatised in Australia and had a long stage run in 1893.

In 1895, after eleven years in Australia, Gould returned to England and began steadily writing an average of four books a year. He wrote over 130 novels and his sales ran into many millions of copies.

Gould was a wonderful raconteur who didn't take himself or his work too seriously. His modesty and sense of humour shine through in the accounts included in this collection of his visits to Melbourne for the Spring Carnival.

While his novels had no great originality of plot, and tended to be melodramatic in the extreme, they were rattling good yarns and stand as proof that racing is a wonderful subject for authors. There is a typical piece of his fiction included here and also a wonderful send-up of his writing by Banjo Paterson.

Under the name 'Knott Gold' Banjo wrote a very funny piece parodying Nat Gould's style. It is titled 'Done for the Double'; a humorous reference to the title of Gould's most famous novel, *The Double Event*, and it still makes me laugh out loud to read it today.

Racing has given me many enjoyable moments and memories. Literature about racing has given me some of my most memorable and satisfying experiences as a reader. As you can imagine, writing, collecting and editing these stories and verses has enabled me to relive many of those experiences. I hope they rekindle some pleasant memories for you.

'*Australians have a particular obsession with racing ...*' Crowd at Randwick 1950s

PART ONE

YOU HEAR BLOKES TALK OF CHAMPIONS

This first section contains stories about particular horses. Some are champions and some are battlers. Some are real and some are fictitious. Some of the real ones are household names while others are long forgotten.

The settings of most of these stories are our more famous racetracks, but the best yarn ever penned about bush racing, in my humble opinion, is also to be found here. It is 'Old Pardon, the Son of Reprieve', which includes that wonderful description of a heavenly racebook entry, 'Angel Harrison's black gelding Pardon, blue halo, white body and wings'.

This selection was made mostly on the basis of which poems and stories I found to be most enjoyable. I also tried to choose pieces that were written from varying points of view and said different things about great horses.

The two 'greats', Phar Lap and Carbine, feature here. Apart from those two I have made no attempt to cover all eras or mention all the 'greats'. Once you start to include stories about the champions of various eras you are open to the 'what about so-and-so' syndrome and then this section would have become a volume on its own.

My only real indulgence in this section is the inclusion of a piece I wrote about my favourite champ, Octagonal, when he retired. It's hardly great literature and probably shouldn't be seen anywhere near Paterson's great poem about Old Pardon, but it was what I wanted to say about my favourite horse at the time.

There is also a very subjective account of ten of my favourite memories from years of race-going. This list isn't based on which horses I thought were the best of their era, or admired most over the years; it's based on the quality of the contest they were involved in.

Generally speaking, however, I wanted to avoid comparisons. As any sensible racing pundit knows, it's impossible to compare champions of different eras. That doesn't stop us from doing it, of course. We all like to ponder the impossible questions in racing. Would Phar Lap have beaten Carbine?

Naturally, no one knows the answer. And when you consider that Carbine was Phar Lap's great-great-granddad it makes you realise that such questions are really a bit silly.

I have an opinion, but I'm not silly enough to put it in print.

DO THEY KNOW?

A. B. ('Banjo') Paterson

Do they know? At the turn to the straight
Where the favourites fail,
And every last atom of weight
Is telling its tale;
As some grim old stayer hard-pressed
Runs true to his breed,
And with head just in front of the rest
Fights on in the lead;
When the jockeys are out with the whips,
With a furlong to go,
And the backers grow white to the lips –
Do you think they don't know?

Do they know? As they come back to weigh
In a whirlwind of cheers,
Though the spurs have left marks of the fray,
Though the sweat on the ears
Gathers cold, and they sob with distress
As they roll up the track,
They know just as well their success
As the man on their back.
As they walk through a dense human lane
That sways to and fro,
And cheers them again and again,
Do you think they don't know?

'Do you think they *don't know?' Champion mare Wenona Girl returns to scale 1962*

VALIANT LADY

J. C. Bendrodt

So you go to the races? You form one of the amazing multitude who follow the Sport of Kings and deadbeats, and all the varied kinds of people in between. Perhaps the siren call of 'easy money', the thrill of a close-fought finish, the love of a satin-coated thoroughbred, the performance of a social duty, brings *you* there.

Whichever it is, there is one thing I do know, and that is that you who see the gigantic stage, set with its tens of thousands close-packed in colossal grandstands, its glorious flowers, its great green stretches where the cream of the equine world sob their hearts out in a game where only the superlative survive, know little of the work and the thoughts and the hopes and the fears of that band of men who produce the four-legged stars you come to see do battle for fame and fortune.

Well, I'll try to tell you why I go to the races. I'll tell you how I, an owner-trainer who loves a thoroughbred, feel from the time I go with a few hard-won shekels to some famous sale ring, to the moment that my colours flash into sight where the field is bunching far up the home stretch for that heart-stirring, heart-breaking run to a little white line on a little black board, and the eagle eye of a judge from whose decision there is no appeal. And if you love a thoroughbred horse, if you really love them, you can read this, and if you don't – well, read something else, because you won't be interested, and you won't understand.

They've come from the four corners of a dozen beautiful pasture lands, from the studs of men who have studied the production of the ultimate in horses for generations. Each of these soft-eyed babies could tell you that his, or her, blood lines could be traced exactly to equine horses who came from their desert homes to Merrie England, along with the fashions Charles the First made à la mode. Believe me! And some of them could speak of ancestors who cropped the grass of Devon when Henry the Eighth displayed his catholic taste in harems.

A little nervous, more than a trifle frightened, they have come from their lovely homes to this noisy, terrifying saleyard, so that you who have burned the midnight oil studying pedigrees may choose and buy a champion. If you can. Yes, indeed! If you can!

Hundreds of them, all well bred, all beautiful, or nearly all, but only a mere handful who will ever become that miracle of speed and courage and stamina that will fling their names in flaunting banners across the sporting pages of a continent.

For days you study them. Hour after hour, you tramp from stable to stable, comparing, measuring, concentrating, and, curiously enough, it is only at night-time that you know you're weary. Then, just a few hours before the auctioneer will call the babies forth to face whatever the future may hold for them, you open the door of a box you have not yet entered and there, in a corner, stands a baby filly.

Now for weeks a colt had been in your mind. You are almost Chinese in your ironclad preference for the male of the species, but here is one little lady you feel you must really have a word with. She is too beautiful to pass by, as you have passed by so many of her sex, because you want a colt. A dark bay, this one – perfect from the points of her tiny black-tipped ears to her almost equally tiny feet. A glorious example of what hundreds of years of careful breeding can produce.

A long five minutes you study her intently, while she gazes fearlessly and just as intently back at you with her soft dark eyes. There is no fear in those eyes – just a quiet curiosity. Marvellous, you say; small, yes, but still – marvellously perfect, and she will grow – just a baby. But you want a colt, not a filly, and then, just as you turn to go, she takes a step towards you.

She is curious, or perhaps Fortune smiles, and you stop and call her softly – encouragingly. She comes and lays her muzzle in your outflung hand, and then, as she stretches her glistening neck, her lovely head comes to rest against your own hard face, and so, for a moment, for you and for her, the world stands still.

And then – well, and then believe me or, as Mr Ripley says, believe me or not – in the quiet of that stable you think you hear a tiny voice say, 'Buy me! Never mind that colt. Buy me!' And instantly you tell her, 'All right, baby, I'll buy you if I have to bust the bank-roll wide open.' And that's a promise! Weeks of study, weeks of tramping, weeks of indecision. Then finality! Just by chance – just like that!

So you go to the ring, and you wait for her, when for weeks you've thought you were going to that ring to wait for a colt, and never did lover wait for sweetheart more anxiously.

You look round those hundreds of intent faces. You study that close-packed amphitheatre. Tier on tier of keen-eyed men – prince and pauper, stable boy and lord of a million acres, cheek by jowl, shoulder to shoulder, but horsemen all, come to buy a champion if they can. Always that 'if' in racing! Will they see what you have seen? How many of them will have picked that soft-eyed filly waiting in her stall for her turn to face the play of Fortune's wheel? Where will the fall of the auctioneer's hammer send her? What sort of a master will guide her destiny?

Well, you made a promise, so you know where she'll go, if the bank-roll will stand it – if some lord of a million acres doesn't make your meagre shekels look like the change he uses for car-fare. What if they bid a figure you can't come up to? But she's very small. Oh yes, of course, that's your chance – she's *very* small.

Well then, here she comes, head held proudly like the tiny princess she is, little hoofs hardly seem to touch the velvet turf she steps upon. Eyes wide with bewilderment as she faces that crowded circle of quiet-faced men.

The auctioneer's voice drones on and on. Her father did this, her mother that, her brother did this, her sister that. The recounting of the miracles of her forebears comes to an end, and eventually the courteous question is asked, 'And now, gentlemen, what am I bid?'

And an optimist says 'One hundred guineas,' and the race is on. Once again Fortune smiles. 'Three hundred and fifty,' someone calls, and instantly you snap back, 'Three hundred and seventy-five,' and there is silence.

It's all you've got to spend on her. It isn't much, I know, but you don't own a million acres. The time will come when you'll spend ten times as much for just one horse, but you don't know that then. Quietly you pray that no one says, 'Four hundred,' and then, after what seems to you to be intolerable aeons of time, that hammer falls, and she belongs to you.

Her attendant leads her back to a stall where you are waiting to praise her and pat her, and tell her everything is OK now. And she puts her head in your arms, and rests it there, which is by way of saying, 'Thank you, master, thank you very much indeed.'

A small boy, who must lose her now, says sadly, 'I've looked after her, mister, since she was knee-high to a grasshopper. You'll take care of her?'

And you say, 'Sure, son, sure, I'll take care of her, never doubt it.'

There is so much to do from that time on. Floats, ships, attendants to take her on the ocean voyage which will bring her to the dock-side at which you wait so anxiously. There has been a cyclone. The papers tell you that the ship on which she travels, tied in a narrow stall deep in a stinking hold, is labouring in a welter of furious seas and howling gales. The Storm Gods chose an awkward time to rave and rant. Two days ago those tumbling seas were calm. Has she been hurt? You've paid a man to guard her well. Has he done the job you paid him for? Well, you'll soon know.

Out of an evil-smelling hold she comes, slung in a crate high above the ship that carried her. Winches rattle, raucous voices spill commands, the crate lands at your feet, and from it, very tired, very sick and very frightened, steps your tiny filly. Wide dark eyes seek yours in that bedlam of shouting stevedores, rattling winches, snarling motors, and your voice is very soft, and your hand is very gentle, as you tell her that she's home now, that everything at last is as it should be.

Then, after you've rattled and bumped through a great city, in a gigantic vehicle they call a float but which has precious little 'float' about it, she is 'home'. A cool, quiet stable, knee-deep in straw, water, food, and your foreman's voice: 'Sure, boss, she's beautiful, but small, strike me, very small!'

And you say, 'Sure! Her grandfather won two Ascot Gold Cups, and her grandmother won the Oaks, and she'll grow.'

Then knowing hands probe and delve as the 'stable' looks her over, and heads are shaken, and 'too small' they say, even if her grandmother won the Oaks with nineteen flaming stone.

Just for a moment you feel a tiny doubt. Perhaps a colt would have been better. There was that one from Star Sapphire, and then you look again at the weary little mite you've gone to so much trouble to get and – shrug your shoulders.

Your foreman's eyes have never left you, and he says suddenly, 'To hell with them, boss. They wouldn't know a racehorse from a Rocky Mountain goat, but me – well, I'll be looking after *her* myself.' And this, you know, is honour *in excelsis*.

'She'll grow,' you've said. Oh, yes, you've said it so many times, but she doesn't grow. And she doesn't eat, and she doesn't do any of the things you had figured on. Instead she becomes very ill. You try everything you know – uselessly. That tiny horse is very sick indeed. So you call in the vets to help you. They come, examine, question, shake their heads. No constitution – colitis, that dread disease – possibly had it for months – probably never race – certainly not 'early'. Still they'll do the best they can. And you know they will, even if their bills are never paid. That's racing. And you'll do your best too. Disappointing? Oh, sure!

Away in the distance a dream, something or other to do with the Gimcrack Stakes – just a dream – a long way off now – a very long way off. Horses bunched at the turn for that battle down that long home stretch. The thunder of the multitude. A name on the lips of thousands in one long roar of sound – your filly's name as she battles with the favourite at that vital furlong pole for mastery, and gains it, goes on, spread-eagles the cream of her age – flashes past that little white line against its little black board, and that judge from whose decision there is no appeal – lengths to the good!

Oh, sure! Just a dream, especially with a weary little horse, despondent and sick, asking to be petted and helped – not trained and harried about for a race a bare six months away.

Her breeder comes to Sydney. A sportsman, this. He hears the vet's report and – offers you another horse if you care to send her back. He will give you that Star Sapphire colt you like so much in her place. You go into your filly's box to say goodbye, and you go when no one else can see you, because it isn't an easy thing to do. I mean easy to say goodbye. And then Fortune, who must take care of all horsemen, if they are ever to own a *race*horse, smiles again. With that little head pressed against yours, you just can't do it, and so that night, you tell the quiet man who bred her that you'll 'carry on'.

You go to work. Day after day, week after week, month after month, the treatment continues. But that little filly is very close to those Happy Hunting Grounds to which all good horses go, before she turns the corner. You do just exactly what those clever vets have ordered – special diet, cunning medicines, warmth, care, kindness. Oh yes, lots of kindness. You feed a racehorse oats, or you feed it nitrogenous food of some sort. You have to. No alternative. But you can't feed this filly oats, or nitrogenous food of any kind. It's pure poison to her with the malady she has.

Three months go by – a coat like polished copper is beginning to glisten again. Symptoms are favourable. You try your first feed of oats. A very small feed of grain, mixed with a very large feed of hope. She eats them, and with no ill effects, praise be. No recurrence of the malady she seems to have overcome.

Well, if she can eat oats, you can train her. Gimcrack Stakes – three months away. You don't like early two-year-old racing, but that was the race you dreamed about for this little lady, because she's pitched and balanced to go like greased lightning, and she's bred to stay. Perhaps, if you're very careful, you can go far enough to let *her* tell you what to do. She'll tell you, never doubt it, if you've sense enough to know her language.

And so now it's work in earnest, but work you love. Your little horse thrives under it. Five in the morning until ten at night, your foreman watches, massages, feeds, exercises, does the thousand and one things one does when a horse is set to win a race. And in the case of this filly, two or three things that are not usually included.

And then one day, with the Gimcrack Stakes six weeks away, you decide to let her 'run down a furlong'. Ah, folks, *there* is a day for you. When, after months of preparation, you bring out the old stopwatch and prepare to learn your fate. Can she run a furlong in twelve seconds? Can she – or will she, as nine out of ten do, take longer? Can she, by some miracle, break twelve with her heavy irons on? Well, well, you'll see in the morning. And if she, as the racing argot has it, 'takes a week', there isn't anything that you can do about it – no, not a thing!

And so, when the older horses have departed, and the trainers have gone where all good trainers go at breakfast-time, when the sun had chased the frost away, you stand, timer in hand, and watch your filly canter gaily to the mark, and breaking away like a flash, run in a blur of speed to a furlong pole. You click your watch, and peek at it, and then, startled, you look again, and you say, 'Well, I'll be …!' and you almost went back on a promise made, in all good faith, to a little horse with black-tipped ears, and you nearly sent her home for something out of Star Sapphire.

Perhaps it's the wind that makes you shiver.

Your watch, which is a perfectly good watch, tells the story. Your filly, in working shoes, carrying 8 stone 10 pounds, and allowed to please herself, flashed over that furlong in eleven seconds and two-fifths, and that, you know, isn't galloping – that, as so many years of trying has so amply taught you, is simply flying! So who can blame you if you start to dream again?

Two weeks go by, and daily your baby horse grows stronger, bigger, faster. Did I say faster? Yes faster, because one fine morning you take her far from prying eyes, and on a track where once years ago a crack sprinter in racing shoes ran two in twenty-three and three-quarters, but on which no horse since has done so well, your filly, in working shoes, flashes over that same two furlongs in twenty-three and one-quarter, and then you know that if she runs true to pedigree, and gets an even break in the race you've set her for, she will be very hard to beat indeed. Oh, very hard!

That evening you go to a great friend who loves to make thousands grow where only one thousand was before, and you tell him, imploring secrecy, that you've got a filly big as a minute, beautiful as a sculptor's dream, faster than chain lightning, and game as an Australian bulldog ant. And he says, as a doctor will say to his patient, soothingly, quietly, 'Sure, Jim, I know. Have a drink.' But you persist, and eventually he becomes enthusiastic, and forecasts that the noble brotherhood of the Ring are due for an outsize dose of sackcloth and ashes, and a notable lack of that legendary fruit of which the resting place is that equally legendary sideboard.

Then he wants to know of her training. How many four-furlong sprints with the pressure on? And you say, 'None at all. Absolutely none at all.' And he laughs, and suggests that you talk of other things, and that's that. You speak nervously of heredity, of the values in pace work, half pace, strong three-quarter pace, of ancestry. You talk in vain. Just over your shoulder when you came into his study, Fortune beckoned him: Fortune who, in the last analysis, governs every little thing there is in racing. Fortune had gone from that room before you left.

The great day grows closer. There are barrier trials now, and daily the young ones who have been 'tried' and who have survived their early preparations thus far (so many don't) spring into flashing life from behind tapes at the starter calls.

Then one day there is a mighty gathering of babies at the official two-year-old trials, and heat after heat thunder down a lightning-fast track under racing conditions. Of the colts and the fillies, the fair sex take all honours. Two of them run four furlongs in forty-eight seconds, and that evening their names get headlines, and you know you'll have opponents worthy of your steel, which is as it should be.

At the trials, someone who knows you have a young one too, asks where your filly is, and you say, 'Having her breakfast, I suppose,' and he shakes his head. 'Great practice this, Jim,' he remarks, 'learns them race conditions.' 'Sure,' you say. 'They're fine. I know other ways.' He grins. 'You've quaint ideas, Jim – how's dancing, or is it skating, nowadays?' You leave it at that!

Ten days before the race, you send your own baby out 'tipped' and with her chosen horseman in silks and satins, in the saddle. And where the world doesn't see, she beats seven others similarly equipped, flying like a little bay meteor over three furlongs from the barrier, and then the crack little horseman on her back has to fight like a tiger to stop her running three furlongs more at that same terrific pace. Bred to stay? Oh sure. I told you that. Or didn't I? That dream is getting closer now!

And from then on? Well no more gallops, no more strain. Just potter about, with a bit of strong three-quarter pace work here and there. Massage, good food, kindness – oh yes, plenty of that. You say she's fit, your friends say you're crazy, your foreman grunts. So what? So someone's crazy! Maybe it's you! You have the courage of your convictions in the racing game – when you've got convictions. So often you just don't know, and neither does anyone else!

But in an education that has encompassed most things, one thing remains to be done. Have you, who watch the babies run, ever thought of their ordeal when first they see the milling thousands, hear the roar of the ring, become a part of that electric atmosphere that is the racecourse? Stage-fright, fear, anxiety, bewilderment, leave many a baby horse half beaten long before the starter's voice sends them thundering away.

And so that she may get used to it, you take your filly to the races – to a meeting where voices bellow, and strangers come to gaze at her. Where men in red coats on white horses canter by, and all the ordered pandemonium of the Sport of Kings surrounds her.

You take your colt too. Oh yes, you have a colt, with a coat like a cloak of burnished brass, and the disposition of a Pirate King.

She takes it well. You parade them both, and your friends come in dozens to see them, and long and loud are the praises for your golden-coated colt, and long and pregnant are the silences that follow your humble suggestion that the filly is lovely too.

'Oh, yes,' they say, if they say anything at all, 'rather small though – a mite miserable – go for a couple like scalded cat – but that colt! Now, mister, *there's* a racehorse!' And the colt, with its burnished-copper coat, and his disposition of a swaggering buccaneer, stands high in the air with his front feet pawing at a point yards above your head, and sends his shrill clear reply over ring and paddock: 'Boy, you've said a mouthful!' But what he doesn't tell them is that the little lady no one cares for could give him a stone and a start and a beating any time you like to call the tune!

And *you* don't tell them either, because you are a little sad, and a wee bit puzzled. Can't they see your lovely filly, or is it *your* eyes that cannot see her imperfections? 'Beauty is in the eye of the beholder.' Well maybe so – maybe so.

Then among the curious ones who wander past, a young 'man about town' stops long enough to remark, 'A fine colt,' and then, turning to where your little horse is standing in her scarlet silken sheet, and her spotless bandages, with the brass and leather of her head collar gleaming because proud hands have worked for hours so that her 'ensemble' may be perfect, the gentleman remarks, 'Don't think much of her,' and your foreman, fed to the teeth, and because he is a little sad too, snarls savagely, 'Mister, which end of her do you think kicks?'

'... *all the ordered pandemonium of the Sport of Kings ...*'

Well, you take them home, and then, presently, lo and behold, the Great Day dawns. That day you dreamed about six long months ago. A dream that, before evening falls again, will have shattered into the oblivion of painful memories, or triumphed into the miracle of a *fait accompli*. That's a day, my race-going friends, that is 'just another day' to you. But for me! Oh, well, I'll try to tell you.

Coffee that morning was hot and strong, and newspapers, race papers, and tipsters' sheets made the bed covering. All that ocean of type that sums up the discoveries of that colossal espionage system that delves with the eye of an eagle, the sagacity of a fox, and the tenacity of a weasel, into the chances of the thoroughbred horse, and out of that multitude of forecasts not one gives your horse a chance! No – not even a place chance, and you think suddenly of that song you sang when you marched to war – 'They're all out of step but Jim!' And then you remember that it was *Jim* who was out of step, and *your* name is Jim.

A hurried toilet, a red-and-white tie, your racing colours. She'll carry them, so you'll carry them too. Then to the stable in a car that must wonder if you think you're Malcolm Campbell. Your foreman's grunted greeting (he's 'strung up' too, though woe betide you if you say so!), the rhythmic swing of his brush massaging muscles like fluid steel beneath a satin coat, that changes in places into little pools of light as a shaft of early morning sun finds her. A velvet muzzle that spares a moment to caress your cheek, before it buries itself in sweet-smelling food. Lips that move with that curious rotary motion, jaws that grind with the even steadiness of a metronome – sweet music to the trainer's ears on race day – I'll say it is.

Dark eyes are clear, untroubled. Under those enormous hot poultice bandages, you know her legs are clean and cool and, best of all, under your inquiring fingertips, her heart beats strong and true, thirty-eight, thirty-nine, maybe forty to the minute. That marvellous muscle from which come all those things you know she's got. Well, little filly, I've done my best, and those who have helped me have done their best, and now – well, now, it's up to *you*!

The rhythmic swing of that brush goes on and on and on. How many thousand hours has he swung a brush like that? How many years has he hissed sibilantly like a disturbed snake, as is the way of all horsemen with a brush? How much of it was worthwhile? Ask him! He wouldn't know what you were talking about. It was all worthwhile from his point of view. Were they not all thoroughbred? They're born and bred that way in racing.

Hours go by, and eventually you stand with your small horse, in a big stall, with a hundred other horses in a long line of stalls on either side of you. The clamour of the racecourse envelops you, and you wish time wouldn't drag so. A famous horse is stabled next your own, and hundreds come to look him over. You step aside so that they can see your filly too. But they don't gesticulate, and they don't admire. They just walk away, and never look in your direction. After all, who are you, and who is your filly? Just one of twenty-one babies entered in an early Classic, some of whom can run half a mile in forty-eight, which is worthy of note. But what can that little one run? Well, nobody knows. Not even you know, though you *think* you do. Hardly anyone ever heard her name. Well, in a little while now, they'll fling her name in banner type across the sporting pages of a nation – well, maybe they will!

Gradually your world grows smaller until the whole of it is concentrated in just one small baby horse. The gamble of the barrier draw has given you nine marble. Not so bad. From the nearby ring an enormous bellow calls your horse at twenty to one. A week ago, that would have seemed philanthropy – almost lese-majesty. Now, on the brink of the Great Ordeal, you're not so sure. But you know the ladies will back her – with a name like that – oh, sure they will! And you'll back her – with what you've got. She won't be friendless! Twenty to one. It's a bonny price, and they say Shylock sired the bookmaker breed. My goodness gracious! Twenty to one!

The parade is on. Twenty-one babies in their flaunting colours. Your jockey comes – smart, capable, cool. You wonder at his coolness. Thank heaven you don't have to ride her. Now you know what courage is! Look at her – calm, unflurried – and *she* knows just as well as *you* know that she's on the threshold of a hard, tough battle. *How* does she know? Bred in her, or course, and in most of those like her, over hundreds of years. How about your own courage? Well, maybe the less said about that, just now, the better. *You* don't need any; you just have to sit and watch!

A pat on a glossy neck, a last word to the jockey and your voice is hard. 'No whip, Bill, no spurs. Let her do it herself. She'll fight it out – bred that way.' And his merry, smiling answer, 'Don't worry, boss. She's home and hosed. Go put the mortgage on her.'

You don't. You couldn't, even if you had a mortgage. Curiously money doesn't seem to matter now. Only one thing matters. You flee to a spot high in a towering grandstand, as far from folk as possible, and through your glasses in the far distance you pick up a huddle of horses who wheel and dive and change in a kaleidoscope of brilliant colour.

And then your entire world narrows down to just one thing. Gone are the crowds, gone the tumult and the shouting, gone any vestige of consciousness of anything or anyone except that distant mass wheeling and diving like a flock of gulls at a five-strand barrier. If you breathe, you don't know it, and you pray for just one thing. That she'll get away when the starter calls, and that she won't be asked to break her heart chasing a field that stole a march on her. That your dream won't go west in a split second of faulty judgement.

You can't see her colours in that shifting huddle. The day is dull, the visibility poor, but you know suddenly that they're off, and then I'll *swear* you do not breathe at all. Your glasses range forward, then backward over that flying field. You can't find her, but two horses on the rails obscure one on the outside of them. Perhaps *she's* running there outside of those you see so plainly.

Then a quarter of a mile away, they swing for home. Desperately your glasses range from the head of that flying field to the tail of it, and back again. A misty rain has blurred your vision so that the blazing colours the jockeys carry are vague and almost indistinguishable. You are conscious of a sense of unbearable urgency. You've got to find her! You've *got* to. Then suddenly you freeze into complete immobility. *That* must be her. There just outside of the chestnut on the rails, is a blood-red bay, with a great white blaze. Going like the wind. *That's* her! Then you're dreaming again.

Horses bunched at the turn for their battle down that long home stretch – the thunder of the multitude – a name on the lips of thousands in one long roar of sound. Your filly's name, as she battles with the favourite at that vital furlong pole for mastery, and gains it, goes on, spread-eagles the cream of her age – flashes past that little white line against its little black board, and that judge from whose decision there is no appeal – lengths to the good!

Then suddenly you realise it's a dream come true, and that that little filly trotting back on dainty feet, black-tipped ears pricked on lovely little head – belongs to you!!

And her name, folks – oh, yes, I forgot to tell you: Gay Romance.

Owned and trained by the author, Gay Romance won the Gimcrack Stakes at Randwick in 1937. She was also the dam of Gay Lover, winner of the 1956 Rosehill Guineas.

PHAR LAP

Anon

How you thrilled the racing public with your matchless strength
    and grace;
With your peerless staying power and your dazzling burst of pace.
You toyed with your opponents with a confidence so rare,
Flashing past the winning post with lengths and lengths to spare.
No distance ever proved too great, no horse or handicap,
Could stop you winning races like a champion, Phar Lap.

With a minimum of effort you would simply bowl along,
With a stride so devastating and an action smooth and strong.
And you vied with the immortals when, on Flemington's green track,
You won the Melbourne Cup with nine stone twelve upon
    your back.
How the hearts of thousands quickened as you cantered
    back old chap,
With your grand head proudly nodding to the crowd that yelled,
    'Phar Lap'.

Who that saw it could forget it – how you won the Craven Plate?
When a mighty son of Rosedale, whom we'd justly labelled 'great',
Clapped the pace on from the start in a middle-distance race,
Just to test you to the limit of endurance, grit and pace.
He was galloping so strongly that the stands began to clap,
For it seemed as though your lustre would be dimmed at last,
    Phar Lap.

But you trailed him like a bloodhound till your nostrils touched
    his rump
Then your jockey asked the question and, with one
    tremendous jump,

'Who that saw it could forget it - how you won the Craven Plate?'
Phar Lap wins his third Craven Plate 1931

'... at Agua Caliente you proved you were the best ...' Phar Lap sets
world record for mile-and-a-quarter at Agua Caliente 1931

Something like a chestnut meteor hurtled past a blur of black
And, before the crowd stopped gasping, you were halfway down
    the track,
And, the further that you travelled, ever wider grew the gap,
And you broke another record – one you'd set yourself, Phar Lap.

The hopes of all Australians travelled with you overseas,
Wishing to inspire you to further victories.
And at Agua Caliente you proved you were the best,
Then your great heart stopped beating – so they brought it home
    to rest.
And Australians won't forget you while the roots of life hold sap,
For the greatest racehorse that was ever foaled was you, Phar Lap.

CONSTANTINE THE GREAT

A. B. ('Banjo') Paterson

The thoroughbred mares in their own exclusive paddock at Limestone Stud were a very aristocratic lot, and as keen on their own dignity and precedence as a lot of patrician dowagers in a Court drawing-room: consequently, they were very much upset when a strange horse was turned in among them one bright December morning, without their permission being asked or their desires considered in any way whatever.

You must understand that these highly pedigreed ladies all figured in the pages of the *Stud Book*, which is the *Debrett's Peerage* of the Turf world, and they knew each other's pedigrees and relationships away back into the days of Charles I.

Not a horse could win an important race in any part of the world, and no mare could produce a Derby winner, but what such of the Limestone ladies as were related to the new celebrity became very proud and arrogant, and those who were not related became jealous – very jealous indeed.

Being a lot of highly bred dowagers, they were divided into as many cliques and coteries as the countesses and duchesses in a Mayfair drawing-room, and the credentials of any new arrival were very closely scanned before she was admitted to any of the more exclusive circles.

'That mare,' a dowager countess would say, on considering the pedigree of a new arrival, 'of course I shall call on her, but I really couldn't make a friend of her. My dear, do you know that her family haven't won a really big race for three generations?'

Besides an infinite number of smaller coteries, there were two clear-cut social sets among the mares – those born in England, and those born in Australia.

The English mares did not actually patronise the others, but they just tolerated them, and on Derby Day the English mares got together and talked about Epsom and Newmarket till the other mares could hardly bear it: and a pert young Australian mare, after listening to as much of this conversation as she could stand, said, 'The Epsom Derby! That's the race where they go up and down hills, isn't it, like our stockhorses go after cattle?', a remark that was passed over in a kind of pitying silence.

But in spite of their bickering among themselves they presented a united front against all outsiders, and they looked upon any horse not in the *Stud Book* in much the same way as a duchess would look upon the bride of a costermonger.

And so, on this beautiful December day, a strange horse was actually being turned into their paddock, a big gaunt bay horse with hair on his fetlocks, a plain head and spur marks on his ribs: a horse that looked as though he ought to be carrying a general at the head of an army, so strong and resolute was his appearance, and so kind and intelligent was his eye, but the hair on his fetlocks, the spur marks on his ribs, and the plainness of his head decided the mares that he could not be a thoroughbred – perhaps something very near it, but not quite born in the purple. So they decided to ignore the intruder, and they cast calm supercilious glances at him as he strolled past them on his way to the river to get a drink.

The two men who had brought him to the paddock stood chatting by the rails. The mares knew one of them well enough, for the tall man with the heavy moustache and the slow soft way of speaking was Gordon Macallister, owner of Limestone Stud, and he was a personal friend of every mare in the paddock. He visited them nearly every day, he looked after them when they were sick and a word from him in praise of one of the foals was enough to make that foal's mother proud and joyful for a week.

The keen-eyed little man with the quick, staccato way of speaking was unknown to the mares and they put him down as not much class anyway; if they had known that he was like Heronshaw, the greatest trainer of the day, they would have been more impressed.

'Well, Ike,' said Macallister, 'this is the best I can do for you. No one goes through this paddock, and no one would dream of looking for him among my crack mares and foals. Why does his owner want him planted?'

'He's broke.'

'Broke! I thought he had plenty of money.'

'So he did have. But he wanted more, so he bought half the wool in Australia and shipped it and struck a misere hand. He's got no ready money, y'understand, and his creditors are after him, and if they can get hold of this horse they'll sell him by order of the court. But the market's rising and if he can hold on for a few weeks he'll be all right again. That's why he wants this horse out of the road.'

'I see. But I'm taking a risk putting him in my mares and foals. I wouldn't dream of doing it for anybody but you. Is he quiet?'

'Quiet! You could bowl hedgehogs at his hind legs all day and he wouldn't kick at 'em. Your daughter could ride him, so then nobody would tumble to it that he is anything more than an ordinary hack. What I'm afraid of is that he might cripple himself if he gets galloping about with these foals.'

'That's what you're afraid of, is it? Well, what about me, taking the risk of turning a stranger into this paddock? He might set the whole lot racing for their lives! If I'll chance my mares and foals, you've got to chance your horse. If I put him anywhere else, somebody's sure to see him and you'll have the bailiffs after him.'

With that, the two men rode away to the homestead and the mares were left to size up the intruder.

Possibly the most aristocratic mare in the paddock was Lady Susan, a descendant of the great St Simon, and with so many other celebrated relatives that her position was almost unchallengeable. True, she was Australian-born, but her grandsire had won the English Derby and she herself had won the Australian Oaks, and, what was more important, her foals had won two Derbies and a Melbourne Cup.

The English mares might affect to despise Australian races, but any foal from Lady Susan was worth five thousand guineas as it stood on its delicate little hoofs alongside her in the paddock. The English mares might talk about Epsom and Newmarket, but none of their foals averaged five thousand guineas, so there was no more to be said: all the mares waited for a lead from Lady Susan in most matters, but in regard to this new horse they thought they were on safe ground in criticising him.

The chorus was led off by Cat's Cradle, a young and pert Australian mare who was inclined to give herself airs because her full sister had won the last big race for two-year-old fillies by three lengths in very fast time. After looking the newcomer over in a very supercilious way she gave a horse laugh, which is a kind of internal laugh you can't see.

'Girls,' she said, 'what have we here with the marks of the harpoons on his ribs, and the whiskers on his fetlocks? I'll bet he's a winner – the winner of the Big Scrub Handicap with the first prize a bees' nest. After you've won the race, they show you the bees' nest in a tree, and you have to cut the tree down and rob the nest for yourself.'

Meanwhile the English mares were muttering among themselves such remarks as 'preposterous', 'wouldn't be tolerated in England', 'you never know what to expect in this extraordinary country', being faintly heard above the singing of Featherbrain, an English mare who was apt to be a bit hysterical, who screamed to her foal and set off up the paddock as hard as she could split, but finding that none of the others followed her, returned in a shamefaced way to the mob.

All this time old Lady Susan had said nothing until her foal, who was quite an important person, for he was expected to fetch at least six thousand guineas at auction, went up to her and said, 'Mother, can I go and speak to the new horse? He seems so lonely, and none of the others will go near him.'

'Yes,' she said, 'you can go. I seem to see a likeness in that horse to somebody I used to know. I think I must have raced against his mother at some time or other. You mustn't say anything rude to him about the hair on his fetlocks, for sometimes that comes to us from the old English horses that were in the pedigrees hundreds of years before the Arabs were ever brought into England. Just be civil to him, and if he tells you anything come back and tell me.'

Even the greatest ladies are not above a little curiosity.

Without the slightest hesitation, Lady Susan's foal marched up to the newcomer and gave him the usual Australian salutation, 'Good day. It looks very dry, doesn't it?'

The stranger, who appeared to be a rough and ready sort of person, said, 'Yes, it's dry all right: and who may you be, young fellow?'

To which the foal, who had a great idea of his own importance though he was only a few months old, answered without any trepidation, 'I'm Lady Susan's foal. Perhaps you've heard of my full brother Gaslight?'

'Gaslight!' said the stranger. 'Why I ran against ...' and here he stopped as though about to say too much. 'I ran against a stone coming up, and bruised my heel a bit. But look here, young fellow, it doesn't matter what you are full brother to. The thing is, can you gallop yourself? The judge don't place any horse first because he's full brother to something, you know.'

'Oh, yes, I know that. But I can go a bit, and when the foals all get together for our gallop round the paddock this evening, you can see me travel. Did you ever do any racing yourself?'

'Oh yes, young fellow, I've raced a bit: not as much as some and more than others. The less you talk about what you can do in racing the better for you, you understand. The handicapper might hear you, and you'd never get the weight off. But I'll watch you go round this evening, and I might be able to give you a wrinkle or two that will do you some good when your time comes to go to the barrier.'

That evening when the foals gathered for their customary sprint round the paddock, the stranger watched them for a while and then tossed up his head and set off after them, going in surprising fashion, his great strides eating up the ground, while the foals with their little nostrils distended and their little hoofs rattling on the stony ridges strove valiantly for the lead. The Featherbrain mare got very excited and said, 'Look, look, he'll kill the foals.'

To which Lady Susan, who had picked up some hard sayings in the training stables, replied, 'Shut your head! The foals are all right.'

You see, her foal was well in front and going like a champion.

After the gallop Lady Susan's foal strolled over to the stranger expecting to get all sorts of compliments, but the stranger was not of the gushing type.

'Very fair,' he said. 'Very fair, but look here, youngster, when you first jump off, don't make too big a jump. It's all right with nothing on your back, but when you've got a jockey there, too big a jump will unbalance him. Just take half a stride as you move out of the barrier, and get the weight on your back under way. Then get down to it and deal it out to 'em all you know. Give my compliments to your mother and tell her I know all about her. Everybody on the Turf knows all about Lady Susan.'

*   *   *

That was the year of the big bushfire, the fire that swept up the river from a hundred miles south, burning all before it. It had been a great season, and the long grass and thistles on the flats were as dry as tinder, and the wind brought the fire along in great leaps, the burning cinders being carried by the wind from the dry trees to start fresh fires half a mile ahead.

When the breeze brought the first scent of the burning gum leaves, and the clouds of smoke appeared over the distant hills, the mares gathered themselves and their foals together sniffling with pointed ears at the new terror – something of which none of them had had any experience whatever.

It so happened that Macallister was away from the head station that day, and he only arrived in his car as night fell, bringing with him his daughter, Jean, a fourteen-year-old girl with just as much interest in the horses as Macallister himself. She had been riding ever since she could remember anything, ever since the days when she was carried as a baby in front of her father's saddle.

Springing from the car, Macallister dragged a bridle out of the tonneau, and walking in a quiet matter-of-fact way he went up to the stranger and slipped the bridle on him, talking to him in a soothing voice all the time. Then he led him up to the car and told his daughter what she must do.

'Jean,' he said, 'that fire will be here in ten minutes and all I've got in the world is in these mares and foals. There's only one thing that can save them, and that is the horse. This is Constantine the

Great, the horse that won both the Sydney and Melbourne Derbies and the Melbourne Cup. You'll have to ride him bareback, for there's no time to go and get a saddle, but they say he's very quiet. Now listen to what I've got to tell you.

'As soon as I let the mares and foals out of this paddock, they'll go like mad things all over the bush, and half of them will be crippled or killed in the darkness: but if you can keep ahead of them for the first mile, they'll follow you and you can lead them up to the big bald hill where there's no grass and no timber. When you get them there, try and keep them there – do your best anyhow. They'll be pretty tired by that time and if you keep on riding round and round, and calling out to them in the darkness they may follow you and it may save the lot.

'And now there's another thing. There's that gate at the Two Mile. You'll have no time to stop and open it or the mares will scatter all over the place. Run him right slap into it, and send it flying. It opens in the middle and his weight will smash it like paper. Don't stop for anything and don't look behind you. The mares will follow you through the gate and the main thing is to keep ahead of them for the first mile. If there's a horse in the world that can keep ahead of those thoroughbred mares with nothing on their backs, this is the one. I did not want him here, but it looks as if he might save us.

'As soon as I get you away, I'll go up to the house and tell your mother to hide in the river if the fire comes, and then I'll go back to try and save that old crippled woman down in the hut on the flat.'

Even as he spoke a red glare showed down at the bend of the river and the mares grew terrified. Swinging the girl onto the big horse's back, he led him towards the gate, patting him on the neck, and talking to him.

'Old man,' he said, 'you're running for a big stake tonight. Bigger than the Melbourne Cup. There's a hundred thousand pounds of money in these mares and there's my little girl's life. It's up to you to save them, so now go to it like a thoroughbred.'

By this time they had reached the gate, the big horse walking quite unconcerned, while the terrified mares crowded behind him.

Giving his daughter a hurried kiss, Macallister threw the gate open, and with the big horse in front, the wild cavalcade swept away into the darkness.

For the first mile Jean knew nothing but the great swinging strides of the horse beneath her, the dimly seen stretch of track in front, and behind her the roaring of hundreds of hoofs, and the mares whinnying and calling to their foals. If she came off, or if the big horse made a false step in the darkness and came down, she would be trodden flat in an instant by the terrified rush of the mares behind her: but there was a wild exhilaration in the ride that banished all thought of fear.

Constantine the Great lay down to work without fear or excitement, for it was nothing new to him to hear the drumming of a field of horses behind him. Some instinct inherited from his Arab ancestors made him reach out and clear in his stride the little waterways that crossed the track. Once or twice in the headlong flight the girl's knee grazed perilously against the trees, and more than once she had to lie flat down on his neck to avoid being swept off by an overhanging branch: but still the great machine-like stride swept him along in front of the mares, and still they followed in close formation at his heels.

After a while the pace slackened and Jean was able to sit up and call out to the mares, who knew her voice and answered her with shrill neighs: but the pace was still fast enough to make any delay risky and Jean knew that if she stopped to open the Two Mile gate the mares would probably swing on down the fence into the darkness and smash themselves up in the scrub.

Having got so far in safety, her spirits rose and she began talking to the big horse as they swept along.

'There's a gate ahead of us,' she said, 'and you've got to smash it or these mares and foals will be killed. Will you do it for me? Don't jump it, or I'll very likely come off, for I'm not very good at jumping fences barebacked, and if the mares follow you over it, that will be the end of me.'

Luckily, the gate was hidden under the shadow of some trees, and the big horse was on it before he saw it.

With no time to jump he gave a snort of defiance and raced straight into it.

Smash! The two by four hardwood battens were splintered like matches under the weight of the blow, and without pause or hesitation he swept on while the mares crowded and crushed through the gap that he had left.

So instantaneous had been the smash that Jean had hardly been shifted on her precarious perch, but with each stride that the big horse took she felt something moist on her hands. She was puzzled to think what it could be, but at last she realised that the horse had cut himself rather badly on the gate and that his blood was splashing up onto her hands and clothes. For the first time in that wild ride she felt utterly miserable, but there was nothing that could be done about it so she held her course through the rough timber for the Bald Hill.

Arriving at the hill, she found that an advanced wing of the fire had nearly cut her off, and everything was red flames, smoke, and confusion. In a sort of sanctuary on top of the hill, all sorts of bush animals had gathered, wallabies and kangaroos bewildered with terror racing madly round and round, while rabbits with their fur on fire rushed screaming across the open.

A mob of emus, all fear of mankind forgotten, trotted up to her and almost stuck their heads in her face as though asking for guidance. Coming up at their ungainly trot, they had cut the mob of mares in two, and for a moment it looked as though one wing of the mares would lose their heads and race into the scrub; but just as things hung in the balance a foal trotted towards her from the outlying mob, his mother followed him, and in another moment all the mares had gathered together again.

By the light of the burning trees Jean recognised the foal that had so unexpectedly come to her help at a critical moment. 'Why,' she said, 'it's Silas! And he seems to know this horse! Aren't you frightened, Silas?' But Silas, with his small nostrils sniffing the smoke, was quite at his ease, and appeared to think that Providence would hesitate before destroying a gentleman of his quality.

Ringed with smoke and fire, and hampered by terrified wild animals, Jean rode backwards and forwards through the night, keeping the mares together and vainly trying to see what injury her mount had sustained. She dared not get off the horse lest she should never be able to get on again, but as daylight broke she was able to see a big raw gash across his chest from which the blood still welled and, overcome with weariness and excitement, she burst into tears.

A few hours later a big gaunt horse with bloodstained chest and forelegs, and ridden by an inexpressibly weary little girl, led the Limestone mares back to the homestead. Here she found the lucerne paddocks had saved the house from destruction, and after receiving the frantically excited greetings of her father and mother, her first thought was of the injury that her horse had sustained at the gate. After examination her father pronounced it only superficial, and it was a thankful girl that tumbled into bed to sleep off the recollections of the night amid the fire.

When things had settled down a bit in the horse paddock once more, Lady Susan marched up to the stranger and said, 'We have to thank you for saving our lives. Do you mind telling me your name? These English ladies and myself are now of the opinion that you must be a far more important person than you look.'

'Well ma'am,' he said, 'I have a name all right. Such as it is you may have heard it, for they call me Constantine the Great. As for importance, well, I've won some races and I've lost others. I've raced against some of your foals and you want to look after that little fellow you have now, for a gamer bit of stuff I never saw.'

When the mares discovered who he was, there was a great excitement in hunting over his pedigree, and it was found that he was first cousin to fifteen of them, and was more or less distantly related to every mare in the paddock. It took them several days to hunt out all the relationships.

A few months later the leading newspaper starred the item: 'Constantine the Great has come back to work, and appears to be in great fettle except that his chest is disfigured by a scar which he no doubt sustained while playing about in the paddock. It does not give him any trouble and he is certain to add to his already imposing record of wins.'

FLYING KATE

Anon

It makes us old hands sick and tired to hear
Them talk of their champions of today,
Eurythmics and Davids, yes, I'll have a beer,
Are only fair hacks in their way.

Now this happened out West before the records were took,
And 'tis not to be found in the guide,
But it's honest – Gor' struth, and can't be mistook,
For it happened that I had the ride.

'Twas the Hummer's Creek Cup, and our mare, Flying Kate,
Was allotted eleven stone two;
The race was two miles, you'll agree with me mate,
It was asking her something to do.

She was heavy in foal, but the owner and me
Decided to give her a spin,
We were right on the rocks, 'twas the end of a spree,
So we needed a bit of a win.

I saddled her up and went down with the rest,
Her movements were clumsy and slow,
The starter to get us in line did his best,
Then swishing his flag he said, 'Go!'

The field jumped away but the mare seemed asleep,
And I thought to myself, 'We've been sold,'
Then I heard something queer, and I felt I could weep,
For strike me if Kate hadn't foaled.

The field by this time had gone half a mile,
But I knew what the old mare could do,
So I gave her a cut with the whip – you can smile,
But the game little beast simply flew.

'Twas then she showed them her wonderful speed,
For we mowed down the field one by one,
With a furlong to go we were out in the lead,
And prepared for a last final run.

Then something came at us right on the outside,
And we only just scratched past the pole,
When I had a good look I thought I'd have died,
For I'm blowed if it wasn't the foal.

THE GREATEST RACEHORSE THE WORLD HAS EVER SEEN

Nat Gould

Carbine was the best racehorse I ever saw during my residence in Australia.

By Musket from Mersey, he was bred in New Zealand, and purchased as a yearling by Mr Dan O'Brien for 620 guineas. His performances, when they come to be carefully considered, were wonderful.

Carbine won thirty-three out of forty-three races in which he started, and was only out of a place once, and he was then suffering from a cracked heel. He won fifteen races in succession, and eighteen races out of twenty, being unluckily second in the two he lost.

As a two-year-old he ran five times in New Zealand, and won each race. He was brought over by his owner to Victoria to run for the VRC Derby in 1888, and was unluckily second to Ensign. He ran third in the Newmarket Handicap to Sedition, a rank outsider, and that good horse, Lochiel; and in the Australian Cup, two miles, he was beaten by Lochiel, who carried 8 stone 7 pounds to Carbine's 8 stone 6 pounds, a real good performance for a three-year-old. He was then purchased by Mr Wallace, a VRC committeeman, for three thousand guineas.

He won the Champion Stakes, three mile, as a three-year-old, beating Abercorn, who was then a four-year-old, at wfa. He won several races that season, including the Sydney Cup, in which he carried nine stone, or within four pounds of Abercorn, who finished third. This race goes far to prove he was a better horse than Abercorn, as he was receiving only four pounds, and giving away a year.

As a four-year-old he ran second to Bravo in the Melbourne Cup, with ten stone on his back, giving the winner 1 stone 7 pounds. He again won the Sydney Cup, carrying 9 stone 9 pounds.

It was in the Canterbury Plate at the VRC meeting he ran the only unplaced during the whole of his career. Space will not permit me giving all his wins, but I can safely say he held the championship as a wfa horse from three years old until he retired from the turf. He beat all the best horses over all distances, and he was as good at seven furlongs or a mile as he was at two or three miles. In these days of sprinters and non-stayers, it is a treat to see a horse of such grand speed and staying powers combined as Carbine.

It was as a four-year-old Carbine performed the great feat of winning five of the principal races at the AJC Autumn Meeting in four days, including the Sydney Cup and four wfa races. No wonder Dan O'Brien heaved a sigh, for he had sold Carbine to Mr Donald Wallace for three thousand guineas some time before. It was a treat to see the way in which Carbine tackled his opponents. The horse fairly revelled in his work, and his rush at the finish was marvellous. I have never seen a horse of his size cover so much ground in his stride.

'It was a treat to see the way in which Carbine tackled his opponents.'
Carbine winning the 1889 Sydney Cup

If Carbine was a wonder up to four years old, what shall we say for his five-year-old career, which fairly eclipsed all that he had previously done? He ran eleven times, and was beaten once, when he ought to have won. He won his memorable Melbourne Cup this season.

When the saddling bell rang before the Cup race there was intense excitement, and Carbine held his position as favourite firm as a rock, and Highborn was at thirty-three to one. Ramage rode Carbine, and Egan, a tiny lad, Highborn. 'Old Jack' was fairly mobbed as he was being saddled, but as usual he took no notice of the crowd. When he came onto the track there was a terrific burst of cheering. Carbine stood still and looked round, and then declined to go to the post.

His trainer, Mr Hickenbotham, gave him a push behind, and Carbine moved a few paces. This was a slow process. At last Ramage threw the reins over the horse's head, and Mr Hickenbotham fairly dragged him up the course. I never saw a more sluggish horse until he commenced to race, and then there was a different tale to tell. Mr Forrester was very confident Highborn would beat him.

I shall never forget that race.

Carbine held a good position throughout, but did not get well to the front until they were in the straight. At the home turn Highborn looked to have a chance second to none, and the hopes of his backers were high. No sooner, however, did Carbine see an opening than he shot through, and after that it was a case of hare and hounds. On came 'Old Jack', with his 10 stone 5 pounds, and at the distance he had the race won.

Cheer after cheer rent the air, and people went almost frantic with excitement. It was a wild scene. For months Carbine had been backed by the public, and at last the suspense was over. It was a glorious victory, and everyone knew it, but none better than Mr Forrester, whose crack Highborn finished a couple of lengths behind him. Not only did Carbine carry 10 stone 5 pounds, but he ran the two miles in 3 minutes 28.5 seconds, the fastest time on record for that distance in the colonies.

I had special opportunities of learning a good deal more about that race before it came off than most people. Mr William Forrester, of Warwick Farm, had in his stable a horse called Highborn that he had specially kept for this event. Mr Forrester was then, and, I am proud to say, still is, a great friend of mine; and I also knew Mr Hickenbotham, the trainer of Carbine, very well.

I went to Warwick Farm from Sydney, about an hour's ride in the train, to have a peep at the horses. Warwick Farm is a snug place, and the house and stables join on to Mr Oatley's private racecourse. Mr Forrester is brimful of hospitality, and a born gentleman if ever there was one. When we came to Highborn's box, Mr Forrester said, 'What do you think of him?'

I was looking at a lanky, flat-sided common gelding, as black as coal, with a wall eye that made him look wicked. Honestly, I could not say I thought much of him. It was wonderful how he improved upon acquaintance. 'He's no beauty,' I replied, or words to that effect.

Mr Forrester smiled, and gave me to understand if I did not have a few pounds on 'the black fellow' in the Melbourne Cup I should regret it. Knowing 'the Squire's' propensity for practical joking, I thought he was trying it on, but I soon found he was serious. He had specially kept Highborn for this particular race, and when the weights came out with Carbine 10 stone 5 pounds and Highborn 6 stone 8 pounds, there was much joy in the Warwick Farm camp.

The preparation of both horses went on satisfactorily, but Carbine's trainer had a lot of trouble with the horse's feet, and had a very anxious time of it. Mr Forrester and some of his friends were quietly putting money on Highborn at very long odds months before the race. Highborn's trial was good enough to win with nearer nine stone up than 6 stone 8 pounds, so no wonder they were sanguine. When I reached Melbourne that year for the Cup meeting, I saw Carbine do his winding-up preparations on the track at Flemington. One morning he easily beat his stable mate, Megaphone, for whom Mr Wallace had given two thousand guineas or more after he ran Carbine such a great race at Randwick.

Meeting Mr Hickenbotham after the gallop, I remarked what a good go it was.

'Yes,' he replied, 'and weight or no weight, bar accidents, he'll win the Cup.'

I had an idea he could go near it, but doubted if he could give 3 stone 11 pounds to a horse like Highborn. About a week before the Melbourne Cup was run, I met Mr Forrester, and he asked me to go up to Oakleigh Park, as they were going to give Highborn a run there. I went, to my sorrow, for Highborn was just beaten by Mr James Redfearn's Malvolio. I remarked to Mr Forrester, after the race, that a beating like that was not good enough to win a Melbourne Cup.

'Don't make any mistake,' was his reply. 'Malvolio's Redfearn's crack three-year-old, and he'll win the next Melbourne Cup with him.'

Sure enough his words came true, for I saw Malvolio win it the following year.

To show how good the performance of Carbine was, I have only to allude to Highborn's performances afterwards. Highborn won the Australian Cup, the Sydney Cup, and the Anniversary Handicap, and ran fourth in the Melbourne Cup the following year with nine stone up. He was sold to go to India, and when the property of the Maharajah of Cooch Behar he won two Viceroy's Cups in succession.

A word as to Carbine's defeat by Marvel at Randwick.

It was a wet day, and the ground was sticky. In the All Aged Stakes, a mile, Carbine ran without plates and could not obtain a hold. It was pitiable to see him floundering and not able to stretch out in his usual grand style. The same afternoon he met Marvel again in the Cumberland Stakes, two miles. This time Carbine ran in shoes.

The race resolved itself into a gallop over the last mile, which was all in favour of Marvel's racing style. Carbine, however, beat him easily, and I think there is no doubt he would have won the other race had he had shoes on.

I saw Carbine win all his big races, and when he was bought by the Duke of Portland for thirteen thousand pounds, I came to London in the same vessel he was on, the Orient liner RMS *Orizaba*.

A few particulars about Carbine's voyage may be of interest.

The horse did not come on board until we reached Melbourne.

Mr Ernest Day, who had charge for him for the Duke, was naturally very anxious to get the horse shipped quietly and a notice appeared in the *Evening Herald*, on Thursday, stating Carbine would be shipped on Saturday morning.

As I happened to have a letter in my pocket stating he would come on board on Good Friday, I smiled. Evidently the paragraph had been inspired to put people off the scent. I was on board when the 'hero of a hundred fights' came to the pier. Carbine was accompanied by one of his sons, a colt out of Novelette, who had been named Lederderg by the Duke of Portland, and who was alongside of him.

'Old Jack' at first seemed inclined to remain ashore. Mr Day endeavoured to persuade him to step onto the gangway, but he declined the invitation. A handful of clover was given him, which he quietly munched, then he looked at the crowd as much as to say, 'What do you think of me?'

Cunningham, the man who had had charge of Carbine at the stud, and who came home with the horses, then went to the rescue. No sooner did Carbine see him coming along the gangway than he stretched out his neck and put one foot forward. Cunningham spoke to him, and then, quietly pulling the head-stall, Carbine followed him like a lamb.

The horse felt his footing carefully all along the gangway and crouched down when he felt the boards creak under him; but he never made the least objection to following his leader. Once in his box Carbine commenced to munch hay quietly, as though a trip to England was an everyday occurrence with him.

The colt took more trouble to get on board, but once in his box he also settled down like an old horse. Not knowing the time Carbine was to go on board, there was not a great crowd there, but on Saturday morning (13 April 1895) the people came down in hundreds to have a last peep at the champion.

When it was found Carbine had been put on board the day before, the crowd commenced to see they had been sold, but they were determined not to be done out of a sight of him. I never saw a more determined mass of people than Carbine's admirers. They crushed up the gangway and jammed up in front of his box, regardless of torn clothes and pickpockets, and there were plenty of the latter about, or what looked like them.

Hundreds of people caught a passing glimpse of Carbine as he stood quietly eating in his box. It was their last sight of 'Old Jack', and there were many present who had won money over him in that memorable Melbourne Cup.

No horse that ever ran in Australia was a greater idol with the public than Carbine, and the pier was crowded with his admirers long before the boat sailed.

When we cast off from Sandridge Pier there was a mighty burst of cheering, and cries of 'Carbine' rent the air. I was near the horse's box at the time with Mr Day, and 'Old Jack' pricked up his ears and raised his splendid head at the sound, as though he fancied there was another race to be run.

A beautiful wreath was sent on board for Carbine. It was in the shape of a horseshoe, and had Donald Wallace's colours on, and written on a card attached to it, 'For dear old Carbine; bon voyage.' Had Carbine got hold of that wreath, I am afraid he would have made short work of it.

Mr Day had several chats with me during the voyage. He is a most entertaining man, and had travelled all over the world in charge of horses. He even took a consignment of horses to India for the Ameer of Afghanistan, and safely conveyed them through the famous Khyber Pass. One morning I went with Mr Day to see Carbine have his breakfast. I pulled a few stalks of green clover out of the bundle and put them between my teeth. 'Old Jack' put his nose between the bars and took them as gently as though he had been my particular pal all his life. I never saw such a quiet, docile stallion, and throughout the voyage the horse behaved splendidly.

At Colombo Carbine had a narrow escape. He was very ill, and Mr Day had to perform an operation on him, which he did successfully, and no man could have paid more attention to the horse than he did. Cunningham held the horse's head during the operation, and Mr Day happening to look up saw blood running down his sleeve. On asking what was the matter, Cunningham said, 'Oh nothing; Old Jack had a bite at my arm.' No wonder, with two such attendants and on board a steady boat as the *Orizaba* undoubtedly is, Carbine should have arrived safely.

At Welbeck, which is also home to the great St Simon, Carbine will be mated with some of the best mares in the world, and he ought to get good stock from St Simon mares. I cannot conclude from this chapter in a more fitting manner than by quoting a portion of a letter I received from Mr W. Forrester after arriving back in England. Dated Warwick Farm, 6 May. He writes:

> So you are a mate of Carbine's. Notwithstanding my thinking him the greatest racehorse the world has ever seen, I wish he had never been foaled, for as you know he cut me out of £28,400 in the Melbourne Cup. Need I say what a surprise, as I thought I could not lose with Highborn carrying so little weight, but old Carbine, with his 10 stone 5 pounds, beat me badly.
>
> Had I won that day I feel sure I would have cleared £50,000 over the meeting, as there were Correze and Muriel in the VRC and Free Handicaps that I looked upon as the best of good things, but I was in hobbles and, without a stake, could not have a dash.
>
> If my mare Rosary has a colt foal by the old horse it may be a second Carbine and I am glad to tell you she is in foal to him, and should it face the starter it will be known as Fatal Bullet.
>
> I have not the slightest doubt he will do well with the Duke of Portland's mares if they give him plenty of work and do not keep him stalled up and keep the shoes off him as much as possible. Most of a stallion's trouble in old age is with the feet, caused by being continually shod. We let them live down here without shoes on. Why not in old England?

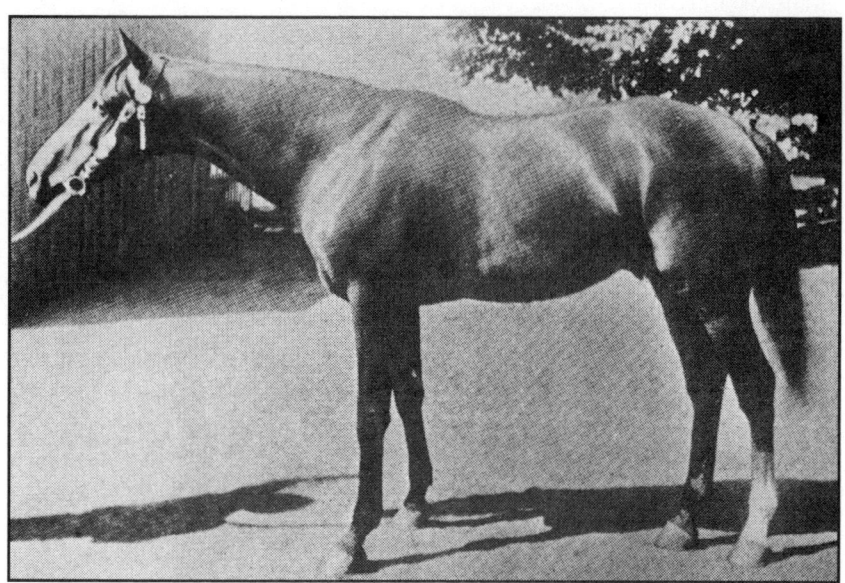

Carbine '... the greatest racehorse the world has ever seen.'

Carbine stood four seasons at stud in Victoria and sired the winners of 203 races in Australia. His first crop included Wallace, who won the Caulfield Guineas, VRC Derby, C. B. Fisher Plate, Sydney Cup and more before retiring to stud himself to sire the winners of 949 races, including two Melbourne Cup winners in Kingsburgh and Patrobas, the great stayer Trafalgar and seven Derby winners.

Carbine also sired Amberlite, who became, in 1897, the first horse to win the Caulfield Cup, AJC Derby and VRC Derby in the same year.

His owner, Donald Wallace, who had made his money in the Broken Hill mineral boom, fell upon hard financial times in the 1890s and Carbine was sold to the Duke of Portland for thirteen thousand pounds, to stand with the great St Simon at the Duke of Portland's stud at Welbeck Abbey. It was thought that he would be a perfect outcross to St Simon's female progeny as St Simon was highly strung and Carbine was placid.

Carbine's son Spearmint won the English Derby in 1906 and went on at stud to sire the dam of the great sire Nearco. Carbine's blood ran in the veins of both Northern Dancer and Star Kingdom and he can be found in the pedigrees of over fifty Melbourne Cup winners.

As Spearmint was the sire of Sentiment, the dam of Nightraid who sired Phar Lap ... the Red Terror was also Carbine's great-great-grandson.

O FOR OCTAGONAL

Jim Haynes

You hear blokes talk of champions, you see 'em come and go,
A real champ maybe comes along each twenty years or so.
I've read of Phar Lap and Carbine, those legends of the past,
And I saw Tulloch and Gunsynd and they were tough and fast,
Kingston Town was brilliant, so strong the mare Sunline,
But for true fighting spirit there was just one champ for mine!
No champion that ever strode the turf could make me feel
The way I felt about that gallant brown son of Zabeel.

O for Octagonal to be racing once again,
O for Octagonal, on him you could depend,
He never gave up trying, he'd stick right to the end,
O for Octagonal, he was the punter's friend.

'*... true fighting spirit ...*' Octagonal passes Saintly and Filante, with
Nothin' Leica Dane in background, to win the 1996 AJC Derby

Derby Day in '96 you should have heard the cheers,
From the biggest crowd the Randwick track had seen for
    thirty years.
With Saintly, Nothing Leica Dane, Filante down the straight,
I won't see another race like that, however long I wait.
It was true grit and courage that wore the others down,
His will to win that drove him on to take the triple crown.
His stamina unparalleled, his action was sublime,
Oh what I'd give to see old 'Ocky' race just one more time!

O for Octagonal to be racing once again,
O for Octagonal, on him you could depend,
He never gave up trying, he'd stick right to the end,
O for Octagonal, he was the punter's friend.

SNOW STAR

J. C. Bendrodt

He had a fabulous speed that horsemen marvelled at.

He held in this matchless body the key to fortune race-folk dream about. I have stood sometimes watching him canter away from me along a bright-green track down which I knew that, in a little while, he would return with his legs like pistons hurling his silver body forward in that fantastic speed that was his hallmark. With his wide nostrils flaring and his black-tipped ears pricked, and his brown eyes laughing at me as he flashed past. And after a bit, as I'd watch him trot towards me, centuries rolled back and there was a narrow street down which, between ranks of genuflecting people, a warrior king rode home amid a gorgeous cavalcade.

There was the flash of jewels, the high clear call the bugles make, the clash of cymbals, and a great grey horse the warrior rode upon. A silver horse with flaming jewels in his headband, and golden fretwork in the crimson bridle that framed his great dark eyes. Then the picture faded until there was only a grey horse left, and I knew it was Snow Star coming home.

And there were so many other dreams built on the flawless courage, the matchless speed this horse possessed. Dreams that began to become realities when the crowds called his name in triumph as he came cantering back towards the judge's box. Dreams that went west as I saw him limp as he trotted in.

I remember that they crowded round me with congratulations and lavish praise for him, and I think my face was still and hard because there was a cold, drear ache in my heart that wouldn't let me smile, though I tried to.

And then I took him home, and when it was quiet and no one watched me, I took his foreleg firmly between my fingers and ran them down the ligaments, and he gave a little gasp and held his leg up as a dog will hold an injured paw.

I looked up, and his wide eyes pleaded with me not to hurt him, and I said, 'So that's it, boy!'

I knew that in the morning his name would flame in headlines in the words they use to tell of coming champions. I knew that after that they would speak of him just once again – when they announced that he was finished. A crippled horse! Broken by the blazing speed that was his heritage.

I remember that in a little while I stood up, and years seemed to have passed by since I'd bent to examine that near foreleg. It seemed then that time laid a hand upon my shoulder, gentle but inexorable – you waited twenty years for him!

Then I went to his stable door and he put his muzzle on my shoulder while we looked out into the quiet night and watched our dreams die – one by one.

Nowadays when the sun is setting behind the quiet mountains that gird his home, he will stand, with his coat a glistening snow-and-silver foil, against their darkening background. With his soft eyes, that still have the look of eagles in them, watching the day go out in a flame of glory.

And as I study him I can see the kings again and the cavalcades, the flash of jewels. I can hear the clash of cymbals and the high clear call the bugles make.

And then it is night, but in the dusk I can still see that snow-and-silver figure. Then I'll call him and he will come to me, and in the darkness I can't see his crippled leg, and the sound of his steps on the emerald turf are like the beat of a metronome, because he isn't lame – when he walks.

He will always put his head down when he reaches me so that my fingers can play over the snowy plain between his eyes, and then in the quiet night it seems to me that he's trying to say, 'I'm sorry, boss.'

But dreams are hard to kill. Perhaps in men growing older dreams are all that are left. I couldn't tell you. But sometimes I sit, when a silver moon rides in a snowy bank of clouds against a background filled with stars, and a mare idles where the soft green grass is short and sweet, and there is a little figure at her side that is as snowy as the clouds are, and as silver as the moon above that watches him, and his legs are strong, and flat, and true.

It is then that the kings and warriors ride again. There are the heralds with their trumpets. There is a racehorse greater than them all. In these dreams I call him Snow Star's son.

OLD PARDON, THE SON OF REPRIEVE

A. B. ('Banjo') Paterson

You never heard tell of the story?
Well, now, I can hardly believe!
Never heard of the honour and glory
Of Pardon, the son of Reprieve?
But maybe you're only a Johnnie
And don't know a horse from a hoe?
Well, well, don't get angry, my sonny,
But, really, a young 'un should know.

They bred him out back on the 'Never',
His mother was Mameluke breed.
To the front – and then stay there – was ever
The root of the Mameluke creed.
He seemed to inherit their wiry
Strong frames – and their pluck to receive –
As hard as a flint and as fiery
Was Pardon, the son of Reprieve.

We ran him at many a meeting
At crossing and gully and town,
And nothing could give him a beating –
At least when our money was down.
For weight wouldn't stop him, nor distance,
Nor odds, though the others were fast,
He'd race with a dogged persistence,
And wear them all down at the last.

At the Turon the Yattendon filly
Led by lengths at the mile and a half,
And we all began to look silly,

While her crowd were starting to laugh;
But the old horse came faster and faster,
His pluck told its tale, and his strength,
He gained on her, caught her, and passed her,
And won it, hands-down, by a length.

And then we swooped down on Menindie
To run for the President's Cup –
Oh! that's a sweet township – a shindy
To them is board, lodging, and sup.
Eye-openers they are, and their system
Is never to suffer defeat;
It's 'win, tie, or wrangle' – to best 'em
You must lose 'em, or else it's 'dead heat'.

We strolled down the township and found 'em
At drinking and gaming and play;
If sorrows they had, why they drowned 'em,
And betting was soon under way.
Their horses were good 'uns and fit 'uns,
There was plenty of cash in the town;
They backed their own horses like Britons,
And, Lord! How we rattled it down!

With gladness we thought of the morrow,
We counted our wagers with glee,
A simile homely to borrow –
'There was plenty of milk in our tea.'
You see we were green; and we never
Had even a thought of foul play,
Though we well might have known that the clever
Division would 'put us away'.

Experience docet, they tell us,
At least so I've frequently heard,
But, 'dosing' or 'stuffing', those fellows

Were up to each move on the board:
They got to his stall – it is sinful
To think what such villains would do –
And they gave him a regular skinful
Of barley – green barley – to chew.

He munched it all night, and we found him
Next morning as full as a hog –
The girths wouldn't nearly meet round him;
He looked like an overfed frog.
We saw we were done like a dinner –
The odds were a thousand to one
Against Pardon turning up winner,
'Twas cruel to ask him to run.

We got to the course with our troubles,
A crestfallen couple were we;
And we heard the 'books' calling the doubles –
A roar like the surf of the sea;
And over the tumult and louder
Rang 'Any price Pardon, I lay!'
Says Jimmy, 'The children of Judah
Are out on the warpath today.'

Three miles in three heats – ah, my sonny,
The horses in those days were stout,
They had to run well to win money;
I don't see such horses about.
Your six-furlong vermin that scamper
Half a mile with their feather-weight up;
They wouldn't earn much of their damper
In a race like the President's Cup.

The first heat was soon set a-going;
The Dancer went off to the front;
The Don on his quarters was showing,

With Pardon right out of the hunt.
He rolled and he weltered and wallowed –
You'd kick your hat faster, I'll bet;
They finished all bunched, and he followed
All lathered and dripping with sweat.

But troubles came thicker upon us,
For while we were rubbing him dry
The stewards came over to warn us:
'We hear you are running a bye!
If Pardon don't spiel like tarnation
And win the next heat – if he can –
He'll earn a disqualification;
Just think over that, now, my man!'

Our money all gone and our credit,
Our horse couldn't gallop a yard;
And then people thought that we did it!
It really was terribly hard.
We were objects of mirth and derision
To folk in the lawn and the stand,
And the yells of the clever division
Of 'Any price Pardon!' were grand.

We still had a chance for the money,
Two heats still remained to be run;
If both fell to us – why, my sonny,
The clever division were done.
And Pardon was better, we reckoned,
His sickness was passing away,
So he went to the post for the second
And principal heat of the day.

They're off and away with a rattle,
Like dogs from the leashes let slip,
And right at the back of the battle

He followed them under the whip.
They gained ten good lengths on him quickly
He dropped right away from the pack;
I tell you it made me feel sickly
To see the blue jacket fall back.

Our very last hope had departed –
We thought the old fellow was done,
When all of a sudden he started
To go like a shot from a gun.
His chances seemed slight to embolden
Our hearts; but, with teeth firmly set,
We thought, 'Now or never! The old 'un
May reckon with some of 'em yet.'

Then loud rose the war-cry for Pardon;
He swept like the wind down the dip,
And over the rise by the garden,
The jockey was done with the whip
The field were at sixes and sevens –
The pace at the first had been fast –
And hope seemed to drop from the heavens,
For Pardon was coming at last.

And how he did come! It was splendid;
He gained on them yards every bound,
Stretching out like a greyhound extended,
His girth laid right down on the ground.
A shimmer of silk in the cedars
As into the running they wheeled,
And out flashed the whips on the leaders,
For Pardon had collared the field.

Then right through the ruck he came sailing –
I knew that the battle was won –
The son of Haphazard was failing,

The Yattendon filly was done;
He cut down the Don and the Dancer,
He raced clean away from the mare –
He's in front! Catch him now if you can, sir!
And up went my hat in the air!

Then loud from the lawn and the garden
Rose offers of 'Ten to one on!'
'Who'll bet on the field? I back Pardon!'
No use; all the money was gone.
He came for the third heat light-hearted,
A-jumping and dancing about;
The others were done ere they started
Crestfallen, and tired, and worn out.

He won it, and ran it much faster
Than even the first, I believe;
Oh, he was the daddy, the master,
Was Pardon, the son of Reprieve.
He showed 'em the method to travel –
The boy sat as still as a stone –
They never could see him for gravel;
He came in hard-held, and alone.

But he's old – and his eyes are grown hollow;
Like me, with my thatch of the snow;
When he dies, then I hope I may follow,
And go where the racehorses go.
I don't want no harping nor singing –
Such things with my style don't agree;
Where the hoofs of the horses are ringing
There's music sufficient for me.

And surely the thoroughbred horses
Will rise up again and begin
Fresh races on far-away courses,

And p'raps they might let me slip in.
It would look rather well the race-card on
'Mongst Cherubs and Seraphs and things,
'Angel Harrison's black gelding Pardon,
Blue halo, white body and wings.'

And if they have racing hereafter,
(And who is to say they will not?)
When the cheers and the shouting and laughter
Proclaim that the battle grows hot;
As they come down the racecourse a-steering,
He'll rush to the front, I believe;
And you'll hear the great multitude cheering
For Pardon, the son of Reprieve.

BEING THERE

Jim Haynes

Memories are unreliable.

The way you remember an event often differs from the reality. You find an old photo and realise you have had the wrong memory of a certain event all along.

You tell a great story and someone who was there says, 'No, it wasn't like that, the favourite was a bay, not a chestnut, and he didn't come along the rail, he came around the field and won easily.'

It's also true that the significant part of an event in your memory may not be the important part historically. You may remember how good the apple pie was at lunch and not remember who won the main race.

It's no good asking your wife, but you do anyway. 'Who won the Metropolitan that year we had lunch in the members with the Johnsons?'

'That grey horse with the funny name with a zed in it ran third that year,' she replies. 'It had green-and-pink silks and Emily Johnson wore that black-and-white empire-line dress and a red hat ... don't know who won ... sorry. I can't remember anything that far back, darling.'

Just how vivid a racing memory is often depends on where your money was at the time.

I have amazingly sharp memories of an old Tamworth-trained, mid-week horse named Mr Mohican winning the last race at Warwick Farm one day when I managed to get twenty to one in the ring from Eric Conlon and also took a box trifecta with the two favourites who dutifully finished second and third. I can see the finish of that race as clearly as I can see my desk and computer right now. I have no idea what year that was though.

Some of the memories that follow in this story go back over forty years and I wouldn't bet my house on them, but they're very real to me.

I've been lucky enough to be present to see some memorable stoushes down the straight at some great racetracks. So I thought I'd test my memory and come up with my top ten, purely subjective, 'battles down the straight'.

Everyone loves a 'countdown' so these are in some sort of order, although so much depends on how distant the memories are, and my mood at the time of recalling them.

Naturally I can't include any races I merely heard on the radio or watched on television. You actually see a lot more on television than when you're on the course, but this is all about being there.

So, here we go, they're off.

Ten

My number ten memory of a battle in the straight is a distant recall from childhood. It's a memory of seeing Tulloch carry sixty-three kilograms up the rise and down the Randwick straight to gallant defeat behind Sharply, carrying 48.5 kilograms, in the 1961 Sydney Cup.

I'm not sure exactly how the struggle unfolded that day but I have a memory of it tucked away in my cerebellum somewhere and I don't want to see the footage of the race; it may not match the way I remember it.

'... *a memory of seeing Tulloch ...*'

Handicaps can be cruel to champions, and nobody who roared for Tulloch that day at Randwick loved him any less when he failed to catch Sharply. It was a fairly sombre crowd after the race though, I remember that, or perhaps it was just that my dad wasn't saying much.

Nine

Randwick is a track that really sorts out the champs from the pretenders down the straight. True front-runners have to be great horses to hold on up the rise, and it takes a great horse to come from behind up that rise and pass another good one.

What you see, more often than a grinding nose-to-nose struggle at Randwick, is a brave front-runner holding on to a lead while a good swooper attempts to run it down. When you do get real nose-to-nose 'knock 'em down, drag 'em out' stoushes at Randwick you tend to remember them.

Which brings us to the next of my top ten 'battles down the straight', Sunline's second Doncaster in 2002. To this day I swear Shogun Lodge won that race. It was certainly a dead heat on the grounds of sheer guts and grit. They raced side by side for two entire furlongs that day. I still can't believe you could get five to one on Sunline in the ring when they jumped. And I still can't believe I didn't take it!

Eight

I have agonised about my next choice. I feel I am cheating with this one because it wasn't really a 'battle down the straight' so much as an act of unbelievable choreography.

Anyway, as I'm making the rules here, I am going to throw in Private Steer's 2004 Doncaster victory as my number eight, although it was really a match race between one amazing horse and the rest of the field.

I can't even remember what I backed to beat her but I distinctly remember being mesmerised as Glen Boss began to weave his way through the entire field. It was like watching the horseracing equivalent of a giant slalom.

They were as good as last on the turn and had no hope, not a hope in the world. Then, as they straightened, Glen Boss just picked her up and balanced her and she sidestepped her way through like a rugby winger against a tiring pack of forwards.

Boss didn't go near the rails and he didn't go around the field. Time seemed to slip into slow motion as I watched Private Steer come down the straight. I remember seeing the dark-blue jacket with the lightning bolt move through the crowd of horses as if it was all being stage-managed by the best stunt director in Hollywood.

The result was never in doubt once the dance began; she moved right through the field and put out her head and won. I was waiting for the pirouette at the end.

It was beautiful to watch. It gave new meaning to the cliché 'poetry in motion'. It was enough to make a grown man cry. In fact it did make a grown man cry. Private Steer's big burly owner, after

'... one amazing horse ...' Glen Boss on Private Steer after she won the 2004 Doncaster

whose grandmother she was named, cried at the presentation and I went a little teary myself; I hadn't backed her.

My own stupidity on the punt often brings tears to my eyes. Private Steer would have won the Miracle Mile at Harold Park if they'd held it that autumn and she'd started in it. I should have known that.

Seven

Rewind my memory-bank tapes now, back twenty years, to Aintree in 1984.

It was my only first-hand experience of the famous English Grand National, a race I'd watched every year from childhood on the newsreels and television, ever since I saw Elizabeth Taylor ride the winner in the movie *National Velvet*, at the old Empire Picture Palace.

Being there is always worth the trip, and the crowd and the excitement of the day itself make such experiences worthwhile, even though you don't see much in a huge crowd at an event like the Grand National or the Melbourne Cup. But, at least you can say you've been there.

Here's another strange quirk of memory: I remember the winner of the first steeplechase on the programme that day, because I backed it due to its name, Little Bay. It was probably a simple descriptive name, but to me it was the name of a Sydney beach, and it was my only winner all day.

I watched the Grand National from a position at the top of the straight, just down from the elbow, which really marks the start of the run in, and opposite The Chair. The Chair is the fifteenth of thirty jumps and the tallest and broadest fence on the course, at five feet two inches. It also has a six-foot-wide ditch on the take-off side.

You get good value watching a Grand National at Aintree. You actually get to see two very different 'battles down the straight'.

On the first circuit of the two-and-a-quarter-mile course the horses jump The Chair and the Water Jump in the straight. On the second circuit these two fences are not jumped and the horses take the last fence just before the elbow and then face an almost five-hundred-yard run to the line.

You can't really understand the incredible rush that comes from seeing a field of forty horses take a jump like The Chair unless you have experienced it. The sound of the horses landing and galloping on from the fence is unforgettable.

The sense of impending chaos and the absolute craziness of what is being attempted, and the courage of the men and horses attempting it, bring a lump to the throat and an adrenalin rush to the spectator that verges on the primeval.

On the second circuit a bunch of some half-a-dozen horses were still in it as they passed my vantage point so there were still many chances on the run in, and to see those brave jumpers, still going hard down the straight after four miles, was a stirring sight.

The leading bunch fighting it out down the straight included the previous year's winner, Corbiere, and the runner up from the previous year, and favourite at nine to one, Greasepaint.

Greasepaint tired on the run in and was eventually beaten by four lengths that day by Hallo Dandy, ridden by Neale Doughty and trained by the great Gordon Richards. Corbiere was third.

'The sound of the horses landing and galloping on from the fence is unforgettable' Eventual winner, Hallo Dandy (No 28), races away from The Chair in the 1984 Grand National

Greasepaint was to be unlucky in the Grand National. He started favourite the following year also, and finished a brave fourth behind Last Suspect, Mr Snugfit and Corbiere, who added another third to his win in 1983 and his third in 1984.

Greasepaint was owned by an Irishman named Michael Smurfit and trained by another Irishman named Dermot Weld. I'd never heard of either of them until 1984, and most Aussies hadn't heard of either of them until nine years later, when Vintage Crop, owned and trained by the same two men, won the Melbourne Cup carrying the same colours that Greasepaint carried that winter day at Aintree.

There's really nothing like Aintree on Grand National day. It's one of those special sporting events like the FA Cup, or the Melbourne Cup, or the Kentucky Derby, or Wimbledon, or the AFL Grand Final: unique events where the actual experience is more important than the result.

Six

If it's unique atmosphere you're after, an event where the experience outweighs the result, may I suggest an Easter visit to Oakbank, in the Adelaide Hills, for the Great Eastern Steeplechase.

You won't be lonely if you visit Oakbank at Easter; about fifty thousand others usually do the same thing.

Many camp for the entire weekend or longer at various vantage points around the track. Others make the day trip to the track and fill the lovely old stands and lawns of the picturesque course.

This event combines the elements of a rural show, fairground, picnic race day and family camping trip into one glorious weekend of fun. Oh yes, and there are horseraces too. In fact, there are several horseraces that are a real blast from the past. At Oakbank you get a glimpse of a bygone age when real horses raced over proper fences in the type of races that Adam Lindsay Gordon wrote about and rode in.

Australian steeplechasers are not as valued and followed and well known to the racing public as their English and Irish counterparts, who have the whole winter racing season to themselves. Still, you can't doubt the courage and character of horses that run in a race like the Great Eastern. These are horses to be admired and remembered.

Australian steeplechasers are often tough old stayers, failures and rejects from flat racing with more endurance in their legs than speed. After a few often less-than-memorable seasons racing on the flat, some have the strength, disposition and character to train on for a jumping career. Without this option, these horses would not have a future. Other horses just love to jump and are born to hurdle and steeplechase.

In those states that still stage jumps races in Australia (the southern states of Victoria, Tasmania and South Australia), hurdles and steeplechases are seen by many as a winter sideshow to each race day, with one or two jumping races on each programme through the colder, wetter months.

The Great Eastern is no sideshow to a race day, although the centre of the course is itself a sideshow alley with rides, carnival attractions and fairy floss for kids of all ages. The Great Eastern is the centrepiece of the whole weekend, the reason we're all there.

The Von Doussa Steeple on Easter Saturday and the Great Eastern on Easter Monday are classic races of a kind now almost gone from the calendar. The course at Oakbank is so long and undulating that two race-callers are required to view the whole racetrack and call the races using a tag-team system.

The Great Eastern features twice in my top ten 'battles down the straight'. Here, in position number six, is a memory of the 1973 event in which the local hero was a black horse called The Cent and the Victorian interloper was a tough grey horse, almost white in fact, called Mystic Moon.

For most of the crowd it really was a case of black and white that year. South Australians don't take kindly to Victorian 'raiders' and The Cent was favourite both in the ring and in the hearts of the majority.

Mystic Moon had won important races in Victoria and, according to many locals, should have stayed there and won some more instead of spoiling a good weekend for South Australian horses.

Now, the Great Eastern, like the Grand National, is not for the faint-hearted.

Horses in the Great Eastern actually pass the winning post three times in their five-kilometre trip. So imagine the exhilaration and excitement that gripped the crowd that day in 1973 when the black horse and the grey horse came neck-and-neck down the straight the third time.

The horses jump a fallen log on a rise above the grandstand area and then race down a long sweeping hill to the straight and the winning post.

Over the fallen log they came, the brave grey and the big local jet-black horse.

Down the hill and along the straight they fought side by side. The roar of the crowd was deafening in the shallow valley where the grandstands, lawn and finish are situated. The tiring horses bumped and fought all the way to the post. The roar of the crowd told you The Cent had won before the judge's cursory glance at the photo confirmed the decision, a short neck.

'... the brave grey and the big local jet-black horse.' The Cent leads Mystic Moon over the last jump at Oakbank, 1973

The local horse was welcomed back with rapturous applause and rousing cheers, but the protest flag was soon flying and it took stewards a long time to dismiss the Victorian protest.

As a New South Welshman and a man who has never managed to back a horse that finished a Great Eastern, let alone won one, I was a truly neutral observer. And I must admit I felt rather sorry for the gallant grey that tried so hard so far from home with so few friends.

South Australians are a loyal lot, and they never forgot the big black horse that defeated the Victorian champ. When The Cent died years later they buried him near the winning post at Oakbank. Fifty thousand people visit his grave every Easter.

Five

Flemington is the classic course for long drawn-out nose-to-nose battles; the long straight there probably produces more of the 'war of attrition'-type finishes than anywhere else in Australia.

My top Flemington memory of a battle down the straight, however, doesn't involve a nose-to-nose tussle.

It was the Melbourne Cup, 1994. Vintage Crop was favourite but was under an injury cloud. The Caulfield Cup winner Paris Lane was also well backed and I fancied a chestnut mare by El Qahira: her name was Alcove and she had won the Oaks at Randwick in the autumn.

It was a typical Melbourne day with drizzle and grey skies for an hour or so followed by pleasant spring sunshine for a while.

I quite like Melbourne but I always lose coats, scarves, pullovers and umbrellas when I'm there. You take clothes off and put them on so often in Melbourne, due to the changeable weather, that I tend to leave a trail of lost property in cabs and restaurants and trams.

The usual loonies, drunks and show-offs were in evidence on Cup Day 1994. I saw at least three different Elvises, a few Batman and Robin combinations, a Phantom or two and, in spite of the cool weather, there were even a few pink tooth fairies about.

I have to admit that I am not a fan of Cup Day on the course: I like racing too much and the holiday revelry gets in the way of my enjoyment. It's one day when I am quite happy to watch the race on television.

Having had a good look at the previous year's winner, that wonderful Irish stayer Vintage Crop, in the exercise yard, I decided the excessive bandaging looked rather ominous, and I plonked heavily on Alcove.

As it turned out Vintage Crop could have won his second Cup that day. The injury didn't seem to worry him and was obviously superficial; perhaps Dermot Weld was up to his usual tricks, talking down the champion's chances.

What stopped Vintage Crop winning was an eccentric ride by Michael Kinnane. Having vainly attempted to push him across to the rail early, the jockey let him race wide for the entire two miles. His effort to finish seventh, carrying sixty kilograms and having covered about an extra furlong in distance, was really quite courageous.

I was standing at the rail about two furlongs out and my memory of the battle down the straight that day is extremely vivid. I have a snapshot of one split second of that race etched in my memory, a colour photograph of one exact moment.

You hear commentators talk every year about the 'wall of horses' as the Cup field swings the corner and straightens for the run in. But to experience that sight first-hand gives meaning to the cliché whenever you hear it afterwards.

The leading bunch seemed to include at least half the field as they thundered past my position. The ground shook and the roar of the crowd, deafening since the jump, reached a painful level of intensity.

At the exact moment when that 'wall of horses' passed my position Alcove put her head in front of the field. I saw Paddy Payne, in the blue and white striped silks, drive her to the lead. Her eyes were wide and her nostrils flared as her chestnut head stretched out. I saw it all in incredible detail and I can still see it clearly now in my mind's eye.

I also had time, somehow, to notice that her bandages were unravelled and discoloured with blood and mud. Then the horses were gone, out of frame.

Jeune outstayed them all to defeat Paris Lane by a length and three-quarters. This came as a surprise to many, including me, who thought the imported stallion was best over a middle distance.

Alcove had been galloped on in the middle stages and ran a brave race to finish fifth.

Four

The best nose-to-nose tussle I ever saw in Melbourne occurred at Caulfield, a track for which I have a particular fondness. The position of the comfortable all-weather grandstand at Caulfield seems to provide a better view than just about anywhere else for watching horses race all the way down the straight.

The Yalumba Stakes of 2002 was a match race between two large and athletic champions in Sunline and Lonhro, with a few other lesser lights making up the numbers. The huge mare was approaching the end of her career while Lonhro was nearing his peak.

Trevor McKee, owner of Sunline, and the Ingham brothers, who owned Lonhro, rate as true enthusiasts and lovers of racing. It is to the credit of McKee that Sunline raced on as a mare to give us all so many wonderful memories. The McKee motto was always, 'we're here to race'.

Mind you, Sunline was as strong and robust a beast as you would ever wish to see. She towered over most of her male counterparts and never looked as if her femininity was likely to lead to any frailty, weakness or delicacy of disposition.

The Inghams were also great believers in racing horses while they were still fit and willing to race. I will never forget Jack Ingham's answer to a question put to him after Lonhro's sire, Octagonal, had won his second Mercedes Classic and broken the stakes winning record.

The reporter asked Jack why he was going to risk running the champion again in the Queen Elizabeth Stakes when he had absolutely nothing to prove and was worth many millions as a stallion. Jack simply looked the reporter in the eye and asked him, 'Don't *you* want to see him race again?'

On Yalumba Stakes Day 2002 the crowd in the members' area mostly fancied Sunline. Not many of us seemed to be supporting Lonhro, just the Ingham family and a few others who had strayed south of the border for the spring racing.

Lonhro's greatest victory was to come eighteen months later when he picked himself up after being checked twice in the straight at Flemington and ran down a good three-year-old in Delzao to win the Australian Cup.

Lonhro was big and strong and a beautiful-looking horse. In the Australian Cup of 2004 and the Yalumba Stakes of 2002 he proved that he had also inherited his sire's incredible will to win.

He moved to the outside of Sunline as they rounded the big tight home bend at Caulfield and was a half-length behind her when they straightened.

It appeared that Darren Beadman knew his mount was a metre faster per furlong on a straight run at weight-for-age. He rode Lonhro out steadily and they made ground on the great mare almost imperceptibly, centimetre by centimetre.

One split second of lost focus or loss of belief by either horse or jockey and the race would have been over, but neither cracked.

I never forgave myself for not backing Sunline six months earlier in the Doncaster, but at least I had the good sense to back Lonhro to beat her that day at Caulfield.

'At the post it was a clear neck victory to the big brown stallion' Lonhro defeats Sunline in the 2002 Yalumba Stakes at Caulfield

At the post it was a clear neck victory to the big brown stallion carrying the famous cerise colours.

Three

The victor in the next epic from my memory bank carried the same famous colours.

The track was Rosehill and it was Golden Slipper Day, 2003.

The great West Australian champion Northerly had never had much luck in Sydney but at weight-for-age against a depleted and pretty ordinary field, he was red-hot favourite to win the Mercedes Classic. It was a matter of 'how far' in most race-goers' minds.

The Mercedes that year was looked upon as a mere appetiser for the Slipper. It would be a chance for Sydney to see the great Northerly going through the motions in a group one event.

It was a chance to salute a champion, an added attraction to the big dash-for-cash by the over-developed babies later in the afternoon.

The problem was that nobody had explained all that to a tough old stayer called Freemason.

Freemason was a real character. A bay gelding by Grand Lodge, he had won the Queensland Derby and the Frank Packer Plate way back in 2000. Since then he had contested most staying events in Sydney and seemed to make a habit of running a place when he started at huge odds, but running nowhere whenever he was fancied.

I made a habit of backing Freemason for a place whenever he got out past twenty-to-one in the betting; the longer the odds the better I fancied his chances. To be honest, I should say that, along with most others, I assumed the Mercedes would be a training gallop for Northerly. Still, I would probably have backed Freemason if I hadn't been playing host to a couple of female friends that day.

Having to be civil and attentive to women at the races is never conducive to backing winners and, whatever the reason, I didn't check Freemason's price and I didn't have a bet.

But I am wandering off topic. This is a list of memories of great races. The list that comprises my memories of lost chances on the punt is much longer.

To return to the story at hand, it appears that Freemason was in the mood to race that day. In fact he seemed so disgusted at the false pace early in the race that he took the lead, which he rarely did. When Northerly came alongside in the back straight, Freemason pushed down his accelerator and decided to take the champ on, almost 1400 metres from home.

The battle that resulted from this has its own unique category in my memory. It was the only time I ever witnessed a nose-to-nose, full-on, no-holds-barred, flat-out, ding-dong stoush for the entire final 1200 metres of a race.

The sheer audacity of Freemason's mad challenge when Northerly came alongside seemed to win the crowd over to support the old Sydney stayer.

After all, he was a local horse and his lack of respect for the interstate hero seemed somehow courageous. Stupid, bound to end in embarrassment, a mere *beau geste* ... but courageous all the same.

'Freemason, racing on the inside, refused to let Northerly past ...'
The 2003 BMW Classic finish

Once Northerly responded to the challenge the two horses just kept daring each other to go faster and faster. By the one thousand-metre point the crowd sensed something weird and wonderful was going on. By the four hundred-metre mark the crowd was in a frenzy. When would this crazy old horse realise he wasn't as good as Northerly?

The answer was … never.

Freemason, racing on the inside, refused to let Northerly past and there was never more than a neck between them over the final 1200 metres. They raced past the post locked together and a photo showed that Freemason had won by a short half-head in the brilliant time of 2 minutes 26.82 seconds for two thousand metres.

Punters and race-goers usually think through their pockets, but sometimes they respond with their hearts when magic occurs. Unwanted in the betting-ring, Freemason was cheered again and again as he returned to scale carrying the colours of a couple of other Aussie battlers, Jack and Bob Ingham.

Two

Those cerise colours seem to feature rather a lot in my greatest racing memories; the winner of the next memorable event also carried them.

When it comes to racing on the flat, this memory is furlongs ahead of all others. It's the unforgettable encounter of four great three-year-olds, Nothin' Leica Dane, Saintly, Filante and Octagonal, in the 1996 AJC Derby at Randwick.

That race really turned the tide for racing in Sydney; people came out in huge numbers in anticipation of the best Derby for years. They got far more than their money's worth that day and it seems to me that racing crowds have been on the increase in Sydney ever since. I reckon that race did it for racing in Sydney; it made racing more than just a form of betting in the public's mind. It made racing a spectator sport once again.

You couldn't get a seat in the stands. The atmosphere was electric. It was the biggest crowd for thirty years and the race lived up to all hype and expectations. In fact, it surpassed anything you could have made up.

The best crop of three-year-olds in years staged a monumental four-way battle. Up the famous rise and down the straight they came, racing nose-to-nose, the VRC Derby winner, a future Cox Plate and Melbourne Cup winner, a future Epsom and Yalumba Stakes winner, all three of them at their peak and flat out trying to stay ahead, or get ahead, of one of the toughest and bravest horses to ever race in Australia.

How Octagonal fought on to win that race is a worthy part of Australian racing folklore. He seemed to race quite low to the ground when he let down and he just ground away, a dark-brown nemesis slowly overhauling the two big chestnut horses on his inside with his neck extended the way it always was, to get his nose to the post first. It was as if he knew where the camera was.

It was inspiring to watch that courage in motion.

I took my dad to the races to see Octagonal's Derby. Dad was pretty old by then and getting a bit frail, but it was only fair. After all, he had taken me to see Tulloch's great attempt to win the Sydney Cup in 1961 with sixty-three kilograms on his back.

I never saw a better contested finish to a race in my life and I never saw a horse with more will to win than Octagonal. I backed him that day too.

What could possibly top the Derby of 1996 as a fighting finish? Not much in my opinion, but I have one memory of a battle down the straight that beats it.

One

It was Oakbank again, 1978. A small field for the Great Eastern that year, as the track was quite heavy and the weather was wet over Easter.

The atmosphere was a little dampened and the ground was soggy underfoot but it was still Oakbank, the great Easter Carnival in the Adelaide Hills. You know about the Oakbank atmosphere already, because the great tussle between Mystic Moon and The Cent was an earlier memory in this countdown.

In 1978 most of the already small field either fell or retired. Oddly enough it was mostly the front-runners who fell or dropped out.

Of those left standing towards the end, three were way back in the field and one, a tough little chestnut gelding with the totally appropriate name of Roughneck, ridden by Pat Hely, was left way out in front.

Now, you might think, 'What a fizzer of a race. How can four horses scattered over a mile of racetrack with one half a mile in front be of any interest?'

You might think that.

You might also think these things demonstrate why jumps races hold little interest and are an anachronism.

You'd be wrong on both counts.

You might think, in a race like that, there's no real contest.

You'd be wrong again.

Unlike 1973 there was no cheering, no roaring of the crowd as Roughneck cleared the fallen log, came down the hill, entered the straight and approached the last two jumps.

There was just an uncanny quiet.

You see ... Roughneck was just about out on his feet. He was visibly exhausted and laying in badly.

At the second last he clipped the jump and almost went down, just about touching his nose on the turf. He regained his footing but staggered sideways as the entire crowd caught its breath. I'd never heard fifty thousand people catch their breath before. It was a sound that filled the valley.

Hely somehow got him balanced again and approached the last jump.

In those few seconds I truly came to believe in something akin to Jung's theory of the collective subconscious, or the power of prayer. Everyone watching was willing that little chestnut gelding to get over that last fence; you could feel it.

He steadied and approached the fence at a speed just fast enough to gain some momentum for a final jump.

Hely seemed to lift him by the reins and he rose to take the last fence ... and he cleared it, landed safely, and galloped on.

Then the crowd roared.

And that's the loudest roar I've ever heard on a racetrack anywhere in the world; it was a roar of relief and admiration. Then the crowd clapped. And they clapped until he cantered past the winning post.

No one had backed him. He was any old price.

The nearest horse wasn't even in the straight when he cleared the last jump. He won by forty lengths.

But I think that's the best battle down the straight that I ever saw.

Mind you, I could change my mind tomorrow. I'm relying on memory, and memories are unreliable.

'... *they clapped until he cantered past the winning post.' Roughneck wins the Great Eastern, 1978*

PART TWO

I'D MUCH SOONER GO TO THE RACES

Racing began in earnest in the new colony of New South Wales on 15 October 1810, when the officers of the 73rd Regiment organised a three-day race meeting in Hyde Park. Of course, there had been unofficial meetings before that and good Arab horses and racing stallions had been imported from America and India as early as 1802.

The records tell us that Captain Ritchie's grey gelding Chase won the very first race. The horses raced clockwise as the course design suited that direction due to the position of the sun in the afternoon. The finish line was about where Elizabeth and Market Streets meet today.

The three-day meeting caused massive drinking and rowdiness and a stray dog brought down D'Arcy Wentworth's good horse, Gig, during a race on the final day. All in all, however, the meeting was deemed to be a huge success and it became a part of the Sydney social calendar until 1814.

In 1814 the 73rd Regiment was transferred to Ceylon and the colony lost its race committee. Racing lapsed into unofficial match races and was banned for a time by Governor Macquarie until a brief revival at Hyde Park. This was followed by a further ban under Governor Brisbane.

In 1825 the Sydney Turf Club was formed and began racing at Captain Piper's racecourse at Bellevue Hill under the patronage of Governor Brisbane, who was happy to see some sort of organised racing replace the mayhem of unofficial meetings and dangerous races around the old dilapidated course at Hyde Park.

Colonial politics and posturing, followed by a public insult at an STC dinner, led to the next governor, Governor Darling, withdrawing his patronage from the STC in 1927. Twenty-nine members resigned in support of the governor and formed the Australian Racing and Jockey Club.

The STC held meetings at Camperdown and the ARJC raced at Parramatta. From 1832 to 1841 racing was conducted on cleared scrubland along the Botany Road. This track was called 'Randwick' but was a different course altogether from the one we know today.

In 1840, in an effort to establish a viable permanent racing calendar and due to the poor conditions of the racetracks in use, a group of leading lights in the colony formed the Australian Race Committee and set up a racetrack at Homebush. This group then decided to form a permanent race club, and the AJC was officially born in 1842. The Homebush track was used until the completion of the 'new' Randwick in 1860.

In Melbourne, racing started at Flemington in 1840 and, in 1848, three hundred and fifty acres were officially designated to be a public racecourse and a committee was set up to regulate racing.

Early meetings differed from today's racing in many ways. Often races were run in heats and most races were over quite long distances. Three heats of two miles was a common sort of racing event in the 1860s and 1870s. The same field raced each time and the results were averaged to find the winner.

The racing phrase 'at the distance' comes from this time. Many people think the phrase means 'at the turn' but it actually refers to a 'distance post', which was set up somewhere, usually in the straight about a furlong out, but not always. Horses who hadn't reached this point when the heat winner passed the winning post were 'distanced' and could not run in succeeding heats.

Many other things we take for granted as part of racing were missing from early race meetings. The AJC introduced colours in 1842 and saddlecloth numbers were not used until the 1870s.

Prior to that time horses involved in the finish would make their way to the judge's stand after a race and the judge would identify the place-getters by their registered racing colours and then announce his decision. The jockeys then went to weigh-in. Flag

'From the early colonial days ...' Old engraving of an early Sydney Cup

starts were used until the 'barrier wire' was introduced around 1870 and the 'barrier stalls' arrived some fifty years later.

From the early colonial days, through the heyday of racing in Australia in the mid twentieth century, when enormous crowds were commonplace, right down to the age of the TAB and racing channels on television, Australians have always loved a day at the races and a bet on the weekend.

The social, sporting and gambling elements of racing exist in a kind of delicate balance today and 'the races' are still a part of the unique fabric of our national character.

'... the heyday of racing in Australia ...' 1951 mile start with jockeys Darby Munro, Jack Thompson, Billy Cook, Ray Selkrig, Arthur Podmore, George Moore, Athol Mulley, Noel McGrowdie and Stan Cassidy

'... enormous crowds were commonplace ...' Hobartville Stakes day Warwick Farm 1962

Above: '... the "barrier wire" was introduced around 1870 ...' A start at Randwick circa 1880

Left: 'The jockeys then went to weigh-in.' Champion jockey Noel McGrowdie on the modern style scales

ROYAL RANDWICK

James Andrew ('Tip') Kelaher

Are the two-year-olds still racing down the Randwick mile,
Do thudding hoofs still shake the Randwick turf,
Do flower-beds and gardens still produce their springtime smile,
Does the ring-roar match the booming of the surf?

Are there still some lovely ladies to beautify the scene,
Is the band still playing marches 'neath the stand,
Is the sunshine just as brilliant and the couch grass just as green
As when we sailed to fight on foreign strand?

Is the stale cigar smell drifting, and do gripping hands denote
Glad meetings and a move towards the bar,
Is there movement, life and laughter from the 'birdcage' to the tote
As the old friends congregate from near and far?

Have you any colts like Gold Rod or Avenger or High Caste,
Or a miler like proud Ajax at his best,
Could the new lot hope to foot it with the champions of the past,
With Eurythmic, Gloaming, Poitrel and the rest?

Oh, the bay, the black, the chestnut – rippling muscles in the sun!
Close finishes! The crowd's loud, vibrant roar!
A day of keen, hard-racing, stirring contests every one,
Brings a tingle to a horseman's blood once more.

Now Randwick stands a symbol of the life we left behind,
And 'twill compensate for loss and parting pain,
When the war is safely over if I have the luck to find
I can spend a day at Randwick once again.

Andrew James ('Tip') Kelaher was born in Sydney in 1914 and attended Sydney Boys' High. He spent much of his short life in north-west New South Wales and enlisted in a machine gun battalion in 1940. He was killed in action at Tel El Eisa in Egypt on 14 July 1942. His commanding officer wrote, 'In the face of heavy machine gun fire, artillery and mortars he stayed by his gun and kept it in action to the last.' He wrote the poem 'Royal Randwick' just before his death.

'Brings a tingle to a horseman's blood once more.' The Randwick 'birdcage'.

'... a miler like proud Ajax at his best ...'

'I can spend a day at Randwick once again.'

RACING

A. B. ('Banjo') Paterson

This being the eve of the Melbourne Cup, I thought I ought to say something about horseracing.

I don't know which is the hardest, the human race or the horserace. You can tell pretty well what a horse will do but when a man starts backing horses you never know what he'll do.

Now, here's an instance. A lady friend of mine, a fine sensible woman, went into a big drapery store just before the last Metropolitan. She bought a lot of goods and they sent a small boy out with her to carry her parcels to the car.

On the way out to the car the boy said, 'Now, listen, lady. If you want a good bet, put all you've got on Strength for the Metropolitan. It's a snip. Now I'm telling you. Don't listen to anybody else. Back Strength.'

If it had been anything except horseracing she'd have given him a lift under the ear and told him to mind his own business, but people think there's some kind of magic about horseracing. She put a pound on Strength and won fifty pounds and then she said to me, 'Now, how did that boy know Strength was going to win?'

I said, 'He didn't know. He was just guessing.'

'Oh,' she said, 'that's nonsense. He must have known. Look how sure he was.'

So then I thought I'd try her on another tack and I said, 'What was the boy like?' She described him and I said, 'Oh, I know about that boy. He's a bit of a phenomenon. They keep him here to tell them what the fashions will be next season.'

'Ah,' she said, 'don't be silly. How could he know what the women's fashion would be? An ignorant little boy like that!'

'Well,' I said, 'how could he know what would win the Metropolitan?'

It was no use. She's going down to that same shop this week to buy the same goods and get the same boy to carry them, and she thinks she'll get the winner of the Melbourne Cup at fifty to one. I've no doubt that ninety per cent of you that are listening to me would do the same thing if you knew what shop it was.

This betting complex is an interesting study in human psychology. People think there's some magic about it. Well, it's like the poetry. It's an inheritance from the old tribal days, when every tribe had its magician. A magician in those days would tell a man that he was going to die in a fortnight and if the man's health continued to be good, the magician would knock him on the head some dark night. Then, when the body was found in the morning, the tribe would say, 'Isn't that magician a wonder! How did he know the man was doing to die?'

Even intelligent people like the Romans would not go into battle until the soothsayers had killed some chickens and studied their entrails to see whether the Romans were going to win the battle. It's not much over a couple of hundred years since the English were burning people for witchcraft, and millions of people believe in fortune tellers, and divining rods for finding water, and quack doctors that can cure anything. You know, even now any quack doctor can go into a country town and take away two or three hundred pounds in cash, while the local professional men can't get in a bob. It's the same complex we have on the turf, the magician complex.

Talking of doctors, a doctor friend of mine started betting pretty heavily and I said, 'What are you betting on, doctor? What makes you think you can beat the books?'

'Oh,' he said, 'I've got hold of a wonderful chap. He knows when they are going to back their horses. They tell him ...' (I thought to myself, 'I'm sure they would') 'and, although I never listen to trainers, who are mostly a lot of mugs, this cove knows.'

So then he went to go away, and I said, 'Where are you going to, doctor?'

'Oh,' he said, 'I'm going down town to pay for a suit of clothes for this fellow. He hasn't got any clothes fit to go to the races in.'

Well, there you are. Can you beat it? The magician complex again.

Coming now to this year's Melbourne Cup, I've been very friendly with Mr Moss, owner of the second favourite, Veilmond, for many years, and I asked him whether he thought Phar Lap could give his horse twenty-five pounds.

Do you know what he said? He said, 'I don't know.' If he'd been a small boy in a shop he'd have known offhand.

About this business of knowing winners, I was at Randwick one day with a lady friend of mine – I seem to have a lot of lady friends, don't I – and she stopped a trainer and she said, 'Oh, Mr So-and-so, tell me what will win this race.'

Now the trainer hadn't been going too well, and he said, 'Look, lady, if I knew the winners of races, do you think I'd train horses for a living? Do you think I'd get up at four o'clock in the morning and get my feet wet, and run to the telephone all day explaining to owners why their horses didn't win? I would not. I'd come down here and win all the money I wanted and I'd go fishing all day, and I'd play cards all night. I wouldn't go to bed till four o'clock in the morning. On with the dance: that'd be my motto.'

So when he went away this lady said, 'There's a nice ungrateful hound for you. My husband used to have horses with that man, and now he won't tell me anything.'

So I said, 'I think he told you a lot.'

Betting is like drinking and card playing; it's all right in moderation but I have seen too many decent fellows got to ruin and some of them got to gaol because they get this betting complex. But the Latin poet Horace says, '*Dulce est desipere in loco* … It is pleasant to make a fool of yourself occasionally,' so I think I'll probably make a fool of myself by betting a bit with Mr Moss on Veilmond mainly for old acquaintance sake.

I think Phar Lap may beat himself by fighting for his head in the early part of the race. But keep that to yourself. Don't tell anybody I told you.

Veilmond did finish ahead of Phar Lap in the 1931 Cup, to which Paterson refers here but, unfortunately for 'The Banjo', he was fifth and Phar Lap eighth behind White Nose. Veilmond was at least a model of consistency in the Cup, having also finished fifth behind Phar Lap in 1930. And, incidentally, although Paterson was an astute judge of horses, it was common knowledge that Phar Lap was prone to over-race and be difficult to ride at times; he probably lost the 1929 Cup by fighting for his head early, and finished third.

SYDNEY CUP DAY

Anon

It was on a Sydney Cup Day,
While strolling round the course,
Joe Thompson he comes up to me
And says, 'Do ya wanna back me horse?
Now if you want to back it
The odds are three to one,
Just give me thirty smackers
And I'll give you back a ton.'

Oh, he may be very tricky,
And he may be very sly,
He can always find his match,
He only has to try,
And what he does is clever,
On that we all agree,
He may have got at one or two,
But he won't get at me.

Now Joe acts the injured party,
And bitterly complains.
Says he's offerin' me a certainty
If I only had the brains,
But if I didn't want it,
Well, he'd find some other bloke.
But in the meantime, while I'm thinkin'
Could I spare a chap a smoke?

Well I looked at Joe before me
And I lit his cigarette,
And gave him one for later on
And a fiver for a bet,
And he sauntered off towards the ring
His hat pushed on the side,
A man of means once again,
With a fiver's worth of pride.

Oh, he may be very tricky,
And he may be very sly,
He can always find his match,
He only has to try,
And what he does is clever,
On that we all agree,
But an old tout who's down and out
Can always count on me!

THREE POETS ... ONE RHYME

Jim Haynes

This is a story about three great writers, legendary Australian literary figures, who loved horseracing and wrote hundreds of poems on the subject.

It is also the story of the fun they all had with a particular rhythm and rhyme scheme, and how two of them parodied the other to produce three of the most exciting and amusing pieces of verse ever written about the racing game.

We are an odd nation. Two of our national icons are a bushranger who wore a homemade suit of armour and a chestnut gelding who raced over fifty years ago. Our national broadcaster uses a famous cricketer's batting average for its Post Office box address in every capital city and we rather enjoy being famous for drinking beer and eating pies, although we don't rate in the top ten nations for doing either.

We think of ourselves as sporty, down-to-earth and anti-intellectual, yet we attend the theatre more regularly than the populations of other English-speaking nations, and read more books than they do. We are also the only country in the world to feature the portraits of two poets on its bank notes.

A Galloping Poet

The Australian love affair with rhymed verse goes hand in hand with our love of racing. It all began with an ex-patriot Englishman who wanted to be taken seriously as a poet, but ended up being remembered for his galloping rhymes and his riding ability.

His disappointment at not having his 'serious' poetry taken seriously, along with financial troubles and injuries sustained while steeplechasing, eventually led to his suicide. Yet the very same factors made him the inspiration for our most famous writers and are the reasons he is revered today as the father of Australian rhymed verse.

Adam Lindsay Gordon was born in the Azores in 1833 while his parents were staying on his grandfather's plantation, probably for the sake of his mother's health. His father was a retired Bengal Cavalry captain who had married his first cousin. The family was an old and famous one, which had produced many distinguished men.

On their return to England young Gordon was sent to Cheltenham College. He had constant trouble at school and was there for only a year before he was sent to a church school in Gloucestershire.

At the age of fifteen he was sent to the Royal Military Academy, Woolwich, where he was good at sports but undisciplined and not inclined to study. In 1851 his father was asked to withdraw him and, after another spell at Cheltenham College, where, rumour has it, he was finally expelled, he finished his education as a private pupil of the headmaster of the Worcester Royal Grammar School.

Gordon lived with an uncle in Worcester but began to lead a wild and aimless life, contracted debts, and was a cause of great anxiety to his father. He also fell in love with, and proposed to, a young woman at this time, but she refused him. Finally it was decided that he should go to Australia and make a fresh start.

This was a common procedure at the time with 'respectable' families. Sons who got into trouble with debt or women were often shipped off to the colonies and sent money at regular intervals to keep them there. Breaker Morant was another of these 'remittance men'.

Gordon was just over twenty when he arrived in Adelaide in 1853. He immediately obtained a position in the South Australian mounted police and was stationed at Mount Gambier. He was a tall man and handsome in the saddle, but out of the saddle his posture was bad and his eyesight very poor. He was shy, sensitive, and inclined to be moody.

In 1855 he resigned his position and took up horse-breaking in the south-eastern districts of South Australia. An interest in horseracing, which he had developed as a youth in England, continued in Australia. He had a reputation for being 'a good steady lad and a splendid horseman'.

His father died in 1857 and his mother about two years later. He received the then massive amount of seven thousand pounds from his mother's estate towards the end of 1861. In 1862 he married seventeen-year-old Margaret Park and bought a cottage at Port MacDonnell, near Mount Gambier, where they lived for two years. This cottage, which the poet gave the rather twee and poetic name of 'Dingley Dell', is preserved to this day.

In 1864 Gordon had his first poetry published and also came third in the Border Watch Handicap Steeplechase, the most famous Mount Gambier horserace. The day after, he made his famous leap on his horse, Red Lancer, over a high fence between Leg of Mutton Lake and the Blue Lake. He landed on a small 1.8-metre ledge with a sixty-metre drop into the Blue Lake below. An obelisk, erected in 1887, now marks the spot.

In 1865 he was asked to stand for parliament and was elected by three votes to the South Australian House of Assembly. He spoke several times but had no talent for speaking in public and made a poor politician. He resigned his seat in November 1866.

He was earning himself a reputation as a rider over jumps and often won or was placed in local hurdle races and steeplechases. He was also contributing verse to various magazines. Around this time, he bought several properties, including one in Western Australia, which he visited in 1867. But he lost money on all his land purchases.

Next he moved to Ballarat in Victoria, where he rented livery stables and set up a general horse business as a dealer and breaker. However, Gordon had no head for business and the venture was a failure. In March 1868 he had a serious accident when a horse smashed his head against a gatepost.

Later that same year he was bankrupted by a fire in his livery stable and, to add to his misery, his infant daughter died just short of her first birthday, and his wife also left him for some time.

In spite of being short-sighted he was becoming very well known as a gentleman rider, and on 10 October 1868 actually won three steeplechase races in one day at the Melbourne Hunt Club meeting at Flemington. He began riding for money but was not fortunate

'He was earning himself a reputation as a rider over jumps ...'
Gordon riding at Dowling Forest

and had more than one serious fall. He sold his business in 1868 and moved to Brighton, in Melbourne.

In Melbourne Gordon succeeded in straightening out his financial affairs, made a little money from race riding and became friendly with literary figures of the day such as Marcus Clarke and Henry Kendall.

In March 1870 Gordon again injured his head in a bad fall while riding in a steeplechase at Flemington and he never completely recovered from the accident.

In June 1870 he learnt that his claim to his family's ancestral land in Scotland had been rejected on a legal technicality.

His last book, *Bush Ballads and Galloping Rhymes*, was published on 23 June 1870. Gordon had just asked his publishers what he owed them for printing the book, and had realised that he had no money to pay them and no prospects.

That day he bought a package of cartridges for his rifle and went home to his cottage at Brighton. Next morning he rose early, walked into the scrub at Brighton Beach and shot himself.

Gordon wrote volumes and volumes of 'serious' poetry. All through his short adult life he wrote poetry in the very ornate literary style of the old ballads and the romantic poets. Most of his verse seems tedious and old-fashioned today, but then so does most of Tennyson's poetry.

He was finally recognised as a literary figure of some standing and, in 1934, his bust was placed in Westminster Abbey. He is the only Australian writer to receive that honour, although he was, of course, actually British.

When he is remembered by the Australian public these days it is generally not for his serious poetry or his place in the literary world. Firstly, he is remembered as the poet who originally wrote galloping rhymes, like 'How We Beat the Favourite', and sentimental verses like 'The Sick Stockrider', and who inspired Paterson, Lawson, Morant, Ogilvie and a host of other verse writers. All four poets mentioned said Gordon was their favourite poet and their inspiration, so it is fair to say that Adam Lindsay Gordon is the father of Australian 'bush' verse.

Secondly, many Australians over the years have used a couplet of Gordon's when writing in their friends' autograph and remembrance books, without even knowing it was Adam Lindsay Gordon they were citing. The lines so often quoted are a fragment of a very long poem titled *Ye Weary Wayfarer*:

Life is mostly froth and bubble, two things stand like stone.
Kindness in another's trouble, courage in your own.

He is also remembered for his daring deeds as a horseman and steeplechase jockey and for his rather romantic and tragic life.

With his knowledge of literary forms and old ballads, Gordon was a master of rhythm and rhyme. One of his most famous galloping ballads is the starting point for this wonderful tale of parodies.

How We Beat the Favourite

Adam Lindsay Gordon

'Aye, squire,' said Stevens, 'they back him at evens;
The race is all over, bar shouting, they say;
The Clown ought to beat her; Dick Neville is sweeter
Than ever – he swears he can win all the way.

'But none can outlast her, and few travel faster,
She strides in her work clean away from The Drag;
You hold her and sit her, she couldn't be fitter,
Whenever you hit her she'll spring like a stag.

'And p'rhaps the green jacket, at odds though they back it,
May fall, or there's no telling what may turn up.
The mare is quite ready, sit still and ride steady,
Keep cool; and I think you may just win the Cup.'

Dark brown and tan muzzle, just stripped for the tussle,
Stood Iseult, arching her neck to the curb,
A lean head and fiery, strong quarters and wiry,
A loin rather light, but a shoulder superb.

'Keep back in the yellow! Come up on Othello!
Hold hard on the chestnut! Turn round on The Drag!
Keep back there on Spartan! Back you, sir, in tartan!
So, steady there, easy!' And down went the flag.

We started, and Kerr made a strong run on Mermaid,
Through furrows that led to the first stake-and-bound,
The Crack, half extended, looked bloodlike and splendid,
Held wide on the right where the headland was sound.

I pulled hard to baffle her rush with the snaffle,
Before her two-thirds of the field got away;
All through the wet pasture where floods of the last year
Still loitered, they clotted my crimson with clay.

The fourth fence, a wattle, floored Monk and Bluebottle;
The Drag came to grief at the blackthorn and ditch,
The rails toppled over Redoubt and Red Rover,
The lane stopped Lycurgus and Leicestershire Witch.

She passed like an arrow Kildare and Cock Sparrow
And Mantrap and Mermaid refused the stone wall;
And Giles on The Greyling came down at the paling,
And I was left sailing in front of them all.

I took them a burster, nor eased her nor nursed her,
Her dark chest all dappled with flakes of white foam,
Her flanks mud bespattered, a weak rail she shattered,
We landed on turf with our heads turned for home.

We crashed a low binder, and then, close behind her,
The ground to the hoofs of the favourite shook,
His rush roused her mettle, yet ever so little,
She shortened her stride as we raced at the brook.

She rose when I hit her, I saw the stream glitter,
A wide scarlet nostril flashed close to my knee,
Between sky and water The Clown came and caught her,
The space that he cleared was a caution to see.

And forcing the running, discarding all cunning,
A length to the front went the rider in green;
A long strip of stubble, and then the quick double,
Two stiff flights of rails with a quickset between.

She came to his quarter, and on still I brought her,
And up to his girth, to his breastplate she drew,
A short prayer from Neville just reached me, 'The Devil!'
He muttered ... locked level the hurdles we flew.

A hum of hoarse cheering, a dense crowd careering,
All sights seen obscurely, all shouts vaguely heard;
'The green wins!' 'The crimson!' The multitude swims on,
And figures are blended and features are blurred.

'The Clown is her master!' 'The green forges past her!'
'The Clown will outlast her!' 'The Clown wins!' 'The Clown!'
The white railing races with all the white faces,
The chestnut outpaces, outstretches the brown.

On still past the gateway she strains in the straightway,
Still struggles, 'The Clown by a short neck at most!'
He swerves, the green scourges, the stand rocks and surges,
And flashes, and verges, and flits the white post.

Aye! So ends the tussle, I knew the tan muzzle
Was first, though the ring men were yelling, 'Dead heat!'
A nose I could swear by, but Clarke said, 'The mare by
A short head.' And that's how the favourite was beat.

The reader will see how the rhyme scheme of two close rhymes, followed by long lines which also rhyme with each other, gives the exact feeling of a galloping horse. The metre is a variation of a form called 'amphibrachic', where three syllables are used and the middle syllable is accented. It really doesn't matter how he did it, what matters is that the rhythm and rhyme sweep the story along at such a galloping pace the reader can't help but get excited and swept along at the same time.

'*A length to the front went the rider in green.*'

Enter 'The Banjo'

A. B. Paterson's strong connection to racing in Australia can be gauged by the fact that he is the only writer in the Australian Racing Hall of Fame, and also because he appears as the major contributor to this collection of racing stories and verses. He always said that Gordon was his inspiration.

Andrew Barton Paterson was born on 17 February 1864, at Narambla, New South Wales, not far from Orange. He was the son of a Scottish immigrant, Andrew Bogle Paterson from Lanarkshire, who had arrived in Australia in the early 1850s, and Rose Barton, daughter of a pioneering family.

Rose's parents had emigrated from England and owned a property in the Riverina. Rose's mother, Emily, was a cultivated woman who had been educated on the continent and wrote verse, which was published privately. Paterson was to spend a lot of his childhood with his grandmother.

His early life was spent on family properties in the Riverina and near Yass in New South Wales. Here he became acquainted with the colourful bush characters that he wrote about so vividly in his later life.

Paterson's early education took place at home under a governess and then at the bush school in Binalong, the nearest township. From about the age of ten years he attended the Sydney Grammar School. He lived with his widowed grandmother in Gladesville and spent the school holidays at Illalong Station with his family.

'Barty', as the family called him, spent much of his early life around horses, and his lifelong love of horseracing and polo is reflected in many of his poems. He was a member of the first New South Wales polo team to play against the Victorians.

He had a very light touch on the reins which he always attributed to the fact that he was dropped by his nurse as a small child and suffered a badly fractured right arm. The nurse was afraid to tell anyone about the accident; she was an Aboriginal girl and doubtless feared the consequences. The damage was not detected for some time and then young Paterson had to undergo a series of operations which left his right arm considerably shorter than his left. He attributed his success at polo and racing to this fact. He won the Polo Challenge Cup in 1892 on his horse, The Shifter, and also competed in races at Rosehill and Randwick as an amateur, or 'gentleman', rider.

After completing school the sixteen-year-old Paterson was articled to a Sydney firm of solicitors, Spain and Salway. He was admitted as a solicitor in 1886 and formed the legal partnership Street and Paterson. His first poem was written in 1885 and he wrote his first 'racing' poem, 'A Dream of the Melbourne Cup', on 30 October 1886. In the poem Paterson dreams that the Cup is won by the New South Wales horse Trident:

But one draws out from the beaten ruck
And up on the rails by a piece of luck
He comes in a style that's clever;
'It's Trident! Trident! Hurrah for Hales!'
'Go at 'em now while their courage fails;'
'Trident! Trident! For New South Wales!'
'The blue and white for ever!'

In the dream Paterson has backed the winner at 'a million to five' but, true to colonial rivalry perhaps, the bookie had not paid him when he finally 'woke with indigestion'. (Several days later Trident ran fourth behind Arsenal in the Cup.)

Paterson's verse began appearing in *The Bulletin* from 1885 under his nom-de-plume, 'The Banjo', which was the name of a racehorse his father had once owned. It was not until 1895, on the publication of *The Man from Snowy River and Other Verses*, that the public finally discovered the name of the man behind the verse.

Even though he was a practising lawyer in Sydney, he always had a hankering for the bush and made numerous trips to remote areas in Queensland and the Northern Territory. His links with *The Bulletin* prompted the *Sydney Morning Herald* and *The Argus* to send him as a war correspondent to the Boer War in South Africa in 1900 and 1901. His vivid and exciting reports were well received.

In 1902, his second collection, *Rio Grand's Last Race and Other Verses*, was published and the following year he became editor of the *Sydney Evening News* and married Alice Walker, a grazier's daughter. In 1908 he and his family left Sydney and ran a grazing property in the highlands near Yass in southern New South Wales.

Paterson was almost fifty when war broke out in 1914, but he enlisted in the AIF and worked in France as an ambulance driver before joining the First Australian Remount Unit as a lieutenant. This was a unit of horsemen from bush and racecourse whose task was to train mounts for the Australian Light Horse in Egypt. Paterson rose to the rank of major and his skills with men and mounts gained him great respect.

After the war, Paterson returned to Sydney as a freelance journalist. In 1922 he became editor of *The Sydney Sportsman*, a weekly sporting newspaper, to which he also contributed ballads and essays, and which became very popular under his direction.

In 1930 Paterson retired from full-time journalism, but remained a freelance sports reporter and feature writer. He also became a regular broadcaster for the Australian Broadcasting Commission. He had published his first novel, *An Outback Marriage*, in 1906 and, in 1936, his racing novel, *The Shearer's Colt*, was completed. Paterson also wrote a long treatise on horseracing, in which he explained breeding, betting, handicapping and all aspects of the racing business.

In 1939 Paterson was awarded the CBE for his services to Australian literature. He died in 1941, just short of his seventy-seventh birthday.

Although he lived much of his life in the city, his stories and verses are written from a true knowledge of the bush and its people, and he had a real grasp of the sense of humour that permeated life in rural Australia, especially on racetracks. The advice he gave race-goers in the poem 'Wisdom of Hafiz', that the only real tip you'll ever get is to see the stable money go on, is as true today as it was in his lifetime.

As has previously been stated, Paterson admired, and was inspired by, Adam Lindsay Gordon. In 1894, Paterson wrote a parody of Gordon's famous galloping rhyme, 'How We Beat the Favourite', which reversed the roles and added the double twist of a betting coup gone terribly wrong. This poem appeared in the racebook for the Rosehill meeting on 9 November, the Saturday following the Melbourne Cup, and used the same rhyme scheme and scansion as the original.

'... the only writer in the Australian Racing Hall of Fame ...' A. B. ('Banjo') Paterson

The poem is called 'How the Favourite Beat Us' and it tells how an owner tries to back his horse, fails to get a price, attempts to get the jockey to pull the horse and is ironically defeated in his trickery by a mosquito ... and his own horse. The poem appears to be set in Newcastle as the mosquito in question is one of the famous 'Hexham greys' from the mangrove swamps near the Hunter River.

How the Favourite Beat Us

A. B. ('Banjo') Paterson

'Aye,' said the boozer, 'I tell you it's true, sir,
I once was a punter with plenty of pelf,
But gone is my glory, I'll tell you the story
How I stiffened my horse and got stiffened myself.

''Twas a mare called the Cracker, I came down to back her,
But found she was favourite all of a rush,
The folk just did pour on to lay six to four on,
And several bookies were killed in the crush.

'It seems old Tomato was stiff, though a starter;
They reckoned him fit for the Caulfield to keep.
The Bloke and The Donah were scratched by their owner –
He only was offered three-fourths of the sweep.

'We knew Salamander was slow as a gander,
The mare could have beat him the length of the straight,
And old Manumission was out of condition,
And most of the others were running off weight.

'No doubt someone "blew it", for everyone knew it,
The bets were all gone, and I muttered in spite
"If I can't get a copper, by Jingo, I'll stop her,
Let the public fall in, it will serve the brutes right."

'I said to the jockey, "Now, listen, my cocky,
You watch as you're cantering down by the stand,
I'll wait where that toff is and give you the office,
You're only to win if I lift up my hand."

'I then tried to back her – "What price is the Cracker?"
"Our books are all full, sir," each bookie did swear;
My mind, then, I made up, my fortune I played up
I bet every shilling against my own mare.

'I strolled to the gateway, the mare in the straightway
Was shifting and dancing, and pawing the ground,
The boy saw me enter and wheeled for his canter,
When a darned great mosquito came buzzing around.

'They breed 'em at Hexham, it's risky to vex 'em,
They suck a man dry at a sitting, no doubt,
But just as the mare passed, he fluttered my hair past,
I lifted my hand, and I flattened him out.

'I was stunned when they started, the mare simply darted
Away to the front when the flag was let fall,
For none there could match her, and none tried to catch her –
She finished a furlong in front of them all.

'You bet that I went for the boy, whom I sent for
The moment he weighed and came out of the stand –
"Who paid you to win it? Come, own up this minute."
"Lord love yer," said he, "why you lifted your hand."

"'Twas true, by St Peter, that cursed "muskeeter"
Had broke me so broke that I hadn't a brown,
And you'll find the best course is when dealing with horses
To win when you're able, and keep your hands down.'

The Laureate of the Larrikin

Clarence Michael James Stanislaus Dennis was born in Auburn, South Australia in 1876, to James Dennis and his second wife, Catherine. Due to the boy's and the mother's ill health and frailty, Dennis was looked after in his early years by his mother's aunts who lived nearby.

In 1883, James Dennis took up the lease on a hotel in Gladstone in South Australia's mid-north and, a couple of years later, moved seven miles further north to run the Beetaloo Hotel in the township of Laura.

Dennis's mother died in 1890 leaving his father with three sons and a hotel to look after. This was never going to work successfully so two of his mother's unmarried sisters moved to Laura to help with the children's upbringing. For some time in his teens Dennis attended the Christian Brothers' College in Adelaide but had returned to Laura by the age of seventeen and took a job as a clerk to a local solicitor.

At nineteen he published his first poem in the local newspaper, *The Laura Standard*. Some time later, after stints as a barman in his father's hotel and a period spent in Broken Hill, he worked as a writer on the staff of the *Critic*, an Adelaide weekly newspaper, finally ending up as the journal's editor.

In 1905 he started a threepenny weekly newspaper called the *Gadfly*, which lasted about three years. After two years of editing the *Gadfly*, Dennis left Adelaide and went to Melbourne.

He worked as a freelance journalist in Melbourne and joined a small community of artists that had been established in a sort of camp in the Dandenong Ranges at a place called Toolangi, about forty miles east of Melbourne. Apart from a brief interlude in Sydney, Dennis lived in this area for pretty much the rest of his life.

Over the next five years Dennis published a series of poems in *The Bulletin* and other magazines and became involved in Labor politics. In 1913 these poems were published in his first book, *Backblock Ballads and Other Verses*.

The book received favourable reviews but did not sell very well and Dennis decided to try his luck in Sydney, where he joined the staff of the union journal *The Call*. Dennis didn't really take to Sydney. He also became disillusioned with the Labor movement and returned to Melbourne, where he took up employment in the Public Service.

On his return to Melbourne he wrote to Angus and Robertson, the Sydney-based publisher with whom he had become acquainted while living in the harbour city. He outlined to them his ideas for a book entitled *The Songs of a Sentimental Bloke* and the book was published in mid October 1915.

The *Bloke* struck a nerve with Australian audiences and by September 1916 had been dramatised for the stage, performed in Sydney and Melbourne, and was probably as popular as it was possible for a work of fiction to be at that time.

The book sold over fifty thousand copies in just nine months. It sold many thousands more copies as the years passed by and continues to sell today as an Australian classic. It was also published in New Zealand, Britain, Canada and the USA.

In 1916 Dennis published *The Moods of Ginger Mick* based on a character from *The Sentimental Bloke,* and it sold over forty thousand copies in six months. By the end of the war C. J. Dennis had become the best selling writer, and the best known poet, in Australia.

In 1917 he married Olive Herron and applied for a lease on the property where he had been living for years at Toolangi. Eventually he gained freehold ownership of the land.

Dennis, or 'Den', as he was called by all who knew him, started work on the staff of the *Melbourne Herald* in 1922 and the bulk of his output from that time on was devoted to pieces for the newspaper.

Over the next sixteen years he produced around three thousand pieces of verse and prose. Some of these were topical comments on the news of the day and all of them display Dennis's sharp wit and wonderful observation of the Aussie character. Most of these pieces were never collected in his lifetime and, while many have not been generally available, some have recently been gathered together and a few are to be found elsewhere in this book.

'The Laureate of The Larrikin', C. J. Dennis

Dennis was a small man who was described as being of 'slight but enduring physique, with an aquiline nose and slate-grey eyes with a half hidden twinkle'. He loved the Aussie character and wrote many pieces of verse about the racetrack and the Australian obsession with punting.

As he wrote almost daily for the *Herald* he tended to write at least one verse concerning the Melbourne Cup each year and some of these forgotten gems feature in this collection. When he died in June 1938 at the age of sixty-one, Joe Lyons, prime minister of Australia at the time, said, 'He created characters which have become immortal and he captured the true Australian spirit. Already his work is world-famous, and future generations will treasure it.'

In 1932, when Peter Pan was a hot favourite for the Cup, Dennis dipped his poetic lid to his two predecessors, Gordon and Paterson, and wrote his parody of 'How We Beat the Favourite'. It is a typical

C. J. Dennis piece, which captures the mood of the day and shows how well Dennis knew the average bloke and how his mind worked. Its title shows how Dennis's emphasis was always on the common punter rather than the actual race itself: it is called 'How We *Backed* the Favourite'.

How We Backed the Favourite

C. J. Dennis

'Sure thing,' said the grocer, 'as far as I know, sir,
This horse, Peter Pan, is the safest of certs.'
'I see by the paper,' commended the draper,
'He's tipped and he carries my whole weight of shirts.'

The butcher said, 'Well, now, it's easy to tell now
There's nothing else in it except Peter Pan.'
And so too the baker, the barman, bookmaker,
The old lady char and the saveloy man.

'You stick to my tip, man,' admonished the grip-man,
'Play up Peter Pan; he's a stayer with speed.'
And the newspaper vendor, the ancient road mender,
And even the cop at the corner agreed.

The barber said, 'Win it? There's nothing else in it.
I backed Peter Pan with the last that I had.'
'Too right,' said the liftman. 'The horse is a gift, man.'
The old jobbing gardener said, 'Peter Pan, lad!'

I know nought of racing. The task I was facing,
It filled me with pain and unreasoning dread.
They all seemed so certain, and yet a dark curtain
Of doubt dulled my mind ... But I must keep my head!

I went to the races, and I watched all their faces.
I saw Peter Pan's; there was little he lacked.
And as he seemed willing, I plancked on my shilling
And triumphed! And that's how the favourite was backed.

So there it is, a wonderful trifecta of poems, all using the same rhyme and metre, by three of the best poets that ever lived in Australia.

They are three of the most recitable of all Aussie verses and are certainly among my all-time favourites. I like the way each verse illustrates so accurately a different aspect of the Australian obsession with thoroughbred racing.

I enjoy the excitement and honesty of Gordon's poem, and I enjoy the two different styles of humour displayed by Paterson and Dennis, and the respect that you sense in their efforts to closely parody the style of the man they both admired so much, Adam Lindsay Gordon.

Parody is, perhaps, the ultimate compliment.

THE WISDOM OF HAFIZ

A. B. ('Banjo') Paterson

My son, if you battle the bookies, there are several things you
    should know,
Remember, it's seldom the pigeon can pick out the eye of the crow;
Remember, they live by the business; remember, my son, and go slow.

If ever an owner should tell you, 'Back mine,' don't you be
    such a flat.
He knows his own cunning, no doubt ... does he know what the
    others are at?
Find out what he's frightened of most ... and invest a few dollars
    on that.

Walk not in the track of the trainer, nor hang round the rails
    at his stall.
His wisdom belongs to his patron, shall he give it to one and to all?
When the stable is served he may tell you ... and his words are
    like jewels let fall.

Run wide of the tipster who whispers that Borak is sure to
    be first,
He tells the next mug that he corners a tale with the placings
    reversed;
And, remember, of judges of racing, the jockey's the absolute
    worst.

When they lay three to one on the field, and the runners are
    twenty-and-two,
Take a pull on yourself; take a pull ... it's a mighty big field to get
    through.
Is the club handicapper a fool? If a fool is about, p'raps it's you!

Beware of the critic who tells you the handicap's absolute rot,
For this is chucked in, and that's hopeless, and somebody ought
*   to be shot.*
How is it he can't make a fortune himself when he knows
*   such a lot?*

From tipsters, and jockeys, and trials, and gallops, the glory
*   has gone,*
For this is the wisdom of Hafiz that sages have pondered upon,
'The very best tip in the world is to see the commission go on!'

Hafiz was a fourteenth-century Persian philosopher and poet whose wisdom was legendary. Whether he actually knew much about the racing game is doubtful; it is not mentioned in his biographies. Paterson is at the game of parody again here: Hafiz wrote 'divinely inspired' verses in the style parodied above by 'The Banjo'.

THE GUDGEONS GO TO RANDWICK

Lennie Lower

(Adapted from *Here's Luck*)

I had a feeling of impending trouble. As the browsing lamb sees the shadow of the hawk on the grass, so I saw trouble.

Gradually the clock forced itself on me. It ticked at me. Its little hand went around. Every tick was a second nearer the grave; my life was ebbing away, ebbing away – second by second. I was in a very bad state.

There was a loud knock on the door, and my son, Stanley, appeared. At the sight of him my fit of abstraction vanished and my mind resumed business at the same old stand.

'Well?' I queried.

'Daisy just phoned and said she's going to the races with Maureen and she wants us to come and meet her out there. You'll have to hurry. I'm almost ready. Don't bother about a shave. Come on, hurry up.'

'Races? What races?'

'Randwick Races. Get a collar on and a coat. I'll have to get you a hat somewhere. Look lively or we'll be late.'

He scurried out of the room, and the bedroom door, the front door and the gate slammed almost simultaneously behind him.

I rose to my feet. I didn't want to go to the races. I just wanted to sit down and think. Besides, I had only about eight pounds and I wasn't going to be financially butchered to make a holiday for the gimme-girls. I was a respectable married man whose wife had merely left to live with her sister. I sat down again. A loud crashing of doors and gates resounded through the house and Stanley suddenly appeared in the room like a stage demon.

'Not dressed yet!' he squeaked breathlessly.

'I'm not ...'

'Here's a hat of Temple's I've borrowed for you from next door,' he gasped, and threw it to me.

'I'm not ...'

'Come on. Get on your coat. I've phoned for a taxi; it will be here any moment.'

'I'm not going!' I shouted.

'Don't be silly, Dad. This collar looks clean enough. I found it in the hall. Got your studs?'

'Listen to me, Stanley. I am not going. Don't try these tornado tactics on me; I'm not going.'

'Aw, be yourself, Dad! You're not working. There's no money coming in. Daisy knows an absolute cert for today. Opportunity only knocks once. Come on!'

The doorbell rang.

'That's the taxi-man!' he exclaimed. 'Here, put your coat on.'

I clambered into my coat as he rushed out of the room. He was back in something under a second with my tie and studs.

'You can put these on in the car,' he gasped, slamming a hat on my head. He grasped me by the arm, swung me out of the room, out of the front door, out the gate and into the taxi.

'Randwick!' he cried. 'Drive like hell!' and the car leapt forward.

'Keep close to that car in front,' I added, 'and if it stops, shoot to kill.'

I struggled out of the hat, which was much too small and jammed down on my ears.

'What are you talking about?' said Stanley. 'What car in front?'

'There's always a car in front,' I replied testily. 'A black closed-in car, and it winds in and out streets until it pulls up at a deserted house and they all get out and carry the unconscious girl into the cellar and we surround the house and capture the Master Mind who turns out to be the butler.'

He stared at me. 'You're mad!' he said.

'Have it your own way,' I replied, and proceeded to adjust my collar.

I made no complaint to Stanley for literally dragging me out of the house and throwing me into a taxi. I had been practically abducted – shanghaied; but the thing was done. It was no use objecting. It was all of a piece with my presentiments and I sensed the presence of the finger of fate.

I am a fatalist and believe that what will be, will be; what is, is; and what was, was; and so on through the verbs. I am not alone in my belief; the modern trend of thought is more and more in that direction and I sometimes suspect that even the Railway Commissioners operate their passenger services on the same principle.

Stanley must have been thinking on similar lines. He had been gazing at the taximeter, a thing I never do in a taxi as it takes half the pleasure out of the ride. He seemed to be fascinated by the cold-blooded inexorableness of the thing.

'You know, Father,' he said, 'all life is a gamble.'

'A highly original remark, my boy,' I replied, 'I suppose then that a Randwick race-meeting is the quintessence of life and a royal routine flush would be the peak of existence?'

'It would be the end of your existence if you were playing at the camp with the boys. Wouldn't it be funny if we won a thousand pounds today?'

'Funny! The braw laddies of the Highland Society would laugh their sporrans off. May I inquire the basis of these hopes for fun? How are we to participate in this huge joke?'

'Don't try to be sarcastic, Father. It lessens my respect for you.'

'Your respect for your poor old father is already a minus quantity. It only appears on pay-days. You haven't answered my question.'

He leaned over and clutched my ear.

'Daisy had a stone moral,' he whispered.

'A stone moral.'

'Ssh!'

'What's a stone moral?'

'Don't talk so loud. It's a certainty. It can't be beaten. There's only one horse in it.'

'Oh, well, in that case,' I said, leaning back in my corner, 'it certainly must win.'

'Of course it'll win; you can put your undies on it.'

'Seems rather strange, though,' I ruminated, 'having only one horse in the race. Any fool ought to see that it must win.'

'Arrgh!'

I relapsed into my corner again.

The taximeter, foaming at the mouth, demolished another shilling and gnashed its teeth in anticipation of the next. The tick menace is not confined to our country districts.

'Who is going to pay this lightning calculator?' I asked, pointing to it.

'That's all right. I'll see to that,' replied Stanley with a contemptuous flirt of his hand that must have greatly disheartened the meter. 'It's only twelve shillings,' he added.

'Where did you get it?' I exclaimed.

'Temple. Good feller your neighbour. Stung him for a couple.'

'Great!' I cried. 'Serves him damn well right!' I had begun to dislike Temple and to hear of his lending money to Stanley was sweet music to mine ears. Anything lent to Stanley can be lined up with the Pyramids, the Sphinx, the national debt and such-like time-defying monuments.

'Leger reserve, sir?'

The driver spoke through the back of his neck after the manner of his kind. The car pulled up and we decanted ourselves onto the pavement. Stanley paid the driver and we walked towards the entrance.

'Synagogue rules,' he said. 'Take yourself in and pay for yourself.'

We clattered through the turnstiles. A horde of racebook sellers detonated in our faces.

'Book! Book! Book! Bookertherazes! Book, sir?'

I bought two and handed one to Stanley.

'That squares us,' I said. 'You paid for the taxi and I've paid for the programmes.'

'If there's a harder man than you,' he said, taking the book, 'I'll bet he stands on a pedestal in Hyde Park, wrought in solid bronze.'

'Where have we to meet Daisy?' I said coldly.

'Over by the first stand – there she is!'

I looked as he pointed, and saw Daisy and Maureen with two men, one of whom seemed to be drunk.

'Who are those men?' I asked, waving my hand at the same time to Daisy.

'Dunno,' he answered in a puzzled voice.

As we drew nearer to them a strange feeling of apprehension stole over me. Their faces left me perturbed. I felt that the only way these men could attain popularity in a civilised community would be for them to become radio announcers, unseen and gravely announcing a glut of onions in the market. Later, when I heard their voices, I was forced to deny them even this faint hope. We doffed our hats and greeted the ladies.

'So glad you came,' said Maureen in an enthusiastic voice. 'I don't think you've met our friends. Mister Simpson; Mister Gudgeon. Mister Stanley Gudgeon – Mister Slatter – Gudgeons. Mix!'

As we shook hands I made a mental note of Stanley's perfidy in divulging my name. Smith is good enough for me.

'Over by the first stand …' Behind the stands at Randwick 1920

'Gonna back all the winners?' asked Mr Slatter pleasantly. Or as pleasantly as he could. He was not the type of man I usually associate with. He was tall and very broad about the shoulders, attired in a silvery-grey suit and a hard hat. His features reminded me of the cliffs at South Head, and his nose, which had evidently been broken at some time, had a disposition to lounge about his face. I pictured him shaving with a hammer and a cold chisel.

'I hope so, Mr Slatter,' I replied.

'Call me Woggo,' he said, spitting over my shoulder. 'All the boys call me that. Where's Dogsbody?' he added, gazing around.

I concluded that 'Dogsbody' was the inebriated Mr Simpson's trade name and turned to see him a little distance away, leaning on Stanley and breathing very confidentially into his face.

'Come on, Dosb'dy,' bawled Woggo. 'We're going inter the ring.'

I took Daisy's arm and moved off towards the betting-ring.

'Your friend has evidently been looking on the wine when it was red,' I remarked to her.

'The frantic clamour of the bookmakers roared around us ...' Randwick *betting ring circa 1930*

'He'd look on it if it was purple and had frogs in it.' She squeezed my arm. 'Glad you came, honey,' she said.

'Have you known Mr Slatter long?' I asked.

'Woggo? He's all right. We get the dinkum oil off him. He knows all the jockeys and trainers and everything. He was born in a horse-trough and carried round in a nosebag when he was a child. You don't want to worry about him.'

'What does he know for this race?'

She stopped and put her mouth close to my ear. 'King Rabbit,' she whispered. 'He's an outsider and he'll be any old price. Put a couple of pounds on for me.'

She kissed me on the ear. She was just a gimme-girl, but twenty years of life fell from me, and I kicked them out of the way as I walked on.

The frantic clamour of the bookmakers roared around us as we entered the ring. Men and women surged about the stands hurling money away with both hands. Punters pleaded to be allowed to lay odds on the favourite and elbowed each other out of the way in their earnest desire to be robbed.

Tip-slingers, urgers and whisperers slunk like jackals through the crowd, and grave and massive policemen placed their furtive bets. I shrunk from the ordeal, but how can man die better than by facing fearful odds? The rest of the gang came up and, with a parting glance at Daisy, I plunged into the riot.

Pausing at a stand, I addressed the open mouth of a bawling bookmaker.

'What price King Rabbit?'

'Oo? King Rabbit? Never 'eard of it. King Rabbit? Ar, yer, four to one, King Rabbit.'

I turned away.

'Well, eight to one,' he bawled. 'Tens!'

I continued on my way.

'Fifteens!' he yelled. 'Twenties! Well, go to blazes!'

I emerged at long last with my head throbbing under Temple's hat and the dust of conflict clinging to my boots. Daisy was waiting for me, with Maureen. I handed her a ticket.

'Sixty-eight pounds!' she shrieked. 'He must have been thirty-three to one!'

'You went to a good school,' I said.

'Gimme half if it wins,' pleaded Maureen.

Daisy impaled her with a glance.

'This is my ticket,' she said coldly. 'Stanley will get yours.'

'But he's only putting ten shillings on for me,' wailed Maureen.

'Faulty work,' said Daisy succinctly. 'Come and we'll watch the race, honey,' she added, taking my arm.

Never, never shall I forget that race. When I am old and peevish, sans teeth, sans hair, and shod with elastic-sided boots, I shall be content merely with the memory of that race. When St Peter asks me my greatest display of charity and fortitude on earth, my answer will be that I refrained from choking Daisy when King Rabbit won the Grantham Stakes.

When the barrier went up, the jockey seemed quite oblivious to the fact that I had four pounds on his mount. He appeared to go to sleep on the horse's neck. They wallowed round the bend behind everything else that had legs. The jockey seemed to be about as useful as a wart on the hip and I groaned aloud.

To this day, I believe the horse heard me. He laid his ears back, opened his mouth and accelerated. He threw his legs about in wild abandon. His hoofs touched the turf merely here and there. He flung himself along like a thing gone mad. His tail stood out. Like a chestnut bullet he sped past the field, past the favourite, past the winning-post, and twice around the course before he could be pulled up. Doped, of course.

The great, beautiful, brave beast, may he live for a hundred years and die in a lucerne paddock surrounded by his progeny.

Hoarse with shouting, my hands sore from beating the railing, I assisted the almost unconscious Daisy out of the crowd. The stricken punters were very, very quiet and the happy laughter of the bookmakers plunged the iron into their souls.

Thirty-three to one! Even now my hand trembles as I write.

One hundred and thirty-six pounds I collected, and sixty-eight for Daisy. If horses have halos when they die, King Rabbit should look like a zebra. We were joined by the rest of the party. I wanted to go home. I was padded with notes. Daisy was crying on my shoulder; Maureen was in the charge of the matron in the ladies' waiting-room; Stanley and the drunken Simpson were dancing like bears in the midst of an interested crowd.

Woggo Slatter stood aloof and not a pore of his skin opened or shut. Not a smile disturbed his granite face. A cigarette hung from the corner of his mouth, and when I sighted him he was buying a packet of chewing gum. Chewing gum! Fancy him being able to chew.

I parked Daisy in the grandstand and went to him.

'Thanks for the tip, old man,' I said, grasping him by the hand. 'Thanks very much.'

''Sall right,' he drawled. 'We has our lucky days. I might want ter put the fangs inter you for twenty or so one er these days. What are you goin' to do now?'

'I'm going home.'

He shifted his cigarette to the other side of his mouth.

'Don't go yet,' he said. 'Got another one. Be a short price, but it's good.'

He tipped his hat over one eye and walked away.

Stanley touched my arm.

'Hello!' I said. 'Corroboree finished?'

'The police stopped it,' he whispered.

'What are you whispering for? Are they after you?'

'No,' he said in an almost inaudible voice, 'it's my throat. I couldn't talk at all a while ago. I don't care if I'm never able to yell again. Wasn't it wonderful?'

'Oh, fair performance, I suppose. What are you going to do now?'

'I'm going home if I can get away from Maureen,' he whispered.

I studied the nail on my little finger for a moment. 'Don't go yet,' I said. 'Got another one. Short price, but good,' and tilting my hat over my forehead I strolled away and left him gaping.

Returning to the stand, I found Maureen and Daisy sitting with their heads close together. Their talk ceased suddenly as I came up to them. I know women. I buttoned my coat and sat down warily.

'Oh, gee!' sighed Maureen. 'Wasn't it just too lovely! Whatever are you going to buy me with all that money?'

'If you'll excuse me, Maureen,' said Daisy in a chilly voice, 'Jack is *my* friend. Go and find Stanley.'

'I like Stan,' murmured Maureen, 'but I don't value his friendship half as much as Jack's. Besides, he's only a boy, really, isn't he?'

I felt that I was being haggled over. Stanley had evidently been weighed in the balance and found to be under the limit.

'What about Woggo?' I suggested.

'Woggo!' they echoed. 'Ha! Ha!'

That let Woggo out. He was either a member of the syndicate or an abandoned mine.

'Do you know what this next winner is going to be?' I asked, to change the subject.

'Dunno,' answered Daisy. 'Woggo will tell you when the time comes. Here he is now.'

Woggo strolled into view and halted before us. Fixing his gaze on the horizon, he slowly stroked his left ear with three fingers, spat aimlessly in the general direction of the betting-ring and moved on. Maureen and Daisy hurriedly turned the pages of their racebooks.

'Number three, Useless Annie!' they gasped in unison.

'What about her?' I queried, looking around.

'That's it,' gabbled Maureen. 'That's the pea. Where's Stanley?'

She jumped to her feet and scurried away.

'What do I do now?' I asked, turning to Daisy.

'All you've got to do now is to empty the roll out on Useless Annie – and make it snappy. Off you go! I'll wait here.'

'The whole lot!' I gasped.

'Absolutely,' she said, giving me a push. 'Put a pony on for me.'

I hurried away and burrowed into the betting-ring. A striving elbow bored into my ear as I squirmed through the crowd. It was Stanley. I might have known that with practically the whole population of Sydney collected in one place, Stanley would single me out for injury.

I stamped heavily on his foot.

'Sorry, Stan,' I said, patting him on the shoulder, 'it's the crowd you know. What's a pony?'

'Thassall right, Dad,' he replied, 'that wasn't my foot. A pony is a little horse.'

He was swept away on a wave of punters before I could land him one. Useless Annie, as Woggo foretold, was a short price. One Hennessy, on the outer edge of the ring, who may possibly have been one of the lost tribe, offered to lay me fifty pounds to forty and I passed up the money. He made a quivering stab with his pencil at the betting-ticket and passed the result down to me.

'What's this?' I asked, staring at the Morse code on the ticket.

'Useless,' he snapped, glaring at me. 'A pony, fifty pounds to forty. That's vat you vant, ain't it?'

'Useless Annie?' I inquired meekly.

'Ah, Gor!' he moaned. 'Can't you read?'

'All right, all right,' I muttered, and wandered away to the bar.

A flying barman, handling glasses like a nervous octopus, extracted the order from between my teeth before I could utter it, and sped away.

'Snappy, eh?' commented Stanley. He was at my elbow. Ubiquitous.

'Stanley,' I said, producing the ticket, 'what do you make of this?'

'Useless Annie,' he said, glancing at it. 'Who put you onto that zoo fodder?'

'Slatter.'

'The urger with the ironstone complexion?'

I nodded uneasily.

'One born every day,' he muttered, shaking his head at his glass. 'One a minute.'

'What's wrong with it?' I demanded.

He leaned towards me. 'Useless Annie's in the bag,' he whispered. 'I've backed Bonser Baby. Get on while you've got time.'

'But ...' I faltered, waving my ticket.

'Well, of course, if you don't want to – don't,' he said, shrugging his shoulders.

'Do you think I ought to?'

He glanced at me pityingly. 'Anyone picked your pocket yet?'

'No.'

'Hmm, funny,' he said. Then fiercely he added, 'Go and get your money on. Leave your drink; I'll look after that.'

I gulped my drink and hurried away with my mind in a whirl.

The bookmakers were howling that they were prepared to lay five to one against Bonser Baby and I took a hundred and fifty to thirty pounds in three bets. I stood to win one hundred and fifty, or flay my thirty pounds' worth out of Stanley. Something seemed to tell me that I would win. I felt confident. I decided to avoid Daisy for the nonce, and took up a position near the track to watch the race.

It wasn't a race. Some dissatisfied gentleman close to me remarked that it was 'a mere sanguinary, lightning-struck, blasted, confounded and unmentionable procession.' Useless Annie might have been sired by a rocking-horse, and as regards its dam, it was damned by all present. The jockey made a ferocious display with his whip and then realistically fell off and left his horse to browse the track.

Bonser Baby was in front, with another horse gaining on it rapidly and for a moment it looked as if the jockey of that horse would have to fall off too. Fortunately Bonser Baby, with the fear of the bone-yard in him, speeded up his lollipop and staggered past the post amid a chorus of congratulatory groans. The race had not the thrill of the previous one, and although I was pleased to collect my winnings, I was not excited. My presentiments were returning.

I sought Daisy and handed her the ticket for Useless Annie. 'I put fifty on for you,' I said with a wry smile, 'the remainder I put on for myself.'

I sat down heavily beside her.

'Oh, what a pity!' cried Daisy. 'You poor thing! Are you absolutely broke?'

'Penniless,' I muttered.

'And you put fifty on for me! That was sporty of you, Jack. Here, you'd better take this fiver.'

I waved it aside.

'Don't be foolish,' she said, pressing it into my hand. I took it and thanked her.

'Hard luck,' I groaned.

'Absolutely.'

The stand was half full, but she put her arm round my neck, and drawing my head close to her mouth kissed me on the chin. 'There's possibilities in you, honey,' she whispered.

''Ullo! Wot's this?' grated a harsh voice.

I looked up and quickly declutched. Slatter was glaring at me and chewing his lip. He looked, to put it mildly, discontented. I felt an empty feeling in my stomach as I rose to my feet. It looked like an even chance of my becoming a co-respondent or a corpse.

'It's all right,' cried Daisy, rising.

Keeping my eyes on Slatter, I edged, crabwise, away from him.

'Well, so long,' I called, waving my arm.

''Ere!' growled Woggo.

I hurried on.

'Come 'ere. I want yer!' he bawled savagely.

I broke into a trot.

''Ell!' he bellowed, and started after me.

It was then that the benefits of living a more or less clean life came to my aid. There, on that day, without thought of honour or reward, I put up a performance that would have given any Olympic Games aspirant a lesson. I flashed past Stanley, who was strolling towards the gates with Maureen clinging to his arm like some parasitic growth.

'Father!' he yelled.

'Pace me, boy,' I gasped.

'Hey!' called a policeman, dashing towards me.

I slowed down as Stanley came beside me.

'Whatever you've pinched,' he panted, 'hand it over to me. They're bound to search you.'

'What's all this?' boomed the constable.

'It – it's his wife,' gasped Stanley. 'She's dying. We must get a taxi.'

I caught a glimpse of Woggo temporarily off the scent in the crowd.

'Dying?' queried the constable.

'Yes,' I gulped.

'While the Spring Meeting's on!' he gasped incredulously.

I nodded vigorously. Woggo had sighted us.

'My gore!' said the policeman. 'You can't beat women.'

'Come on, Stanley!' I cried, and bounded towards the gate.

''Ere!' shouted Woggo.

'Stop!' bawled another policeman.

'Taxi, sir,' queried an angel in uniform, as we dashed out the gate.

I hurled Stanley in and threw myself on top of him.

'Woollahra!' I yelled. 'Drive like hell!'

Stanley sat down and straightened his tie as the car bounded away. 'Referring to the car in front,' he said, 'do we shoot to kill, in the event of its stopping?'

'If you're trying to be funny, Stanley,' I said, scrambling to my knees, 'you have selected an inopportune time and run a grave risk of disfigurement for life.'

'Well, what's it all about?'

'Woggo was going to assault me,' I hissed, seating myself.

'Was he? And yet when I first saw him I didn't like him. Funny how you can be mistaken about a feller.' He shook his head and sighed. 'And I helped you to get away,' he muttered.

THE RIDERS IN THE STAND

A. B. ('Banjo') Paterson

There's some that ride the Robbo style, and bump at every stride;
While others sit a long way back, to get a longer ride.
There's some that ride like sailors do, with legs and arms, and teeth;
And some ride on the horse's neck, and some ride underneath.

But all the finest horsemen out, the men to Beat the Band,
You'll find amongst the crowd that ride their races in the Stand.
They'll say, 'He had the race in hand, and lost it in the straight.'
They'll show how Godby came too soon, and Barden came too late.

They'll say Chevalley lost his nerve, and Regan lost his head;
They'll tell how one was 'livened up' and something else was 'dead'.
In fact, the race was never run on sea, or sky, or land,
But what you'd get it better done by riders in the Stand.

The rule holds good in everything in life's uncertain fight;
You'll find the winner can't go wrong, the loser can't go right.
You ride a slashing race, and lose, by one and all you're banned!
Ride like a bag of flour, and win, they'll cheer you in the Stand.

'… they'll cheer you in the Stand.' Paddock Stand at Randwick from the now extinct flat enclosure

PASSELLA

J. C. Bendrodt

You wouldn't have known when the police came in, but I did.

To you the giant dance-hall would have seemed about as usual. But your big-time dance-hall operator always knows. Sometimes I've wondered if there isn't some affinity between a showman and a wild forest creature. Neither of them needs much warning when unusual things occur.

I took a golden cigarette case from the pocket of a coat my tailor said was faultless. I opened it and chose a cigarette, and my men came past and didn't stop, but whispered as they passed me from the corners of their mouths, 'It's the cops, boss,' and I answered softly, 'Sure, I know.'

I lit my cigarette, and looked out over the dance floor where undulating thousands moved to the music of a waltz. I shifted my gaze casually to the shadows near the doorways and watched the big men take position. I knew the phones were covered and the exits and the stairs. I knew that in the avenue outside the patrol cars and the wagons would be waiting. The stage was set.

I lit another cigarette and turned away. A deep voice said, 'So it's selling sly grog now, Jim, is it. Well, you can come along with me.'

Then another voice bit into the silence like a file, 'Forget it, copper. It wasn't 'im that sold it. It was me.'

Well, there it was. Liquor is worse than dynamite in public dance-halls. You had to have it at a function such as this one was, but you didn't sell it. You had good sense enough for that. You let your patrons bring it in, and then you watched them. You limited the quantity they could take.

You didn't have the profit motive, so you didn't care. But someone had sold liquor here tonight for profit, that was certain. Someone who couldn't smell 'Police' beneath a tailed coat and white bow-tie. And here at my side was a tiny chap with high-bridged nose and myopic eyes who said in his acrid voice, ''E didn't sell it, copper, I did.'

I hadn't spoken. This was a situation when I thought a still tongue might pay dividends. The big inspector didn't know that he was wrong. It wouldn't have been the slightest use my telling him that I hated grog in a place like this just as much as he did.

He looked at me for a long time. He knew the tricks of evidence, the difficulties in a court of law. I knew he had to take the little man in all the circumstances. There wasn't any other thing for him to do.

I smiled and said gently, 'Well, Inspector, I couldn't tell the answer. It's up to you.'

He glared at me, then beckoned with a finger, and two large, good-humoured fellows ranged up on either side of the little man, and he walked away between them with his head at about the level of their knees. I noticed that his legs were bowed, and that he had little narrow feet.

In the morning an unsympathetic magistrate told him, 'Ninety pounds or thirty days,' but in the meantime my big boys had found the real culprit, so my cashier peeled the notes off, and brought the little fellow back to me.

I told him to sit down, and smiled at him while he picked with stubby fingers at a pack of cigarettes.

'What's the name, lad?' I inquired.

'Tom,' he said. He didn't say Tom White or Tom Some-other-thing, he just said, 'Tom.'

'Well, Tom,' I went on, 'what did you do it for? You didn't sell the wine, and you don't know me. But you thought I had sold it, didn't you?'

'Sure.' He grinned. 'Why wouldn't you?'

'Well, Tom,' I said, 'the answer to that one would probably be very involved from your point of view. We'll skip it. Now tell me, why did you say you sold it?'

He looked at me with his hard little face set stubbornly, and then he grinned.

'Well, I'll tell you, boss. Your caterer put me on the casual waiter staff last night. I knew the set-up when the cops came in, and I figured you'd be generous if I took the rap for you.'

I nodded. 'An opportunist, eh, Tom? And apparently an honest one. That's very interesting.'

So that was it. He had come from a hard school, this one. You only had to look at him to know that. 'But, Tom,' I continued, 'you're no waiter. Now tell me just what are you?'

'Waiter be damned!' he said indignantly. 'I was broke, so I took the job to get a feed. I'm a jockey.'

'Jockey? But, Tom, if you're a jockey, why don't you work at it?'

He shuffled his feet uneasily, and peered at me with his round myopic eyes, and then he grinned.

'The stewards 'ad me in,' he said, 'and afterwards I figured I might as well buy a one-way ticket out of town.'

He grinned again, but looked at me in astonishment when I asked, 'But why one way only, Tom?'

He studied me suspiciously, and then he asked, 'Say, boss, do you know anything about horses or jockeys?'

'Nothing, Tom. I've never seen a racecourse.' His face cleared as if a great light had burst upon him.

'Well,' he said, 'I've 'eard of folks like you, but you're the first I've ever met. Whadda you do on Saturdays? Perhaps you'll understand when I tell you I rode forty-two favourites in succession and got beat on every one. Does that mean anything to you?'

'Not a thing, Tom.'

He peered at me again. 'Well, I'll be damned!' he said. 'I don't believe it does, boss,' and he shook his head in a puzzled way.

'Well, Tom,' I said, 'let's forget it. For reasons best known to yourself, you have become a waiter and you don't like it. Now what would you like to do if you had a choice?'

He answered instantly, 'Train a 'orse.'

I looked at him. His object had been purely mercenary, but the fact remained that but for him my name would have figured prominently in the morning papers in connection with sly grog.

'How would you go about that, Tom?'

He looked at me disgustedly for a time before he answered. 'Buy a 'orse I know of,' he said at last. 'A pony mare by Passing By out of Sweet Ella. 'Er name's Passella. A 'undred quid will buy 'er. Then I'd rent a stable and ...' He paused. 'Aw, hell,' he finished indignantly, 'anyone but you would know the rest of it! It don't seem possible that *you* don't.'

I laughed. Then I said, 'OK, Tom. Perhaps I *should* know. There's a stable behind this building. Take it. Here is a hundred pounds. Go and buy your mare. By Passing By out of Sweet Ella, I think you said. If there's anything else you want to train her, just let me know.'

Well, that was the start of it. A queer entrance to the Sport of Kings.

It wasn't long before Tom had her ready. She was a pretty mare with a sweet true head, just 14.1 hands.

'Now, boss,' Tom said in the inevitable highly confidential manner of all trainers of a horse, 'this mare's in at Kensington tomorrow with 8 stone 1, and she's a moral. What I want you to do is just go out quiet like and put about four 'undred on 'er, and she'll come 'ome smoking her pipe.'

The old, old story in the same time-honoured vernacular. How many men have fallen for a yarn like that! The confidence, the bland assurance, the fantastic triumph of hope over experience these little fellows always have.

'But, Tom,' I said, 'four hundred is a lot of money. What makes you so sure she'll win?'

'Sure?' Tom exclaimed with considerable asperity. 'Sure? Of course I'm sure.' Then with the crackpot logic of his kind, ''Aven't I told you she's a moral? Run three in thirty-seven she did this morning, touching the outside fence, with 'er 'eavy irons on. There's a thing called Pretty Sweet in it, which of course Passella will leave for dead, but they'll make a price for us. Well, 'ow about it, boss? 'Aven't lost your nerve, I 'ope?'

I remember that I felt a little bit ashamed. After all, this lad should know. Hadn't he been beaten on forty-two favourites in a row? Wasn't he steeped to his very ears in the chances of the racecourse? He had gone to what seemed to me a prodigious amount of trouble to get this mare ready. He was so confident. He spoke with such finality about so many intriguing aspects of the art of training horses. It appeared almost ludicrous to imagine this horseman wouldn't know. Moreover, he was an amateur psychologist. He'd said, "Aven't lost your nerve, boss, I 'ope?' A remark like that to a man like me! Just dynamite!

Well, I went to Kensington, and Tom hovered at my elbow.

'Now what do I do?' I asked.

Tom said, 'There's Jack Shaw, he'll bet you. 'E's a 'eavy better, 'e'll take the lot.'

'The lot, Tom?'

'Yes, ask 'im for the odds to four 'undred quid.'

So I did as I was told, and Mr Shaw bet me eight hundred pounds to four hundred, and I put the indecipherable ticket in my pocket.

'Now what, Tom?'

He looked at me as a mother will a backward child.

'Get into the stand,' he answered, 'and watch 'er win it.' And he trotted off.

So I sat down in the stand and they brought the ponies out, and the jockeys mounted in their flaunting colours. And there was a chap called Bill Cook in *my* colours, which I'd never seen before.

I didn't know it then because I didn't know thoroughbreds, but she was a bonny little mare, this Passella. I could see the way she fought to reach the bay mare, Pretty Sweet, all the long way up that straight. I didn't know a horse, but I knew a fighter when I saw one. I heard the crowd roar, and I saw the sign hoisted on the signal box. It read, 'Dead Heat'.

I went to look for Tom, and when I found him I asked in some puzzlement, 'What now, Tom?'

'We'll run it off,' he said.

'Run what off, Tom?'

He glared at me. 'Yeah, run it off in an hour's time. 'Ere, you go and 'ave a drink.'

He muttered something under his breath I couldn't catch, and hurried off as if he wanted to get away from me, which was unusual.

Well, they came up that straight a second time, locked together, in a bitter struggle, those two game midget horses with their nostrils flaring, and their ears resting in their straining necks, with the jockeys flailing at them with their whips and the people shouting.

They were very close together, so very close that in the last few desperate yards they seemed to lean over at an angle as if sheer weariness forced them to seek support. But Pretty Sweet won. No doubt of that. By the bare three inches. Her number showed in the signal box, and Tom came running and whispered urgently, 'Protest.'

'Protest, Tom?' I echoed. 'About what? To whom?'

'Aw, hell!' he snarled, and scuttled off, and as the ponies came trotting in I heard the crowd roar, 'Protest!' I looked at the signal tower where a green flag fluttered, and under it the word 'Protest' showed in black and white.

I waited, and in a little time I saw another flag go up, and another legend underneath, 'Protest upheld'.

I saw Tom coming at a run, with a grin upon his face, and when he reached me I asked him, 'What now, Tom?'

His excited chatter stopped as if I'd hit him with a board.

He took his hat off, and ran his stubby fingers through the remnants of his hair, and then in a voice devoid of hope, he said disgustedly, 'Aw, hell! You run and collect your eight 'undred quid and then go 'ome.'

The story's true. You can read the records if you want to.

BOTTLE QUEEN

Trad/Jim Haynes

We bred her in the suburbs and we trained her after dark,
Sometimes down the Botany Road and sometimes in the park,
And the way we used to feed her, it often led to rows,
We pinched the chaff from stables and the green stuff from the
    Chows.

Now her sire was imported, but we never knew from where
And her mother, 'Black Moria', was a bottle dealer's mare.
We bought a set of colours, they were second-hand and green,
And we had to call her something, so we called her 'Bottle Queen'.

In the evenings when we galloped her I usually took the mount,
We didn't have a stopwatch, so me mate, he used to count.
She showed us four in forty-nine, one-forty for the mile,
But she coulda done much better, she was pulling all the while.

Now that's something like a gallop, on the sand with ten stone up,
It'd win the English Derby! Or the Wagga Wagga Cup!
And when we thought we had her just as fit as she could be,
Me mate, he bit his sheila for the nomination fee.

We bunged her in a maiden and they dobbed her seven stone,
Talk about a 'jacky', she was in it on her own!
So we worked her on the bottles when the cart was good and light,
It was bottles every morning and training every night.

We walked down to Kenso on the morning of the race,
The books had never heard of her, we backed her win and place,
Then we rubbed her down and saddled her and led her to the track,
And told that hoop his fee was good … if he brought a winner back!

Well, they jumped away together but 'The Queen' was soon
in front,
As for all the others, they were never in the hunt!
She was romping past the Leger, she was fighting for her head,
When some bastard waved a bottle ... and our certainty
stopped dead!

Now when folks who know hear, 'Bottle-Oh', they say, 'There's
poor old Jim,
He mighta made a fortune, but the bottle did him in.'
Yes we shoulda made a motza, my bloody oath we should,
Except, I guess, you might say that 'The Queen' was trained
too good!

So, don't talk to me of racing, you can see I've had enough.
It's a game for men with money and for blokes who know
their stuff.
And if someone tries to tell you that the racing game is clean ...
Just remember what I told you, my tale of 'Bottle Queen'.

DONE FOR THE DOUBLE

A. B. ('Banjo') Paterson
(Writing as 'Knott Gold',
author of *Flogged for a Furlong, Won by a Winker*, etc.)

Wanted, a Pony

Algernon de Montgomery Smythers was a merchant, wealthy and beyond the dreams of avarice. Other merchants might dress more lavishly, and wear larger watch chains, but the bank balance is the true test of mercantile superiority, and in trial of bank balances Algernon de Montgomery represented Tyson at seven stone. He was unbeatable.

He lived in comfort, not to say luxury. He had champagne for breakfast every morning and his wife always slept with a pair of diamond earrings worth a small fortune in her ears. It is things like these that show true gentility. All others are shoddy.

Though they had been married many years, the A de M Smythers had but one child – a son and heir. He was brought up in the lap of luxury. No Christmas Day was allowed to pass by his doting parents without a gift to young Algy of some trifle worth about £150, less the discount for cash. He had six playrooms, all filled with the most expensive toys and ingenious mechanical devices. He had a phonograph that could hail a ship out at the South Head, and a mechanical parrot that sang 'The Wearing of the Green'. And still he was not happy.

Sometimes, in spite of the vigilance of his four nurses and six under-nurses, he would escape into the street, and run about with the little boys that he met there. One day he gave one of them a sovereign for a locust. Certainly the locust was a 'double-drummer', and could deafen the German Band when shaken up judiciously; still, it was dear at the price of a sovereign.

It is ever thus.

What we have we do not value, and what other people have we are not strong enough to take from them.

Such is life.

Christmas was approaching, and the question of what should be given to Algy as a present agitated the bosom of his parents. He had nearly everything a child would want, but one morning a bright inspiration struck Algy's father. Algy should have a pony.

With Mr Smythers to think was to act. He was not a man who believed in allowing grass to grow under his feet. His motto was, 'Up and be doing – somebody'. So he put an advertisement in the paper that same day.

> Wanted, a boy's pony. Must be guaranteed sound, strong, handsome, intelligent. Used to trains, trams, motors, fire engines, and motor buses. Any failure in above respect will disqualify. Certificate of birth required as well as references from last place, when calling. Price no object.

Blinky Bill's Sacrifice

Down in the poverty-stricken portions of the city lived Blinky Bill the horse dealer. His yard was surrounded by loose boxes made of any old timber, galvanised iron, sheets of roofing felt, and bark that he could gather together. He kept all sorts of horses, except good sorts. There were harness horses that wouldn't pull, and saddle horses that wouldn't go – or, if they went used to fall down; nearly every animal about the place had something the matter with it.

He kept racing ponies, and when the bailiff dropped in, for the rent, as he did every two or three weeks, Bill and the bailiff would go out together, and 'have a punt' on some of Bill's ponies, or on somebody else's ponies – the latter for choice. But the periodical punts and occasional sales of horses would not keep the wolf from the door. Ponies keep on eating whether they are winning or not and Blinky Bill had got down to the very last pitch of desperation when he saw the advertisement mentioned at the end of the last chapter.

It was like a ray of hope to him. At once there flashed upon him what he must do. He must make a great sacrifice; he must sell

Sausage II. What, the reader might ask, was Sausage II? Alas, that such a great notability should be anywhere unknown!

Sausage II was the greatest thirteen-two pony of the day. Time and again he had gone out to race when, to use William's own words, it was a blue duck for Bill's chance of keeping afloat unless the pony won; and every time did the gallant race pony pull his owner through. Bill owed more to Sausage II than he owed to any of his creditors.

Brought up as a pet, the little animal was absolutely trustworthy. He would carry a lady or a child, or pull a sulky; in fact, it was quite a common thing for Blinky Bill to drive him in a sulky to a country meeting and look about him for a likely 'mark'; if he could find a fleet youth with a reputedly fast pony, Bill would offer to 'pull the little cuddy out of the sulky and run yer for a fiver'. Sometimes he got beaten but, as he never paid, that didn't matter. He did not believe in fighting, except under desperate circumstances, but he would always sooner fight than pay.

But all these devices had left him on his uppers in the end. He had no feed for his ponies, and no money to buy feed; the corn merchant had written his account off as bad, and had no desire to make it worse. Under the circumstances, what was he to do? Sausage II must be sold.

With heavy heart Bill led the pony down to be inspected. He saw Algernon de Montgomery Smythers and measured him with his eye. He saw it would be no use to talk about racing to him, so he went on the other tack.

He told him that the pony belonged to a Methodist clergyman, who used to drive him in a 'shay'. There are no shays in this country; but Bill had read the word somewhere, and thought it sounded respectable. 'Yus, sir,' he said, ''e goes lovely in a shay,' and he was just starting off at twenty words a second, when he was stopped.

Mr A de M Smythers was brusque with his inferiors, and in this he made a mistake. Instead of listening to all that Blinky Bill said, and disbelieving it at his leisure, he stopped his talk. 'If you want to sell this pony, dry up,' he said. 'I don't believe a word you say, and it only worries me to hear you lying.'

Fatal mistake! You should never stop a horse dealer's talk. And call him anything you like, but never say you doubt his word.

Both these things, Mr Smythers did; and though he bought the pony at a high price, yet the insult sank deep into the heart of Blinky Bill.

As the capitalist departed leading the pony, Blinky Bill muttered to himself, 'Ha! Ha! Little does he know that he is leading Sausage II, the greatest thirteen-two pony of the century. Let him beware how he gets alongside anything. That's all! Blinky Bill may yet be revenged!'

We shall see.

Exit Algy

Christmas Day came. Algy's father gave orders to have the pony saddled, and led round to the front door. Algy's mother, a lady of forty summers, spent the morning superintending the dinner. Dinner was the principal event in the day with her. Alas, poor lady! Everything she ate agreed with her, and she got fatter and fatter and fatter.

The cold world never fully appreciates struggles of those who are fat – the efforts at starvation, the detested exercise, the long, miserable walks. Well has one of our greatest poets written, 'Take up the fat man's burden.' But we digress.

When Algy saw the pony he shouted with delight, and in half a minute was riding him up and down the front drive. Then he asked for leave to go out in the street, and that was where the trouble began.

Up and down the street the pony cantered, as quietly as possible, till suddenly round a corner came two butcher boys racing their horses. With a clatter of clumsy hoofs they thundered past. In half a second there was a rattle, and a sort of comet-like rush through the air. Sausage II was off after them with his precious burden.

The family dog tried to keep up with him, and succeeded in keeping ahead for about three strides. Then, like the wolves that pursued Mazeppa, he was left yelping far behind.

Through Surry Hills and Redfern swept the flying pony, his rider lying out on his neck in Tod Sloan fashion, while the ground seemed to race beneath him. The events of the way were just one hopeless blur till the pony ran straight as an arrow into the yard of his owner, Blinky Bill.

Running the Rule

As soon as Blinky Bill recognised his visitor, he was delighted. 'You here,' he said, 'Ha, ha, revenge is mine! I'll get a tidy reward for taking you back, my young shaver.' Then from the unresisting child he took a gold watch and three sovereigns, which he had in his pocket. These he said he would put in a safe place for him, till he was going home again. He expected to get at least a tenner ready money for bringing the child back, and hoped that he might be allowed to keep the watch into the bargain. With a light heart he went down town with Algy's watch and sovereigns in his pocket. He did not return till daylight, when he awoke his wife with bad news.

'Can't give the boy up,' he said. 'I moskenoed his block and tackle, and blued it in the school,' meaning that he had pawned the boy's watch and chain, and had lost the proceeds at pitch and toss. 'Nothing for it but to move,' he said, 'and take the kid with us.'

So move they did.

The reader can imagine with what frantic anxiety the father and mother of little Algy sought for their lost one. They put the matter into the hands of the detective police, and waited for the Sherlock Holmeses of the force to get in their fine work. They heard nothing.

Years rolled on, and the mysterious disappearance of little Algy was never solved. The horse dealer's revenge was complete. The boy's mother consulted a clairvoyant, who said, 'What went by the ponies, will come by the ponies,' and with that they had to remain satisfied.

The Tricks of the Turf

It was race day at Pulling'em Park, and the ponies were doing their usual performances. Among the throng the heaviest punter is a fat lady with diamond earrings. Does the reader recognise her? It is little Algy's mother. Her husband is dead, leaving her the whole of his colossal fortune, and, having developed a taste for gambling, she is now engaged in 'doing in on the ponies'. She is one of the biggest betters in the game.

When women take to betting they are worse than men.

But it is not for betting alone that she attends the meetings. She remembers the clairvoyant's 'What went by the ponies will come by the ponies.' And always she searches in the ranks of the talent for her lost Algy.

Here comes another of our *dramatis personae* – Blinky Bill, prosperous once more. He got a string of ponies and punters together. The first are not much use to a man without the second; but, in spite of all temptations Bill has always declined to number among his punters the mother of the child he stole. But the poor lady regularly punts on his ponies, and just as regularly is 'sent up' – in other words, loses her money.

Today she has backed Blinky's pair, Nostrils and Tin Can, for the double. Nostrils has won his race, and Tin Can, if on the job, can win the second half of the double. Is he on the job? The prices are lengthening against him, and the poor lady recognises that once more she is 'in the cart'.

Just then she meets Tin Can's jockey, Dodger Smith, face to face. A piercing scream rends the atmosphere, as if a thousand school children drew a thousand slate pencils down a thousand slates simultaneously. 'Me cheild! Me cheild! Me long-lost Algy!'

It did not take long to convince Algy that he would be better off as son to a wealthy lady than as a jockey subject to the fiendish caprices of Blinky Bill.

'All right, Mother,' he said. 'Put all you can raise on Tin Can. I'm going to send Blinky up. It's time I had a cut on me own, anyway.'

The horses went to the post. Tons of money were at the last moment hurled onto Tin Can. The books, knowing he was 'dead', responded gamely, and wrote his name till their wrists gave out. Blinky Bill had a half-share in all the bookies' winnings, so he chuckled grimly as he went to the rails to watch the race.

They're off. And what is this that flashes to the front, while the howls of the bookies rise like the yelping of fiends in torment? It is

Dodger Smith on Tin Can, and from the grandstand there is a shrill feminine yell of triumph as the gallant pony sails past the post.

The bookies thought that Blinky Bill had sold them, and they discarded him for ever. He is now a bottle-oh!

Algy and his mother were united, and backed horses together happily ever after; and sometimes out in the back yard of their palatial mansion they hand the empty bottles, free of charge, to a poor old broken-down bottle-oh. It is Blinky Bill. Thus has his revenge recoiled upon himself.

BETTING AND BEER

J. G. Medley

Put three or four quid on the horses,
And a couple of pounds on the trots;
Ten bob for the dogs in their courses,
And something or other for spots –
And if there is anything over
That hasn't been got by the cats,
What ho! For a future in clover
By way of a ticket in Tatts.

Oh! Betting and Beer are the basis
Of the only respectable life.
Much better to go to the races
Than moulder at home with the wife.
I'd much sooner go to the races
Than take all the kids to the sea.
My family knows what their place is,
And that is at home – without me.

Extract from JOCKEY JACK

Nat Gould

A bitter night. The rain falling in a pitiless torrent, flooding the streets and filling the broad Melbourne gutters with a rush of water. It was evident the Theatre Royal in Bourke Street had been exceptionally full, judging by the crowds streaming from the various entrances.

Coming down the dress circle stairs might be noticed a man who was evidently known to many of the fashionable crowd present, although it could be guessed he was not one of them. At his side, holding his hand, and looking the picture of happy childish glee, was a young girl, not more than ten years of age. The men nodded to her father in a familiar manner, and several ladies smiled at the child's excited eager face. Most people knew Teddy Dalton.

'It's a fearful night, Hettie. We must have a hansom, and get home as fast as we can,' said the man.

They had reached the pavement now, and he was looking about for a cab, but there were very few there, and they were engaged.

'We shall have to take a waggonette,' he said.

Hettie pouted, and said: 'I don't like them, Dad. Do get a hansom.'

'I'll get yer a hansom, sir,' said a voice close at his elbow.

He turned, and saw a ragged little urchin shivering in the cold, and wet to the skin. 'Poor little fellow,' said Hettie, with tears starting to her eyes; 'how cold he must be, Dad.'

The youngster was a pitiful object to look at. He was very small, and lightly made. His face was intelligent, and he had a pair of bright-blue eyes which looked wistfully under Hettie's hood into her pretty face. His clothes were ragged and torn, and his hat barely protected him from the wet. His little feet were bare, and he rubbed his small hands together to warm them.

'I'm a bit cold, missy, I can tell yer,' he said. 'Let me run for a 'ansom, sir, it'll warm me up.'

'All right, young 'un, be sharp,' was the reply, and off the urchin darted at top speed.

'He can run, anyway,' said Dalton.

'What a little chap he is, Dad,' said Hettie. 'I wonder has he any home?'

The lad was not long away, and returned with a cab, and a decent-looking nag in the shafts.

'That'll do, boy. You've not been long. Here's a shilling for you.'

He put his little girl in the cab, and turned to look at the boy.

'Where's your home?'

'Got none, sir.'

'How old are you, my lad?'

'Dunno exactly, sir, but expects I'm about ten.'

'My lassie's age,' he thought.

'Come along, Dad,' came from the cab.

'This poor little lad says he's no home, Hettie. Fancy leaving him out here all night.'

'Oh, I'm so sorry. Take him home, Dad. He can sleep in the boys' rooms,' and Hettie's head, with the red hood over it, peered out of the front of the cab.

'Here, my lad, jump in here, and curl yourself up on the floor in the corner, and we'll see if we can't bed you down for the night in a stable or somewhere.'

The lad opened his eyes wide, but he scrambled into the cab without the slightest hesitation, and snuggled down in the corner.

'Home,' said Dalton.

The cab pulled up at a neat-looking house, and Dalton flung open the doors. As he did so the lad rolled against the splash-board, and the shock woke him up.

'Been asleep, young 'un? Dare say you're tired,' said Dalton. 'Come, wake up, and tumble out.'

Hettie ran into the house, and was soon in her mother's arms. 'Dad's brought a poor little starved lad home, Mother,' she said. 'He's such a mite.'

'Drat him!' said Mrs Dalton, but not at all bad humouredly. 'He's a heart as big as a melon. He ought to have been a charity organisation.'

Dalton came up the walk, the lad following him. 'Well, he's a nice beauty,' said Mrs Dalton. Then, after a good look at him, she said: 'He's hardly any clothes on. Bless my soul, Ned, how uncommon cold he must be.'

'I should say he wasn't over warm,' said Ned, divesting himself of his overcoat, 'and he looks as if a meal would do him good. Give him some beef and ham, and some hot coffee, that'll settle him.'

The lad's mouth fairly watered, and such an eager expectant look came into his eyes, that Mrs Dalton, good motherly woman that she was, caught him by the neck, and calling out, 'Sarah, Sarah,' took him in the direction of the kitchen.

Sarah, a demure, prim maid, held up her hands aghast at the sight.

'Feed him, Sarah. He's starving,' said Mrs Dalton. 'Are you hungry, my lad?'

'Ain't I jest,' he said. 'You try me.'

'Come along,' said Sarah, and in a very short space of time the homeless wanderer of the Melbourne streets was pitching ham and beef and bread into himself at a rate to make Sarah stare.

'Yer can't have had much ter eat, lad,' she said.

'No – n – no, – not – much,' he got out with difficulty, as his mouth was chock full. The urchin seemed ravenous. Would he never stop eating? Then he poured three large cups of hot coffee down. At last he laid his knife and fork down, and gave a deep sigh, while tears almost came into his eyes.

'What's the matter, my lad?' said Sarah, who seemed to possess a heart of somewhat the same tender material as her master and mistress.

'I'm sorry I can't eat no more,' said the lad, with such a doleful expression of countenance that Sarah laughed.

'Have you had a good feed, youngster?' said Dalton, as he entered the kitchen.

'Yes, sir, thank yer kindly.'

'Then come with me, and I'll fix you up for the night,' and he led the way by aid of a lantern out at the back door. He had a blanket on his arm, and some old boys' clothes. He pulled open the door, and called 'Bob'.

'Hallo, sir,' said the individual addressed, in a half sleepy voice.

'There's a lad in the loft, don't disturb him in the morning.'

'All right, sir,' said Bob.

'There, young 'un, make yourself comfortable. Pull those wet togs off, and roll yourself up in this blanket, and put these clothes on in the morning. If you're a good lad, maybe I'll find a job for you, and you can earn a bit of money.'

'You're very good, sir,' said the lad. 'I'll be ever such a good lad. My, ain't it nice and warm here. Ain't it, just. You bet I'll sleep here, sir.'

'That's right. Now turn in. By the bye, what's your name, my lad?'

'Jack, sir,' was the reply.

'Jack. What's your other name?'

'Ain't got none that I knows of, sir,' said the lad.

'Poor little chap. Well, lie there till you're called in the morning.'

'All right, sir,' and, rolled in his blanket, Jack was fast asleep on his bed of clean straw almost before Dalton had reached the house again.

'Have you fixed him, Ned?' said Mrs Dalton. 'Hettie's gone to bed tired out.'

'Bless the lass. I've put him right, Mag,' said Dalton. 'There's something about that little chap I like. I'll bet he'd be honest.'

'Do you mean to keep him?' said Mrs Dalton.

'If he turns out handy. I want a couple more lads, and he's just the make. He's young, too, and I can teach him better,' said Dalton.

'It's my belief, Ned, you'd make room for forty boys if they asked you. But he does look an intelligent lad. What's his name?'

'Jack, he says, and hasn't got another.'

'The old tale, I expect,' said Mrs Dalton. 'A stray child cast on the world to live or die as Providence sees fit.'

Little Jack lay snug and warm in his blanket. He slept like a top, and for once in his life had pleasant dreams in which a confused mass of ideas floated through his mind. The rain dashed against the building furiously, but he heard it not. Homeless, outcast, street arab Jack had struck a piece of luck which was about to change the whole course of his life.

IMPORTANT
GEORGE DRINKS WATER
USE THE PICKER

DONT BACK-ANSWER

ASK NO QUESTIONS

THERE IS ONLY ONE TRAINER PER S

EVERYTHING HAS A PROPER PLACE

SILENCE IS GOLDEN

TURN OFF THE LIGHTS

'If you're a good lad, maybe I'll find a job for you ...'

When Jack opened his eyes next morning, the sunlight was streaming in at the windows of the loft and almost blinded him, so dazzling was its brilliancy. He rubbed his eyes and stared about him, unable at first to comprehend where he was. He felt so warm and snug, he had half a mind to turn over and go to sleep again. Then he recollected the scene of the night before, and how he had been taken out of the wet, cold street by a kind gentleman and beautiful young girl. At the remembrance of the supper his mouth watered, and he smiled quietly to himself.

Jack was not half a bad-looking chap. True, he was not very clean, and his long, curly hair was unkempt, but he had clear blue eyes and an honest face, which, when lighted up with a happy smile, looked pleasant and attractive. He wondered if he would be allowed to remain in his present quarters, or be turned out into the street again. At the latter prospect he shivered, and snuggled down into his blanket on the straw bed. This stable loft seemed a perfect paradise to homeless little Jack after the hardships he had undergone. He was roused from a half-doze by a voice shouting: 'Now then, you young brat, get up. It's time you came down if you want any breakfast.'

A head appeared at the top of the ladder, and Jack, looking up, saw for the first time Bob Sharpe, Ned Dalton's head lad.

Jack liked that face although the voice was gruff. Bob Sharpe was designated 'head lad', but as a matter of fact he was several years past the age when individuals are usually addressed by that term. He was no lad, but a miniature man well developed, strong, but small.

Jack smiled at him, and didn't seem a bit alarmed.

He said: 'Boss told me to stop here till I were called. If there's any breakfast about, you bet I'll get up.'

This speech from such a child, 'a mere baby' Bob called him, surprised Mr Sharpe, and he said: 'You're uncommon smart with your tongue, youngster, but you're none of the worse for that, although if you don't look out it may get you into trouble here.'

'May I stop here?' said Jack, eagerly.

'Get up and let's look at you,' said Bob Sharpe.

Jack scrambled to his feet and stood erect, and a very small fellow he seemed.

Sharpe eyed him over, then climbed up into the loft, and lifted Jack up in both arms. He put him down somewhat gently, and again scanned him critically.

'How old are you?' he asked.

'Reckon I'm about ten,' said Jack.

'You're just the build. Master must keep you here. Now mind what I say, young 'un, if you're a good lad I'll be your friend, if not, well I'll make things mighty unpleasant for you.'

'I'll be good,' said Jack. 'Only let me stop here. It's so cold out in the streets at night.'

'Come down to breakfast as soon as you're dressed,' said Bob, as Jack commenced to scramble into the dry clothes Dalton had given him the previous night.

He then climbed down the ladder, and went out. He ran across to the kitchen, and opened the door, where he saw four lads sitting at a table having their morning meal.

'Well, Mop,' said one of the lads to Jack, 'what are you staring at?'

The mop was evidently an allusion to the state of Jack's head, and the 'staring' to the ardent gaze he cast upon the eatables.

'I reckon that's good,' said Jack, pointing to a nice pie of considerable dimensions.

'Yes, it's passable,' said the lad who had spoken before.

'Passable!' said Sarah, who was present. 'Well things is comin' to a pretty pass when stable brats can talk in this fashion.'

'Never mind, Sally, you're a good sort,' said another of the 'boys', 'Toddy's a bit off this mornin'. He got chucked off old Primrose, and didn't come a cropper neither.'

This was Sarah's chance for revenge, so she said: 'He never could ride. He'll have to take a few lessons from this little chap before long, or I'm mistaken,' she said, pointing at Jack.

'Much you know about ridin',' said Toddy, angrily. 'As for that kid, he's not pluck enough to get on a horse, I'll bet, much less ride one.'

'Ain't I,' said Jack. 'You jest try me.'

'Bravo, little man,' said Ned Dalton, who had just come upon the scene, and heard his words. 'We'll try you after breakfast and see what sort of stuff you are made of.'

After Jack had had a good meal, he went into the yard again, and saw the lads busily engaged grooming down several horses, and he looked on, evidently delighted.

'Now youngster, come here,' said Dalton. 'Have you ever been on a horse?'

Now as it happened, young though Jack was, he had been several times on horseback, for he was constantly hanging about livery stables and cab-yards, and the men used him to walk their horses about occasionally, and at times he had been put up on a roughish customer 'just for a lark', so Jack answered: 'Yes, I've been on horses, but I can't ride much, sir. But I ain't afraid,' he added, quickly.

'Come along, we'll try you.'

Primrose was brought out, and Jack lifted into the saddle. He hadn't been much used to a saddle, but he said nothing, and looked determined.

The horse walked quietly into the paddock, and then cantered about in high good humour. Jack held firmly on, and stuck his knees in tight.

Dalton eyed him closely.

'Canter him,' he said.

Jack gave Primrose a kick, and the horse lashed out and threw his tiny rider onto his neck, but he was quickly in the saddle again.

Primrose cantered round the grass ring, and Jack sat firmly in his seat. He felt quite elated. Suddenly, without warning, Primrose swerved quickly round, and threw Jack heavily to the ground. He was up in a minute, and looked ruefully after the horse, which had trotted to the gate.

Dalton laughed, as Jack came up and said: 'Put me up again, sir. Let me have another ride.'

Dalton lifted him into the saddle, but said nothing. As Primrose walked away, he quietly switched his behind. The horse lashed out, but Jack kept his seat. He then swerved round again, but this time his rider was ready for the move, and did not come off. The horse, seemingly satisfied, cantered gently along, and Jack pulled him up at the gate again.

Dalton lifted him off, as Sharpe took the horse, and said: 'You'll do, young 'un. I think I can make a rider of you some day. Would you like to be a jockey?'

'Shouldn't I,' said Jack, with his eyes shining with delight.

'Then I'll try and make you one. You've no parents, my little man, so they can't object,' he said. 'Well, Sharpe, what do you think of him?'

'He'll make a rider one of these days, sir. He's just built for it. He's the sort of cove to ride about seven stone when he's nearly a man,' said Bob.

'Then I'll keep him, at any rate,' said Dalton. 'He'll have a good show here, I reckon.'

'He's lucky to get into your stable, Mr Dalton,' said Bob.

'Please, sir,' said Jack, 'are you Teddy Dalton?' and he looked quite awestruck.

Dalton laughed outright, the lad looked so much in earnest.

'Teddy Dalton,' he said. 'What do you know of Teddy Dalton?'

'Why, he won the Cup with Daystar,' said Jack, in a trembling voice, as though such an event must be the height of ambition.

'So he did,' said Dalton. 'How did you know? It's before you were born.'

'But I've heard the lads talk about it, and Jimmy at Inglis' said Teddy Dalton were the best trainer in Australia, and that no man alive could have won the Cup with Daystar but him.'

In spite of himself Dalton looked pleased at such praise even from 'Jimmy at Inglis'. That victory of Daystar had made him for life. 'Yes, I'm Teddy Dalton, young 'un,' he said.

Jack looked thunderstruck as he wonderingly said: 'And you had Daystar?'

'Yes,' said Dalton, smiling.

'And you'll take me here, sir?' said Jack.

'I will, my lad,' said Dalton, patting his head.

This was too much for Jack. He did not cry or express his thanks in coherent words, but he capered about and shouted for joy.

'That'll do,' shouted Dalton, as Jack turned a somersault in his glee.

When Dalton had gone, Sharpe said to Jack: 'The master's taken up with you. I think it's because you're about the same age as

Master Willie when he died. I'll teach you what I can, young 'un, if you behave yourself.'

Jack had indeed found a home at last, and how good a one he was to experience in the future. So Jack was established at Hairbell Cottage, and became a stable lad in the crack racing establishment at Newmarket.

Some weeks afterwards Jack was grooming down his old friend Primrose when Hettie looked in at the door of the box, and her father stood close behind.

'Good morning, Jack,' she said.

'Good mornin', miss,' said Jack, touching his hair.

'That's Primrose, isn't it?'

'Yes, miss.'

'That's such a nice name, Dad,' she said. 'What's Jack's other name?' she asked. 'I've never heard it, what is it, Jack?'

'Don't know as I ever had another name, miss,' he said.

'Oh, but you must have another name.'

'Never heard of one, miss,' he replied.

'Then we must give you one. Let me see,' said the demure young ten-year-old lassie, meditatingly.

'You're to be a jockey, aren't you?'

'Yes please, miss,' said Jack.

'I've got it, Dad,' she said, as she clapped her hands and startled Primrose. 'I'll christen him Jockey Jack.'

Her father laughed, as he replied: 'Capital, Hettie. That name will stick to him, you see if it doesn't. How do you like it, Jack?'

'Grand, sir,' said Jack. 'I hope I'll be a real Jockey Jack some day.'

It was soon whispered about the yard that Jack had been given a nickname by Miss Hettie. The news travelled to Flemington training-ground, and in a very short time the poor little shivering waif Ned Dalton had taken out of the streets that pouring wet cold night was known to all the stable lads around Newmarket as Jockey Jack.

*　　*　　*

'Jockey Jack', as he was called in a moment of childish fun by Hettie Dalton, had no reason to ever regret the day he was taken care of by Ned Dalton.

Within several years of starting in the trainer's stables, he had already commenced to earn fame as a smart, reliable rider.

As a youth, he was small, and built on exceedingly light lines, but for all that he was a neat young man, and by no means tainted with stable slang. Jack had been educated at Dalton's expense. He was eager to learn and he quickly became a very fair scholar. He could write well, and soon learnt to speak in an orthodox fashion.

As a horseman he became proficient, and Ned Dalton was heard to remark upon several occasions that if he had a crack he wanted well and honestly ridden he'd as soon put Jockey Jack up as any man he knew.

'... a stable lad in the crack racing establishment ...'

ONLY A JOCKEY

A. B. ('Banjo') Paterson

> Richard Bennison, a jockey, aged fourteen, while riding
> *William Tell* in his training, was thrown and killed. The
> horse is luckily uninjured.
>
> *Melbourne Wire*

Out in the grey cheerless chill of the morning light,
Out on the track where the night shades still lurk;
Ere the first gleam of the sungod's returning light,
Round come the racehorses early at work.

Reefing and pulling and racing so readily,
Close sit the jockey-boys holding them hard,
'Steady the stallion there – canter him steadily,
Don't let him gallop so much as a yard.'

Fiercely he fights while the others run wide of him,
Reefs at the bit that would hold him in thrall,
Plunges and bucks till the boy that's astride of him
Goes to the ground with a terrible fall.

'Stop him there! Block him there! Drive him in carefully,
Lead him about till he's quiet and cool.
Sound as a bell! Though he's blown himself fearfully,
Now let us pick up this poor little fool.

'Stunned? Oh, by Jove, I'm afraid it's a case with him;
Ride for the doctor! Keep bathing his head!
Send for a cart to go down to our place with him –'
No use! One long sigh and the little chap's dead.

Only a jockey-boy, foul-mouthed and bad you see,
Ignorant, heathenish, gone to his rest.
Parson or Presbyter, Pharisee, Sadducee,
What did you do for him? – bad was the best.

Negroes and foreigners, all have a claim on you;
Yearly you send your well-advertised hoard,
But the poor jockey-boy – shame on you, shame on you,
'Feed ye, my little ones' – what said the Lord?

Him ye held less than the outer barbarian,
Left him to die in his ignorant sin;
Have you no principles, humanitarian?
Have you no precept – 'go gather them in?'

Knew he God's name? In his brutal profanity,
That name was an oath – out of many but one –
What did he get from our famed Christianity?
Where has his soul – if he had any – gone?

Fourteen years old, and what was he taught of it?
What did he know of God's infinite grace?
Draw the dark curtain of shame o'er the thought of it,
Draw the shroud over the jockey-boy's face.

BERT

C. J. Dennis

Did you ever meet Bert? 'E's all over the town,
In offices, shops an' in various places,
Cocky an' all; an' you can't keep 'im down.
I never seen no one so lucky at races.
Backs all the winners or very near all;
Tells you nex' day when the races are over.
'E makes quite a pot, for 'is wagers ain't small;
An' by rights 'e 'ad ought to be livin' in clover.

But, some'ow or other – aw, well, I dunno.
You got to admit that some fellers is funny.
'E don't dress too well an' 'is spendin' is low.
I can't understand wot 'e does with 'is money.
'E ought to be sockin' a pretty fair share;
An' tho' 'e will own 'e's a big money-maker,
'E don't seem to save an' 'e don't seem to care
If 'e owes a big wad to 'is butcher an' baker.

'E don't tell you much if you meet on the course;
But after it's over 'e comes to you grinnin',
Shows you 'is card where 'e's marked the first 'orse,
An' spins you a wonderful tale of 'is winnin'.
Can't make 'im out, 'e's so lucky an' that.
Knows ev'ry owner an' trainer an' jockey;
But all of 'is wagerin's done on 'is pat.
Won't spill a thing, even tho' 'e's so cocky.

Oyster, that's Bert. 'E's as close as a book.
But sometimes I've come on 'im sudden an' saw 'im
Lip 'angin' down an' a reel 'aggard look,
Like all the woes in the world come to gnaw 'im.
But, soon as 'e sees you, 'e brightens right up.
'Picked it again, lad!' 'e sez to you, grinnin'.
'A fiver at sevens I 'ad in the Cup!
That's very near sixty odd quid that I'm winnin'.'

Mystery man – that's 'is style for a cert,
Picks the 'ole card, yet 'e's shabby and seedy;
'E must 'ave some sorrer in secrit, old Bert –
Some drain on 'is purse wot is keepin' 'im needy.
A terrible pity. Some woman, no doubt.
No wonder 'e worries in secrit an' souses.
If I 'ad 'is winnin's, year in an' year out,
Why I'd own a Rolls-Royce an' a terris of 'ouses.

THE ORACLE

A. B. ('Banjo') Paterson

No tram ever goes to Randwick Races without him; he is always fat, hairy, and assertive; he is generally one of a party, and takes the centre of the stage all the time – collects and hands over the fares, adjusts the change, chaffs the conductor, crushes the thin, apologetic stranger next him into a pulp, and talks to the whole compartment as if they had asked for his opinion.

He knows all the trainers and owners, or takes care to give the impression that he does. He slowly and pompously hauls out his racebook, and one of his satellites opens the ball by saying, in a deferential way: 'What do you like for the 'urdles, Charley?'

The Oracle looks at the book and breathes heavily; no one else ventures to speak.

'Well,' he says, at last, 'of course there's only one in it – if he's wanted. But that's it – will they spin him? I don't think they will. They's only a lot o' cuddies, any'ow.'

No one likes to expose his own ignorance by asking which horse he refers to as the 'only one in it'; and the Oracle goes on to deal out some more wisdom in a loud voice.

'Billy K— told me' (he probably hardly knows Billy K— by sight) 'Billy K— told me that that bay 'orse ran the best mile an' a half ever done on Randwick yesterday; but I don't give him a chance, for all that; that's the worst of these trainers. They don't know when their horses are well – half of 'em.'

Then a voice comes from behind him. It is that of the thin man, who is crushed out of sight by the bulk of the Oracle.

'I think,' says the thin man, 'that that horse of Flannery's ought to run well in the handicap.'

The Oracle can't stand this sort of thing at all. He gives a snort, wheels half round and looks at the speaker. Then he turns back to the compartment full of people, and says: 'No 'ope.'

The thin man makes a last effort. 'Well, they backed him last night, anyhow.'

'Who backed 'im?' says the Oracle.

'In Tattersall's,' says the thin man.

'I'm sure,' says the Oracle; and the thin man collapses.

On arrival at the course, the Oracle is in great form. Attended by his string of satellites, he plods from stall to stall staring at the horses. Their names are printed in big letters on the stalls, but the Oracle doesn't let that stop his display of knowledge.

''Ere's Blue Fire,' he says, stopping at that animal's stall, and swinging his racebook. 'Good old Blue Fire!' he goes on loudly, as a little court collects. 'Jimmy B—' (mentioning a popular jockey) 'told me he couldn't have lost on Saturday week if he had only been ridden different. I had a good stake on him, too, that day. Lor', the races that has been chucked away on this horse. They will not ride him right.'

A trainer who is standing by, civilly interposes. 'This isn't Blue Fire,' he says. 'Blue Fire's out walking about. This is a two-year-old filly that's in the stall ...'

'Well, I can see that, can't I,' says the Oracle, crushingly. 'You don't suppose I thought Blue Fire was a mare, did you?' and he moves off hurriedly.

'Now, look here, you chaps,' he says to his followers at last. 'You wait here. I want to go and see a few of the talent, and it don't do to have a crowd with you. There's Jimmy M— over there now' (pointing to a leading trainer). 'I'll get hold of him in a minute. He couldn't tell me anything with so many about. Just you wait here.'

He crushes into a crowd that has gathered round the favourite's stall, and overhears one hard-faced racing man say to another, 'What do you like?' to which the other answers, 'Well, either this or Royal Scot. I think I'll put a bit on Royal Scot.' This is enough for the Oracle. He doesn't know either of the men from Adam, or either of the horses from the great original pachyderm, but the information will do to go on with. He rejoins his followers, and looks very mysterious.

'Well, did you hear anything?' they say.

The Oracle talks low and confidentially.

'The crowd that have got the favourite tell me they're not afraid of anything but Royal Scot,' he says. 'I think we'd better put a bit on both.'

'What did the Royal Scot crowd say?' asks an admirer deferentially.

'Oh, they're going to try and win. I saw the stable commissioner, and he told me they were going to put a hundred on him. Of course, you needn't say I told you, 'cause I promised him I wouldn't tell.' And the satellites beam with admiration of the Oracle, and think what a privilege it is to go to the races with such a knowing man.

They contribute their mites to the general fund, some putting in a pound, others half a sovereign, and the Oracle takes it into the ring to invest, half on the favourite and half on Royal Scot. He finds that the favourite is at two to one, and Royal Scot at threes, eight to one being offered against anything else. As he ploughs through the ring, a Whisperer (one of those broken-down followers of the turf who get their living in various mysterious ways, but partly by giving 'tips' to backers) pulls his sleeve.

'What are you backing?' he says.

'Favourite and Royal Scot,' says the Oracle.

'Put a pound on Bendemeer,' says the tipster. 'It's a certainty. Meet me here if it comes off, and I'll tell you something for the next race. Don't miss it now. Get on quick!'

The Oracle is humble enough before the hanger-on of the turf. A bookmaker roars 'Ten to one Bendemeer,' he suddenly fishes out a sovereign of his own – and he hasn't money to spare, for all his knowingness – and puts it on Bendemeer. His friends' money he puts on the favourite and Royal Scot as arranged. Then they all go round to watch the race.

The horses are at the post; a distant cluster of crowded animals with little dots of colour on their backs. Green, blue, yellow, purple, French grey, and old gold, they change about in a bewildering manner, and though the Oracle has a cheap pair of glasses, he can't make out where Bendemeer has got to. Royal Scot and the favourite he has lost interest in, and secretly hopes that they will be left at the post or break their necks; but he does not confide his sentiment to his companions.

They're off! The long line of colours across the track becomes a shapeless clump and then draws out into a long string. 'What's that in front?' yells someone at the rails. 'Oh, that thing of Hart's,' says someone else. But the Oracle hears them not; he is looking in the mass of colour for a purple cap and grey jacket, with black arm bands. He cannot see it anywhere, and the confused and confusing mass swings round the turn into the straight.

Then there is a babel of voices, and suddenly a shout of 'Bendemeer! Bendemeer!' and the Oracle, without knowing which is Bendemeer, takes up the cry feverishly. 'Bendemeer! Bendemeer!' he yells, waggling his glasses about, trying to see where the animal is.

'Where's Royal Scot, Charley? Where's Royal Scot?' screams one of his friends, in agony. ''Ow's he doin'?'

'No 'ope!' says the Oracle, with fiendish glee. 'Bendemeer! Bendemeer!'

The horses are at the Leger stand now, whips are out, and three horses seem to be nearly abreast; in fact, to the Oracle there seem to be a dozen nearly abreast. Then a big chestnut sticks his head in front of the others, and a small man at the Oracle's side emits a deafening series of yells right by the Oracle's ear: 'Go on, Jimmy! Rub it into him! Belt him! It's a cake-walk! A cake-walk!'

The big chestnut, in a dogged sort of way, seems to stick his body clear of his opponents, and passes the post a winner by a length. The Oracle doesn't know what has won, but fumbles with his book. The number on the saddle-cloth catches his eye – number 7; he looks hurriedly down the page. Number 7 – Royal Scot. Second is number 24 – Bendemeer. Favourite nowhere.

Hardly has he realised it, before his friends are cheering and clapping him on the back. 'By George, Charley, it takes you to pick 'em.' 'Come and 'ave a wet!' 'You 'ad a quid in, didn't you, Charley?' The Oracle feels very sick at having missed the winner, but he dies game. 'Yes, rather; I had a quid on,' he says. 'And,' (here he nerves himself to smile) 'I had a saver on the second, too.'

His comrades gasp with astonishment. 'D'you hear that, eh? Charley backed first and second. That's pickin' 'em if you like.' They have a wet, and pour fulsome adulation on the Oracle when he collects their money.

After the Oracle has collected the winnings for his friends he meets the Whisperer again.

'It didn't win?' he says to the Whisperer in inquiring tones.

'Didn't win,' says the Whisperer, who has determined to brazen the matter out. 'How could he win? Did you see the way he was ridden? That horse was stiffened just after I seen you, and he never tried a yard. Did you see the way he was pulled and hauled about at the turn? It'd make a man sick. What was the stipendiary stewards doing, I wonder?'

This fills the Oracle with a new idea. All that he remembers of the race at the turn was a jumble of colours, a kaleidoscope of horses and of riders hanging on to the horses' necks. But it wouldn't do to admit that he didn't see everything, and didn't know everything; so he plunges in boldly.

'O' course I saw it,' he says. 'And a blind man could see it. They ought to rub him out.'

'Course they ought,' says the Whisperer. 'But, look here, put two quid on Tell-tale; you'll get it all back!'

The Oracle does put on 'two quid', and doesn't get it all back. Neither does he see any more of this race than he did of the last one – in fact, he cheers wildly when the wrong horse is coming in. But when the public begin to hoot he hoots as loudly as anybody – louder if anything; and all the way home in the tram he lays down the law about stiff running, and wants to know what the stipendiaries are doing.

If you go into any barber's shop, you can hear him at it, and he flourishes in suburban railway carriages; but he has a tremendous local reputation, having picked first and second in the handicap, and it would be a bold man who would venture to question the Oracle's knowledge of racing and of all matters relating to it.

HARD LUCK

A. B. ('Banjo') Paterson

I left the course, and by my side
There walked a ruined tout –
A hungry creature, evil-eyed,
Who poured this story out.

'You see,' he said, 'there came a swell
To Kensington today,
And, if I picked the winners well,
A crown at least he'd pay.

'I picked three winners straight, I did;
I filled his purse with pelf,
And then he gave me half a quid
To back one for myself.

'A half a quid to me he cast –
I wanted it indeed;
So help me Bob, for two days past
I haven't had a feed.

'But still I thought my luck was in,
I couldn't go astray –
I put it all on Little Min,
And lost it straightaway.

'I haven't got a bite or bed,
I'm absolutely stuck;
So keep this lesson in your head:
Don't over-trust your luck!'

The folks went homeward, near and far,
The tout, oh! Where was he?
Ask where the empty boilers are
Beside the Circular Quay.

'... *keep this lesson in your head: Don't over-trust your luck!*' *Discarded betting tickets after the last race*

PART THREE

A HORSE FOR THE BUSH RACES

Bush races and picnic races are a great Australian pastime and anyone who has never attended such events is probably poorer for not having enjoyed the experience.

It is also true that Australian literature abounds with stories in which the central theme is 'the city versus the bush'. It is a well-loved myth that we are divided into either city slickers or country bumpkins.

In reality there was little truth in this idea until the great waves of migration occurred in the 1940s and 1950s. Most city-dwelling Australians up until that time had connections with the bush in some form or another and most of those who lived in rural areas were not strangers to the city.

Even today, in the eastern suburbs of Sydney for example, institutions such as boarding schools, Randwick Racecourse and, until recently, the Agricultural Show, have meant that country people are much in evidence and feel quite comfortable in the city environment. Cities such as Brisbane and Adelaide have even stronger connections to the bush.

It is also not that long ago that the city environment was not entirely dissimilar to the rural environment. Banjo Paterson and Norman Lindsay took Sunday rides together through the northern suburbs in the 1920s and '30s, and I can remember horses and carts and farms and dairies in inner Sydney as late as the 1960s.

Some of our best loved stories and literary characters, however, have perpetuated the myth of 'the city or the bush'. Dad and Dave, the Sentimental Bloke, the Man from Ironbark and many others reinforced the idea that Australia was really two nations, one rural and one urban.

If there is any truth at all in this myth it is, perhaps, apparent in the way racing was conducted in the city compared to the bush in days gone by.

It is certainly true that this particular section of the book is full of stories which seem to suggest that bush racing is a crazy, haphazard activity and the bush is inhabited by cheats, drunks and comic book characters.

Let me apologise in advance to all my rural friends. All I can say, in defence of my selection here, is that some of these stories are very funny and others capture the spirit of the time.

Today many country race clubs are thriving due to the TAB and events at provincial tracks like Grafton, Oakbank, Warrnambool, Wagga Wagga and Toowoomba are second to none. Smaller well-run clubs like Wallabadah, which is the oldest rural racing club in Australia and has conducted meetings since 1852, give the lie to many of the malicious myths propagated in this section.

'Wallabadah ... is the oldest rural racing club in Australia'

AN IDYLL OF DANDALOO

A. B. ('Banjo') Paterson

On western plains, where shade is not,
'Neath summer skies of cloudless blue,
Where all is dry and all is hot,
There stands the town of Dandaloo –
A township where life's total sum
Is sleep, diversified with rum.

Its grass-grown streets with dust are deep,
'Twere vain endeavour to express
The dreamless silence of its sleep,
Its wide, expansive drunkenness.
The yearly races mostly drew
A lively crowd to Dandaloo.

There came a sportsman from the East,
The eastern land where sportsmen blow,
And brought with him a speedy beast –
A speedy beast as horses go.
He came afar in hope to 'do'
The little town of Dandaloo.

Now this was weak of him, I wot –
Exceeding weak, it seemed to me –
For we in Dandaloo were not
The Jugginses we seemed to be;
In fact, we rather thought we knew
Our book by heart in Dandaloo.

We held a meeting at the bar,
And met the question fair and square –
'We've stumped the country near and far
To raise the cash for races here;
We've got a hundred pounds or two –
Not half so bad for Dandaloo.

'And now, it seems, we have to be
Cleaned out by this here Sydney bloke,
With his imported horse; and he
Will scoop the pool and leave us broke
Shall we sit still, and make no fuss
While this chap climbs all over us?'

The races came to Dandaloo,
And all the cornstalks from the West,
On ev'ry kind of moke and screw,
Came forth in all their glory dressed.
The stranger's horse, as hard as nails,
Look'd fit to run for New South Wales.

He won the race by half a length,
Quite *half a length*, it seemed to me,
But Dandaloo, with all its strength,
Roared out 'Dead heat!' most fervently;
And, after hesitation meet,
The judge's verdict was 'Dead heat!'

And many men there were could tell
What gave the verdict extra force:
The stewards, and the judge as well –
They all had backed the second horse.
For things like this they sometimes do
In larger towns than Dandaloo.

They ran it off; the stranger won,
Hands down, by near a hundred yards
He smiled to think his troubles done;
But Dandaloo held all the cards.
They went to scale and, cruel fate!
His jockey turned out underweight.

Perhaps they'd tampered with the scale!
I cannot tell. I only know
It weighed him OUT all right. I fail
To paint that Sydney sportsman's woe.
He said the stewards were a crew
Of low-lived thieves in Dandaloo.

He lifted up his voice, irate,
And swore till all the air was blue;
So then we rose to vindicate
The dignity of Dandaloo.
'Look here,' said we, 'you must not poke
Such oaths at us poor country folk.'

We rode him softly on a rail,
We shied at him, in careless glee,
Some large tomatoes, rank and stale,
And eggs of great antiquity,
Their wild, unholy fragrance flew
About the town of Dandaloo.

He left the town at break of day,
He led his racehorse through the streets,
And now he tells the tale, they say,
To every racing man he meets.
And Sydney sportsmen all eschew
The atmosphere of Dandaloo.

'*The yearly races mostly drew a lively crowd ...*' *Individual seating at a bush meeting (Wallabadah 1940s)*

A HORSE FOR THE BUSH RACES

Jim Haynes

A horse for the Bush Races, that's what we wanted more than anything. A real horse, not the kind we sometimes got to ride out at our cousins' places; a real horse, a horse for the Bush Races.

My mate Brian Stafford and I thought that would be the best thing that you could have, a horse that you could actually race in the unregistered grass-fed hack races at the local meetings held by the Weelabarabak and District Bush Race Club. This was a few years before we discovered girls and cars.

Neither of us knew much about keeping a horse but that wasn't the point; it was the 'Romance of the Turf' that mattered to us back then. Brian was almost fourteen and rode fairly well. He was still quite small and talked about being a jockey.

I was twelve and talked about being a jockey too, but only to keep him company really; I was kidding myself. I was skinny but I was already tall and probably too heavy to be a jockey even then. If I had become a jockey my rides would have been limited to top-weighted horses in Welter Handicaps – not a lot of scope there for a steady income. Besides, I was a lousy rider. I was flat out staying on anything at full gallop.

Brian and I used to hang around the stables at the back of his dad's produce store. Brian's uncle, Bindi Williams, kept a small string of racehorses there and we were allowed to pretend we worked for him. That entailed us doing a lot of work nobody else wanted to do around the stables and being allowed to ride in the horse float to local race-meetings and wear a little cardboard triangle tied to a shirt button that meant we could go into the horse stalls and tell people we were 'working for Bindi Williams'. Our official remuneration for all this was that Bindi would give us a quid each if any of the horses won – we loved it.

Brian was allowed to ride some half pace trackwork for Bindi occasionally as long as his mother, Bindi's wife's sister, didn't find out. All I got to do was ride the stable pony over to the track with the other horses to keep the more inexperienced thoroughbreds quiet. My real racing forte was doing phantom calls of the Melbourne Cup or the Golden Slipper or the Great Eastern for everyone at the stables. I knew the colours and breeding of just about every horse racing back then. For an eighteen-month period, in between realising I'd never be a jockey and discovering girls, I was going to be a famous race-caller like Ken Howard.

Anyway that was the background to us wanting to own a horse for the Bush Races. We knew we couldn't own a real racehorse at that age; that would come later when Brian was a retired famous jockey and I was either a retired specialist heavyweight jockey or a famous race-caller.

The Bush Races, however, were different. Local station owners and farmers and businessmen and even ladies could own grass-fed hacks that raced at the Bush Races – and they could ride them themselves at catch weights in all but the most important races. Imagine that, we thought, owning and riding a horse on a real racetrack.

Ah, the Romance of the Turf!

Mind you, there wasn't a lot of 'turf' involved on the Bush Race tracks. The majority of the bush meetings were held on properties outside town and these had mostly six-furlong dirt tracks with an inner running rail all the way around and an 'outer' for the final furlong or so. There were, however, two Bush Race days on the official town track just before Easter – and that track had a grandstand and everything!

It only dawned on me many years later that the Bush Race days were really social events, a chance for the local station owners and town businessmen and their wives and old stockmen and friends to get together and enjoy themselves. The Bush Race Club Ball was really the feature event on the programme – but Brian and I were blinded by the rosy glow of the 'Romance of the Turf'; we thought the Bush Races were all about horseracing!

So we wanted a horse for the Bush Races – and eventually we got one.

'The majority of the bush meetings were held on properties outside town.'

'... that track had a grandstand and everything!'

His name was Student Prince, a real 'racehorse' sort of name, even though he was more of a stockhorse than a racehorse really. He had, we were assured, some racing experience way back in his dim past and was 'part-thoroughbred', like the brave pony in Banjo Paterson's famous poem, 'The Man from Snowy River'.

Just the name, Student Prince, was enough to convince us that he must have been some sort of a racehorse once – we knew no one in their right mind would call a stockhorse 'Student Prince'.

We bought him from a mate of Bindi's called Snowy Thompson. Bindi bought lucerne from Snowy and rested his horses out at Snowy's place sometimes.

Snowy Thompson was part-Aboriginal and had a far-away look in his eyes and loved pulling your leg. The thing I remember most clearly about him is that he always laughed when he spoke to you, whether things were funny or not.

Auntie Maude told me years later that Bindi was part-Aboriginal too. 'Only a bit,' she said, 'way back on his mother's side, that's why he's so good with horses. You should have seen him ride when he was young, could have been a top jockey down in the city if the weight hadn't caught up with him.'

There was nothing unusual about finding out that sort of thing 'years later' when I was a kid. There were funny little secrets like that all over the place in Weelabarabak. The really sad part of it was that people thought that sort of thing was significant, or that it shouldn't be said ... probably because Bindi was married to the daughter of a local businessman.

And it certainly didn't matter to Brian and me that Snowy was part-Aboriginal. We were only concerned with the fact that this wonderful man was being unbelievably generous and virtually giving away such a noble creature. We had to find twelve quid quickly, before he came to his senses and refused to allow himself to be robbed by these two young con men in such an unfair deal. Six quid each, that was all we needed to raise to fulfil our dreams of being real men of the turf ... 'racing identities'!

Brian summoned up all his courage and asked his uncle did we have any pay owing to us. Bindi said no, he hadn't had a winner for months, but maybe he could manage ten bob each if the stables got a real good clean-out regularly for the next few weeks. I had some money of my own but it was mostly in my Commonwealth Bank savings account at school and I knew I was really kidding myself if I thought Mum would let me take it out to buy a racehorse.

I managed to make another two pounds by selling the bantams I had raised to Auntie Maude and my prize billycart to the two eldest O'Shea boys.

The second transaction almost got me into trouble when the two eldest O'Shea boys went close to getting themselves killed going down the One Mile Hill the Saturday after I sold them the billycart. Selling such a lethal vehicle to the O'Sheas could almost be considered a criminal act in Weelabarabak. I should have been ashamed of myself, almost contributing to the death of the O'Shea boys, but I couldn't help it if I made really good billycarts. Anyway, the O'Sheas' recklessness was an inherited characteristic which outweighed any contribution I might make to their near-destruction.

I did feel a sense of shame about the fact that I raised at least another pound by stealing soft drink bottles from the yard behind the Paragon Cafe and handing them back in to collect the deposit from old Mrs Papadopoulos when she was serving in the cafe on her own.

You had to wait until she was on her own in the shop because her husband was much more suspicious of large quantities of soft drink bottles arriving in a short space of time and was prone to ask the question, 'Where you get these, huh?' before going out the back to check on his stockpile of empties.

Anyway, we were getting towards having the money to buy our dream horse when Bindi managed to get a fairly long-priced winner up in a maiden at Coopers Junction and paid us each our ten bob back-pay plus another ten bob for all the work we'd do until his next winner. In other words he gave us the quid he usually gave us when he had a winner.

On top of that we got Old Nugget, who sometimes came to the races with us 'just for the ride', to put two and sixpence each way on for us. Bindi pretended he didn't know about us having a bet so he wouldn't have to lie to our mothers if they asked him if we were betting when he took us to the races. He didn't want to lose two willing workers who had no idea about award wages and conditions.

So we finally had the money and could take possession of Student Prince. I doubled-dinked Brian out to Snowy's place on my pushbike one day after school to pick up our future champion. Student Prince was a tough and alert dark-brown gelding, about fifteen hands in height and a similar number of years in age. He was a true 'brown', not a bay, and if you squinted he looked almost black, which was terrific, we thought. Everyone knows that black is the fastest colour for a racehorse and he was almost black if you squinted – we reckoned we were halfway home already!

So we had our horse and we had a receipt from Snowy so everything was official. Snowy very generously threw in a bridle as well. We soon found out the reason for this generosity – Student Prince had a tendency to be a bit bridle-shy at times. If he was in a bad mood and he saw the bridle coming he'd roll his eyes back and curl his lip and get ready to rear. It was much easier to approach him with the bridle down low or behind your back and slip it up under his neck while you stroked his muzzle.

He was fine once he was used to you, but it was a good policy to hand him over to anyone with a bridle already on him. We soon discovered Student Prince also had a hard mouth. Sometimes you had to wheel him savagely to the left to make him stop from a trot, just spin him in circles a few times, but only if he was in a bad mood or really wound up.

All in all, though, he was a terrific buy – twelve quid well spent.

He was fast and tough enough and anyone could ride him once you knew his little quirks, even me. He was destined to run at Bush Race Meetings too, but all that was in the future the day we picked him up.

Our problems were more immediate as we trotted him into town that afternoon. Our main difficulty was that we had neglected to tell our parents we were buying a horse and we had no idea where our future champion of the turf was going to reside in order to prepare for what we were sure was to be an illustrious racing career.

Brian and I were taking it in turns to ride the horse and my pushbike, switching over every half-mile or so, and we started to debate several issues during these changeovers.

The argument about where he was going to spend his first few days of new ownership was actually preceded by the argument over who owned which end of 'The Prince'. (He soon became known as 'The Prince' when we were talking about him to other people in the racing business. He was known as 'Stewie' on less formal occasions when you were alone with him feeding him apples or carrots and he nuzzled you behind the ear.)

Anyway, the first argument to test our racing partnership was the one about who owned which end of The Prince. It had suddenly occurred to us that we were now responsible for accommodating and feeding a rather large horse that was just about to go into rigorous training in order to become a champion of the turf!

Admittedly he was going to make both of us very wealthy but, until that time, Student Prince might actually like the odd meal or two.

My solution to the problem was simple. I reasoned that the horse needed to be divided into two halves geographically in order that we could have defined areas of responsibility for grooming and health care. Therefore, I reasoned, he should be divided into a back section and a front section and, because I was younger and not such a good rider, I would do the right thing and consent to own the back half, thus giving my friend Brian the obviously better half.

I did point out, as an addendum to this arrangement, that Brian would naturally have to feed the horse and I would, so to speak, get some return on his money.

The manure would be great for Mum's roses and I could already see a possible way out of the dilemma of having to tell her what we had done.

'Mum, I was thinking about your roses and tomatoes and I reckoned you could really do with a regular supply of horse manure. So, with Mothers' Day coming up ...'

Things were looking brighter all the time!

It was odd that Brian couldn't see the good sense of this argument. He wasn't impressed at all by my selfless offer to grant him ownership of what was clearly the better half of any horse.

What's more, on top of this ingratitude, he insisted that we should take The Prince directly to my place rather than his place. He was, he informed me, selflessly willing to let me have our prize possession at my place first.

His argument, that I deserved to have the thrill of having The Prince at my place for the first week or so, seemed strangely reminiscent of my argument that he could own the front half of our future champion.

So there we were, alternately riding and peddling, getting closer and closer to town, and still arguing about our actual destination. What was it to be, Brian's place or mine?

In retrospect it does seem odd that, in all the weeks of anticipation and daydreaming about owning a racehorse, not one second had been spent considering where we would keep the horse, or how we'd feed him, or whether or not we should tell our parents.

It was apparent, as we neared town, that we were beginning to realise the consequences of our actions. The vehemence of our arguments increased as we passed the outlying houses and ten-acre blocks on the edge of town and our generosity towards each other became more selfless with every cross street we passed!

Brian was two years older than me, and that counted for a lot in those days. Two years isn't much in the big scheme of things but it's quite a lot when you're twelve and fourteen; it's almost seventeen per cent more life experience for a start. True, I was bigger than Brian but that was cancelled out by the fact that he was a lot tougher than me.

We took Student Prince to my place.

I must say my dad was a lot calmer about the whole thing than I'd suspected he would be. I've often thought about it since and I'm not sure that he didn't know what was going on all along. I'm fairly convinced that he at least had some very accurate suspicions about our horse-dealing activities.

It would have been better in some ways if he'd been angry. His calm attitude and laconic remarks were far more humiliating to two gentlemen of the turf like Brian and myself than his anger could ever have been.

'What's that?' my father asked as we stopped in front of the fence at our place, me on my bike and Brian on The Prince. I felt this arrangement was a far less provocative way to arrive in case my dad was there. In fact I had only finally agreed to proceed to my house if I wasn't actually riding The Prince when we arrived.

'It's a horse,' I replied as bravely as I could under the circumstances, 'Brian and I bought him.' There, I'd said it.

'And what are you gonna do with him?' my dad inquired calmly, as if he was discussing the weather.

'We're gonna race him,' Brian put in, some trace of returning enthusiasm evident in his voice in the face of my father's controlled demeanour.

My father's reply was totally deadpan, and we both thought it unnecessarily cruel.

'Well I don't know if that's fair, Brian,' he said, 'because judging by the look of him, I reckon you'd both beat him easily!'

'He's a real racehorse, Dad,' I argued weakly, 'he's got a real racehorse name and we're gonna race him.'

Then, just for good measure I played my other trump card. 'The manure will be real good for Mum's garden. I bet it'll make the tomatoes grow real well.'

My father looked at me quietly for about half a minute. He then pointed out, in his laconic style, that the manure wouldn't be much use if the horse ate all the tomato bushes, not to mention the other vegies and all the flowers. He went on to say that, as we didn't really have anywhere to keep a horse just now except the front yard, where the flowers were, or the back yard, where the vegies were, it would be pretty much impossible to keep the horse and not lose the flowers or the vegies.

If the horse was to stay *tonight*, my dad emphasised *tonight*, it would only be on the condition that it was tied up securely and fed and watered properly and taken somewhere else in the morning.

So The Prince spent his first night of his new career tied up at our place. He spent the second night tied up under the big mulberry tree at Brian's place. The rest of his time under our co-ownership, which ended up being almost a year, he spent either at Bindi's stables or back at Snowy's place 'on agistment'.

The price of keeping him in Bindi's stables was that we got to work for Bindi doing all the things we already did but forfeiting the quid we would have got when any of Bindi's horses won. The agistment fee at Snowy's turned out to be very similar: we got to work for Snowy cutting lucerne and helping fix fences. We also had to do extra work at home to pay for Bush Race Club entry fees and extra bits and pieces we couldn't borrow from Bindi.

All this was worked out by our parents, in consultation with Bindi and Snowy.

I must say it was rather humiliating for two racing identities like Brian and me to have so little control over the destiny of our future champion of the turf. We were made to do an enormous amount of work that year – far more, I felt, than was really required to pay for the accommodation and feeding of Student Prince.

I had the sneaking suspicion, later in life, that we did far more than Bindi or Snowy would have really wanted us to do had it been left to them. I think Brian's dad and my dad were the real architects of the work schemes and schedules that we endured for the twelve months until we decided that The Prince probably deserved to be retired from the racetrack.

This decision just happened to coincide with old Mr Myer, a station owner from out Yandaloo way, offering us ten quid for him after he finished fourth in a field of seven at the Tantala Creek meeting. Old Mr Myer still rode horses on his place. He had just lost a good horse to snake bite and was looking for a stockhorse to move cattle around.

'I'll give you ten quid for him if I can take him now,' Mr Myer said. 'My neighbour's got a space in his float; he could take him home for me. What do you reckon, boys? He looks like he'd be a fair stockhorse.'

'He's a good racehorse, Mr Myer,' Brian replied. 'You could race him like we do.'

Old Mr Myer pushed back his hat and looked at the two kids standing in front of him.

I'd like to tell you that a dewy look came into his eyes. I'd like to tell you that he said something kind, something that indicated an understanding of our boyish dreams, an affinity sparked perhaps by his own childhood memories of the 'Romance of the Turf'. What he actually said, however, was, 'Well, son, I saw him run in that last race and I reckon he looks like an average sort of stockhorse to me. I'll give you ten quid for him.'

It turned out that Bindi had previously 'mentioned' to old Mr Myer that Student Prince might be the answer to his little problem of the immediate lack of a useful stockhorse. I'm pretty sure that our parents had also told Bindi to be on the lookout for just such a situation. We were sad to see The Prince go but we were also secretly relieved. We'd just about killed ourselves working for various parties to sustain the high-living lifestyle of racing identities. It would be nice to have a rest for a while, not to mention a few bob in our pockets for a change.

We took the saddle off to return to Bindi, hosed The Prince down one last time, and handed him over to his new owner ... with the bridle still on him.

'You can keep the bridle too, Mr Myer,' Brian said as he pocketed the ten quid. It was no use splitting the money into two fivers because we owed it to Bindi anyway for feed and farriers' bills. Then we watched our faithful champion of the turf led away to where the horse floats were parked at the back of the tearoom.

The tearoom and bar were the only buildings at the Yandaloo track. There was no grandstand at Yandaloo. In fact, we never got to see Student Prince race from a grandstand. Weelabarabak was the only track in the district with a grandstand and he had the scours when the Weelabarabak unregistered meeting was on, and didn't race. Of course, Brian never got to see him race at all, because he rode him on the three occasions when we did get him to race at local bush tracks. We borrowed a set of faded colours from Bindi, and Brian looked real flash sitting up there ready to race, and he rode pretty well too.

The results? Well, Tantala Creek was actually the highlight of our racing career with The Prince, fourth in a field of seven.

There were plenty of excuses for him at the other two meetings. Brian missed the start the first time we raced him at Booroolong and, at the Bandanna Downs meeting, a big clod of dirt hit Brian in the face early in the race and it was all he could do to hold on. We actually ran him twice that day, which was a fairly normal practice back then. Brian borrowed a set of goggles for the second race but The Prince was pretty tired; one race a day was his limit, we decided after that. Whatever Student Prince had to give you got the first time round.

Student Prince never quite fulfilled our expectations I suppose, but Brian and I certainly didn't think his career efforts warranted the abusive and derisive comments we had to put up with from Brian's father every time the subject came up. He insisted on referring to our graceful steed as 'The Stupid Prince'. What was even worse was that he dubbed us 'The Two Stupid Princelings'.

'How's "The Stupid Prince"?' he'd ask with mock sincerity as we dragged ourselves through the back door after a full day's work at the stables or out at Snowy's, 'and what can we do for the "stupid princelings" this evening? How about a bale of hay each?'

My father's efforts at humorous disparagement were even worse. His favourite trick was to refer to The Prince as 'The Half-a-horse'. This was usually a response to my proud claim that I owned 'half a horse'. When I told Auntie Maude this, for example, she replied, 'Really, dear, that's nice, who owns the other half?'

Dad jumped in straightaway with, 'There is no other half, Maudie, it really is half a horse, you should see it!'

So I had to put up with, 'How's that Half-a-horse going, son? Has he made half an effort to win half a race yet?' and 'I hope Brian's half the jockey his uncle was so he can give that Half-a-horse half a chance.'

We got more sympathy down at the stables and out at Snowy's and we learnt a lot that year from people like Bindi and Snowy and Old Nugget. They were, perhaps, a little soft-hearted and more understanding about the trials and tribulations of two young racing identities whose heads were full of the 'Romance of the Turf'.

Then again, they didn't have to live with us like our parents did.

As an adult, it's still a dream of mine to own a horse. And when I say 'own a horse' I still mean a real horse, a racehorse. If I ever strike it rich you can keep the Caribbean cruises and the Rolls-Royce. I just want my very own horse, racing in my very own colours (something arresting yet dignified – like pink with a purple sash and cap) on a real racetrack.

I don't even care what it wins – the Cup or the Slipper would be nice, but a Maiden at Moe, Gawler, Toowoomba or Kembla Grange would be all right too.

Maybe I'll track down my old mate Brian Stafford and we'll go halves.

And if it never happens?

Well, at least I have the satisfaction of knowing that, many years ago, for a time (twelve long, hard months) I was a racing identity, living out my dream of the 'Romance of the Turf' by owning half a horse, a real horse too ... a horse for the Bush Races.

'... fourth in a field of seven.'

THE JUDGE'S DECISION

J. W. Kevin ('Arthur Ferres')

'Twas years ago on the Barcoo when flashy jockey clubs
Were few and far and far between, likewise the flashy pubs;
The pioneers two race days had, the stakes were fat and rich
And the meeting was a roarer and went off without a hitch.

The rum was strong as kerosene, 'twas a hundred in the shade,
The dust was thick as London fog, of grass there was no blade.
The grimy crowd, they didn't mind, they came to see the fun,
Men had brought their prads for leagues to race and see
    them run.

The judge he had no stand to grace, his stand was on the
    ground,
And when the handicaps were run the crowd came surging
    round
To hear his verdict straight and true, the winner that he saw,
The crowd believed the upright judge, the judge's word was law.

The judge he was a German bold, Herr Lyndorf was his name,
He was the local medico, a man of learned fame.
For him the two-day meeting came as quite a welcome treat,
There was no German lager, so he drank Jamaica neat.

'Twas near the close of the second day, the last event was on,
The sun had set, the air was thick with language bold and
    strong.
Some had arranged a white horse called Snowflake should win the
    race,
But Ethiope, as black as jet, had strength and nimble pace.

Away they went, the jockeys jostled, each one on his own,
As on they come 'mid prayers and dust, past rock and tree and
stone.
But now into the straight they turn, the white horse leads them all,
The thirsty crowd begins to yell and whoop and madly call!

Some cry out, 'The white horse wins,' and some cry out, 'The
black!'
As on they flog in straining stride, right down the dusty track.
And now the black has caught the white, he creeps up inch by inch,
But white is game and struggles on, from his place he won't flinch.

And on they come, both locked as one, a roar comes from the
throng,
And bets are made and threats are heard, and language strange
and strong.
And none can tell which horse as yet has caught the judge's eye,
And 'White' and 'Black' and 'Black' and ' White' resound across
the sky.

The race is run, the stakes are won, the still-excited crowd,
Comes reeling round the judge's stand and all are calling loud,
To know which horse the winner was, for some 'dead heat' declare,
And some yell 'White!' and some yell 'Black!' and some just stand
and swear.

The judge, with duplicated sight, stands on an old gin-case
And prepares to tell the yelling crowd the winner of the race.
'Der vinning horse (hic) vas not vite, nor black (hic) as some has
called!
Der vinner of dis (hic) handicap vas (hic) dat damned piebald!'

'... which horse as yet has caught the judge's eye ...' A modern
judges stand

RINGING IN RAINBOW

Thomas Alexander Browne ('Rolf Boldrewood')
(Adapted from *Robbery Under Arms*)

Starlight and Rainbow

Here is an account of how my brother and I met Captain Starlight.

One day, when we were both not yet twenty years of age, Father took Jim and me into a steep gully almost a day's ride from home and led us to a sort of cave by the side of the track, where one man, with a couple of guns and a pistol or two, could have shot down a small regiment as they came down one at a time. After about half an hour we heard the two horses coming down slowly, step by step, kicking the stones down before them.

The leading horse held up his head and snorted as he came into the open in front of the cave. He was one of the grandest animals I'd ever seen, and I afterwards found he was better than he looked. He came stepping down that rocky goat-track, he, a clean thoroughbred that ought never to have trod upon anything rougher than a rolled training track, or the sound bush turf. And here he was with a heavy weight on his back, a half dead, fainting man, that couldn't hold the reins – and him walking down as steady as an old mountain bull, or a wallaroo on the side of a creek bank.

I hadn't much time to look him over. I was too much taken up with the rider, who was lying forward on his chest across a coat rolled round and strapped in front of the saddle, with his arms round the horse's neck.

He was as pale as a ghost.

Then we saw he had been wounded. There was blood on his shirt, and the upper part of his arm was bandaged.

We lifted him off after undoing some straps and a rope. When we laid him down his head fell back, and he looked as much like a corpse as if he had been dead a day.

'It's too late, Father,' said I, 'he's a dead man. What pluck he must have had to ride down here!'

'He's worth two dead 'uns yet,' said Father, who had his hand on his pulse. 'Hold his head up one of you while I go for the brandy. How did he get hit, Warrigal?'

'That damn Sergeant Goring,' said the second rider. He was part-Aboriginal, a slight, active-looking chap, about sixteen, who looked as if he could jump into a gum tree and back again, and I believe he could.

'We got a lot of old Jobson's cattle when he came on us. He jump off his horse when he see he couldn't catch us, and very near drop Starlight. My word, he very nearly fall off – just like that' (here he imitated a man reeling in his saddle); 'but the old horse stop steady with him, my word, till he come to. Then the sergeant fire at him again; hit him in the shoulder with his pistol. Then Starlight come to his senses, and we clear off. My word, Sergeant Goring couldn't see the way the old horse went,' he laughed, 'we gallop different ways, too, and met at the old needle-rock. But they was miles behind then.'

Before the boy had come to the end of his story the wounded man had proved that it was only a dead faint, as the women call it, not the real thing. And after he had tasted a pannikin full of brandy and water, which Father brought him, he sat up and looked like a living man once more.

'Better have a look at my shoulder,' he said. 'That damned fellow shot like a prize-winner at Wimbledon. I've had a squeak for it.'

Father carefully cut off the shirt; it was stiffened with blood where the bullet had passed through the muscle, narrowly missing the bone of the joint. We washed it, and relieved the wounded man by discovering that the other bullet had only been spent, after striking a tree most like, when it had knocked the wind out of him and nearly unhorsed him, as Warrigal said.

'We'll all be shopped if you run against the police like this,' said Father as he worked at bandaging, 'and next thing lead them on to the Hollow by making for it when you're too weak to ride.'

'What would you have me do? Pull up and hold up my hands? There was nowhere else to go; and that new sergeant rode devilish well, I can tell you, with a big chestnut well-bred horse, that gave old Rainbow here all he knew to lose him. Now, once for all, no more of that, I'm the superior officer in this ship's company – you know that very well – your business is to obey me, and take second place.'

Father growled out something, but did not offer to deny it. We could see plainly that the stranger was or had been far above our rank, whatever were the reasons that had led to his present kind of life. We knew him only as Captain Starlight.

We stayed for about ten days, while the stranger's arm got well. With care and rest, it soon healed. He was pleasant enough, too, when the pain went away and Jim and I got to know him as the days passed. He had been in other countries, and told us all kinds of stories about them.

By and by, the day came when the horses were run in for Father and Mr Starlight and Warrigal, who packed up to be off for some other part.

When they were in the yard we had a good look at his own horse – a good look – and if I'd been a fellow that painted pictures, and that kind of thing, I could draw a middlin' good likeness of him now.

He was a dark-bay horse, nearly brown, without a white hair on him. He wasn't above fifteen hands and an inch high, but looked a deal bigger than he was, for the way he held his head up and carried himself. He was deep and thick through behind the shoulders, and girthed ever so much more than you'd think. He had a short back, and his ribs went out like a cask, long quarter, great thighs and hocks, wonderful legs, and feet of course to do the work he did. His head was plainish, but clean and bony, and his eye was big and well opened, with no white showing. His shoulder was sloped back that much that he couldn't fall, no matter what happened to his forelegs. All his paces were good too. I believe he could jump – jump anything he was ridden at, and very few horses could get the better of him for one mile or three.

Where he'd come from, of course, we were not to know then. He had a small private sort of brand that didn't belong to any of the big studs; but he was never bred by a poor man.

I afterwards found out that he was stolen before he was foaled, like many another plum, and his dam killed as soon as she had weaned him. So, of course, no one could swear to him, and Starlight could have ridden past the Supreme Court, at the assizes, and never been stopped, as far as this horse was concerned.

The Turon Grand Handicap

Here is an account of a great adventure with Captain Starlight and Rainbow at the Turon Races sometime later, when Jim and I had embarked upon a life of bushranging with the Captain.

After numerous scrapes and an escape from custody, we were laying up at home. We hadn't been there long, just long enough to get tired of doing nothing, when we got a letter from my sister's friend Bella, who had several times helped us escape the police. The letter informed us that the Turon Races were to be a very grand affair that particular year, and reminded Starlight that Sir Ferdinand would be there, but there'd be such a crowd anybody would pass muster, and so on.

In a 'PS' she told us there was to be a big handicap, with five hundred guineas added; and she asked hadn't we a horse good enough? She signed off, 'Yours sincerely, Isabella Barnes.'

'Well done, Bella!' says Starlight. 'I vote we go, Dick. I never went to a race-meeting with a price on my head before. A thousand pounds too! Quite a new sensation. It settles the question. And we'll enter Rainbow for the handicap. He ought to be good enough for anything they're likely to have.'

'Captain Starlight's Rainbow, 9 stone 8 pounds,' I said, 'with wanted Bushranger Dick Marston to lead him up to the judge's box. How will that wash? And what are the police going to be about all the time? Bella's gone out of her senses.'

'You're a good fellow, Dick, and staunch, but you're like your father,' said Starlight, 'you haven't any imagination. I see half-a-dozen ways of doing the whole thing. Fancy running our horses under the noses of the police – the idea is delicious!'

'I daresay you're about tired of your life,' I said. 'I'm pretty sure I am; but why we should ride straight into the lion's mouth, to please a silly girl, I can't see. I haven't over much sense, I know, or I shouldn't be here; but I'm not such a dashed fool as all that comes to.'

'My mind is made up, Dick,' Starlight replied, 'I have decided irrevocably. Of course, you needn't come, if you see objections; but I'll bet you my Dean and Adams revolver and the Navy Colt against your repeating rifle that I do all I've said, and clear out safe.'

'Done!' I said. 'I've no doubt you'll try; but you'll make Sir Ferdinand's fortune, that's all. He always said he'd die happy if he could only bag you and the Marstons. He'll be made Inspector-General of Police.'

Starlight smiled in his queer, quiet way.

'If he doesn't rise to the top of the tree until he takes me – alive, I mean – then he's bound to die a sub-Inspector. But we'd better sleep on it. This is an enterprise that requires no end of thought.'

Next morning I expected he'd think better of it; we'd had a glass or two of grog; but no, he was more set on it than ever, and full of dodges to work it to rights. He certainly was wonderful clever in all sorts of ways when there was any devilment to be carried out. Half as much in the straight way would have made a man of him. But that's the way of the world all over. He ain't the only one.

As for Father, he was like me, and looked on the notion as rank foolishness. He swore straight on end for about twenty minutes, and then said he expected Starlight would have his own way as usual; but he'd play at that game once too often. He supposed he'd be left in the Hollow all by himself, with Warrigal and the dog for company.

'Warrigal goes with me, I might want him,' says Starlight. 'You're losing your nerve, governor. Perhaps you'd like to go to the races too?'

Father gave a sort of growl, and lit his pipe and wouldn't say no more. Starlight and I talked it out, and, after I'd heard all he had to say, it didn't look quite so impossible as it did at first. We were to work apart. He was to get in with some of the betting men or sporting people that always came to country races, and I was to find out some of our old digger mates and box up with them. Warrigal would shift for himself and look after the horses, and have them ready in case we had to clear at short notice.

And who was to enter Rainbow and look after him?

'Couldn't we get old Jacob Benton? He's the best trainer I've seen since I left home. Billy the Boy told us the other day he was out of a job, and was groom at Jonathan's; had been sacked for getting drunk, and so on. He'll be all the more likely to keep sober for a month.'

'The very man,' I said. 'He can ride the weight, and train too. But we can't have him here, surely!'

'No, but I can send the horse to him at Jonathan's, and he can get him fit there as well as anywhere. There's nearly a month yet; he's pretty hard, and he's been regularly exercised lately.'

Jacob Benton was a wizened, dried-up old Yorkshireman. He'd been head man in a good racing stable, but drink had been the ruin of him – lost him his place, and sent him out here. He could be trusted to go right through with a job like ours, for all that.

Like many men that drink hard, he was as sober as a judge between one burst and another. And once he took over a horse in training he touched nothing but water till the race was run and the horse back in his box. Then he most times went on an awful perisher – took a month to it, and was never sober day or night the whole time.

When he'd spent all his money he'd crawl out of the township and get away into the country more dead than alive, and take the first job that offered. But he was fonder of training a good horse than anything else in the world; and if he'd got a regular flyer, and was treated liberal, he'd hardly allow himself sleep or time to eat his meals till he'd got him near the mark. He could ride, too, and was an out-and-out judge of pace.

When we'd regular chalked it out about entering Rainbow for the Grand Turon Handicap, we sent Warrigal over to Billy the Boy, and got him to look up old Jacob. He agreed to take the old horse, the week before the races, and give him a last bit of French polish if we'd keep him in steady work till then. From what he was told of the horse he expected he would carry any weight he was handicapped for and pull it off easy. He was to enter him in his own name, the proper time before the races. If he won he was to have ten per cent of winnings; if he lost, a ten pound note would do him. He could ride the weight with some lead in his saddle, and he'd never wet his lips with grog till the race was over.

So that part of the work was chalked out. The real risky business was to come. I never expected we should get through all straight. But the more I hung back the more shook on it Starlight seemed to be. He was like a boy home from school sometimes – mad for any kind of fun with a spice of devilment in it.

About a week before the races we all cleared out, leaving Father at home, and pretty sulky too. Warrigal led Rainbow; he was to take him to Jonathan Barnes's, and meet old Jacob there. He was to keep him until it was time to go to Turon. We didn't show at Jonathan's ourselves this time; we were afraid of drawing suspicion on the place.

We rode right into Turon, taking care to be well after dark. A real pleasure it was to see the old place again. The crooked streets, the lighted-up shops, the crowd of jolly diggers walking about smoking, or crowding round the public-house bars, the din of the stampers in the quartz-crushing machines going night and day. It all reminded me of the pleasant year Jim and I had spent here. I wished we'd never had to leave it.

We parted just outside the township for fear of accidents. I went to a little place I knew, where I put up my horse – I could be quiet there, and asked no questions. Starlight, as usual, went to the best hotel, where he ordered everybody about and was as big a swell as ever. He told all and sundry he had been out in the north-west country, and was going to Sydney to close for a couple of stations that had been offered to him.

That night he went to the barber, had his hair cut and his beard shaved, only leaving his moustache and a bit of whisker like a ribbon. He put on a suit of tweed, all one colour, and ordered a lot more clothes, which he paid for, and were to be left at the hotel till he returned from Sydney.

Next day he starts for Sydney; what he was going to do there he didn't say, and I didn't ask him. He'd be back the day before the races, and in good time for all the fun.

The gold was better even than when we were there. A lot of men who were poor enough when we were there had made fortunes. The field had never looked better, and the hard-driving, well-paid, jolly mining life was going on just the same as ever, everyone making money fast – spending it faster – and no one troubling themselves about anything except how much the washdirt went to the load, and whether the sinking was through the false bottom or not.

At first I had a notion of mating in with some diggers, but when I saw how quiet everybody took it, and what thousands of strangers there were all over the place, I gave myself out for a speculator in mining shares from Melbourne. So I shaved off most of my beard, had my hair cut short, and put on a tall hat. I thought that would shift any sort of likeness there might be to my old self, and, though it was beastly uncomfortable, I stuck to it all the time.

I walked about among the stables and had a good look at all the horses that were in training. There were two or three good ones, as usual, and a lot of duffers. If Rainbow wasn't beat on his condition, he had pace and weight-carrying for the best of them. I hardly thought he could lose it, or a bigger stake in better company. I was that fond of the horse I thought he was good enough for an English Derby.

Well, I kept dark, you can be sure, and mooned about, buying a share at a low price now and then just to let 'em see I had money and meant something. My name was Mr Bromford, and I lived at Petersham, near Sydney.

The day before the races there was a lot of excitement in the town. Strangers kept pouring in from everywhere round about, and all the hotels were crammed full. Just as I was wondering whether Starlight was going to turn up till next day I saw a four-in-hand drag rattle down the street to the principal inn, and a crowd gather round it as three gentlemen got out and went into the inn.

'You'll see after all our luggage, will you, ostler?' says one of them to the groom, 'and whatever you do don't forget my umbwella!'

Some of the diggers laughed.

'Know those coves?' I said to a man that stopped at the same house as I did.

'Don't you know? Them's the two Mr Dawsons, of 'Wideview', great sporting men, native-born, and ever so rich. They've some horses to run tomorrow. That's a new chum from England that's come up with 'em.'

I hardly knew him at first. His own mother wouldn't, I believe. He'd altered himself that wonderful as I could hardly even now think it was Starlight; and yet he wasn't a bit like the young Englishman he had pretended to be last year, or the Honourable Frank Haughton either.

He had an eyeglass this time, and was a swell from top to toe. How and when he'd picked up with the Mr Dawsons I couldn't tell; but he'd got a knack of making people like him – especially when they didn't know him. Not that it was worse when they did.

He was introduced to the town's gentry by the Dawsons as Mr Lascelles, holding a commission in an Indian regiment of Irregular Horse, and now on leave, travelling chiefly for health.

Just sufficiently sunburned, perfect in manner, full of information, humorous and original in conversation, and with all the 'prestige' of the unknown, small wonder that 'The Captain' was regarded as a prize, socially considered, and introduced right and left. Ha! Ha! What a most excellent jest, albeit rather keen, as far as Sir Ferdinand is concerned! We shall never, never cease to recall the humorous side of the whole affair.

Well, next day was the first day of the races. I never saw such a turn-out in the colony before. Every digger on the field had dropped work for the day; all the farmers, and squatters, and country people had come in for miles round on all sides. The Commissioner and all the police were out in full uniform, and from the first moment the hotels were opened in the morning till breakfast-time all the bars were full, and the streets crowded with miners and strangers and people that seemed to have come from the ends of the earth.

When I saw the mob there was, I didn't see so much to be wary about, as it was fifty to one in favour of anyone that was wanted, in the middle of such a muster of queer cattle as was going on at Turon that day.

About eleven o'clock everyone went out to the course. It wasn't more than a mile from town. The first race wasn't to be run till twelve; but long before that time the road was covered with horsemen, traps of every kind and sort, every horse and mare in the whole district.

Most of the miners went in four-horse coaches and buses that were plying all day long from the town and back; very few walked. The country people mostly drove in spring-carts, or rode on horseback. Any young fellows that had a good horse liked to show him off, of course; the girls in habits of their own make, perhaps, and now and then a top hat, though they looked very well too.

I began to wonder how Starlight was getting on with his friends, when I saw the Dawsons' drag come up the straight, with four upstanding ripping bay horses in top condition, and well matched. There was Starlight on the box seat, alongside of Jack Dawson, the eldest brother, who could handle the ribbons in style, and was a man every inch of him, only a bit too fast; didn't care about anything but horses and dogs, and lived every day of his life. The other brother was standing up behind, leaning over and talking to Starlight, who was 'in great form', as he used to say himself, and looked as if he'd just come out of a bandbox.

He had on a silk coat buttoned round him, a white top hat with a blue silk veil. His eyeglass was stuck in his eye all the time, and he had kid gloves on that fitted his hands like wax. I really couldn't hardly take my oath he was the same man, and no wonder nobody else couldn't. I was wondering why Sir Ferdinand wasn't swelling about, bowing to all the ladies, and making that thoroughbred of his dance and arch his neck, when I heard someone say that he'd got news that Moran and his ruffians had stuck up a place about forty miles off, towards Forbes. Sir Ferdinand had sworn at his luck for having to miss the races; but started off just as he was, and taken all the troopers but two with him.

'Who brought the news?'

'Oh! A youngster called William Jones – said he lived out there. A black boy came with him that couldn't hardly speak English; he went with 'em to show the way.'

'Well, but how did they know it was true?' says I. 'It might have been only a stall.'

'Oh, the young fellow brought a letter from the overseer, saying they might hold out for a few hours, if the police came along quick.'

'It's a good thing they started at once,' says I. 'Them boys are very useful sometimes, and blackfellows too.'

I went off then, and had a laugh to myself. I was pretty middling certain it was Billy the Boy and Warrigal. Starlight had wrote the note before we started, only I didn't think they'd be game to deliver it themselves.

Now the police was away, all but a couple of young fellows that didn't know any of us by sight, I thought we might enjoy ourselves for once in a way without watching everyone that came nigh us. And we did enjoy ourselves. I did, I know; though you'd think, as we carried our lives in our hands, in a manner of speaking, the fun couldn't have been much.

But it's a queer world! Men like us, that don't know what's to happen to them from one day to another, if they can only see their way for a week ahead, often have more real pleasure in the bit of time they have to themselves than many a man has in a year that has no call to care about time or money or be afraid of anybody.

As for Starlight, if he'd been going to be hung next week it would have been all one to him. He'd have put off thinking about it until about an hour before, and then would have made all his arrangements and done the whole business quietly and respectably, without humbug, but without any flashness either. You couldn't put him wrong, or make him do or say anything that was out of place.

However, this time nobody was going to be hung or took or anything else. We'd as good as got a free pardon for the time being, now the police was away; no one else would have meddled with us if we'd had our names printed on our hats. So we made the most of it, I expect. Starlight carried on all sorts of high ropes. He was introduced to all the nobs, and I saw him in the grandstand and the saddling-paddock, taking the odds in tens and fifties from the ringmen. He'd brought a stiffish roll of notes with him and was backing the Dawson stable right out.

It turned out afterwards that he'd met them at an inn on the mountains, and helped them to doctor one of their leaders that had been griped. So they took a fancy to him, and, being free-hearted sorts of fellows, asked him to keep them company in the drag, and let one of the grooms ride his horse. Once he started he kept them alive, you may be sure, and by the time they got to Turon they were ready to go round the world with him, and swore they'd never met such a man in their lives – very likely they hadn't, either. He was introduced to the judge and the stewards and the Commissioner and the police magistrate, and as much fuss made over him as if he was the Governor's son. It was as good as a play. I got up as near as I dared once or twice, and I couldn't hardly keep from bursting out laughing when I saw how grave he talked and drawled and put up his eyeglass, and every now and then made 'em all laugh, or said something reminded him of India, where he'd last come from.

Rainbow had been entered in proper time and all regular by old Jacob, under the name of Darkie, which suited in all ways. He was a dark horse, sure enough; dark in colour, and dark enough as to his performances – nobody knew much about them. We weren't going to enter him in his right name, of course.

Old Jacob was a queer old fellow in all his ways and notions, so we couldn't stable him in any of the stables in Turon, for fear of his being 'got at', or something. So when I wanted to see him the day before, the old fellow grinned, and took me away about a mile from the course; and there was old Rainbow, snug enough – in a tent, above all places! – but as fine as a star, and as fit as ever a horse was brought to the post.

'What's the fun of having him under canvas?' I said. 'Who ever heard of a horse being trained in a tent before? – not but what he looks first-chop.'

'I've seen horses trained in more ways than one,' says he, 'and I can wind 'em up, in the stable and out of it, as mighty few in this country can – that is, when I put the muzzle on. There's a deal in knowing the way horses is brought up. Now this here's an excitable horse in a crowd.'

'Is he?' I said. 'Why, he's as cool and steady as an old trooper when –'

'When powder's burning and bullets is flying,' says the old chap, grinning again; 'but this here's a different crowd. When he's got a training saddle and seven or eight stone up, and there's two or three hundred horses rattling about this side on him and that, it brings out the old racehorse feeling that's in his blood, and never had a chance to show itself afore.'

'I see, and so you want to keep him quiet till the last minute?'

'That's just it,' says he; 'I've got the time to a second' – here he pulls out a big old turnip of a silver watch – 'and I'll have him up just ready to be weighed out last. I never was late in my life.'

'All right,' I said, 'but don't draw it too fine. Have you got your weight all right?'

'Right to a hounce,' says he, 'nine stun four they've put on him, and him an untried horse. I told 'em it was weighting him out of the race, but they laughed at me. Never you mind, though, he can carry weight and stay too. My ten per cent's as safe as the bank. He'll put the stuns on all them nobs, too, that think a racehorse must always come out of one of their training stables.'

'Well, goodbye, old man,' says I, 'and good luck. One of us will come and lead you into the weighing yard, if you pull it off, and chance the odds, if Sir Ferdinand himself was at the gate.'

'All right,' says he, 'I'll look out for you,' and off he goes.

Well, that first day was a regular fizzer of a spree, if we never had another. The racing was very fair, and, as luck would have it, the Dawson horses won all the big money, and, as they started at longish odds, they must have made a pot of money, and Starlight too, as he'd gone in a docker for their stable. This made them better friends than ever and it was Dawson here and Lascelles there all over the course.

Well, the day went over at last, and all of them that liked a little fun and dancing better than heavy drinking made it up to go to the race ball. It was a subscription affair – guinea tickets, just to keep out the regular roughs, and the proceeds to go to the Turon Jockey Club Fund. All the swells had to go, of course, and, though they knew it would be a crush and pretty mixed, as I heard Starlight say, the room was large, the band was good, and they expected to get a fair share of dancing after an hour or so.

Starlight and the Dawsons dined at the goldfields officials camp, and were made a good deal of – their health drunk and what not – and Starlight told us afterwards he returned thanks for the strangers and visitors; said he'd been told Australia was a rough place, but he never expected to find so much genuine kindness and hospitality and, he might add, so much refinement and gentlemanly feeling. Speaking for himself, he had never expected, considering his being a total stranger, to be welcomed so cordially and entertained so handsomely, more particularly at the mess of Her Majesty's goldfields officials, whose attention on this occasion they might be assured he would never forget. The events of this particular day would never be effaced from his memory. (Tremendous cheering.)

Next day was the great excitement of the meeting. I rode out to the racecourse, thinking myself safer on horseback, for fear of accidents. Starlight, of course, went in the Dawsons' drag, and was going to enjoy himself to the last minute. He had his horse ready at a moment's notice, and Warrigal was not far off to give warning, or to bring up his horse if we had to ride for it.

The 'big money' was all in the handicap, and there was a big field, with two or three cracks up from Sydney, and a very good local horse that all the diggers were sweet on. It was an open race, and every man that had a note or a fiver laid it out on one horse or another.

Starlight slipped away in the crowd from his two friends and managed to get a quiet few minutes with me and Bella and Aileen just before the race. There wasn't much more time and we all had to move off. He had just time to catch up with his new friends and the Dawsons bullied him a bit for keeping them waiting.

'You're not to be trusted when there's temptation going,' Jack Dawson said. 'Saw you talking to that Marston girl. If you don't mind you'll have your head knocked off. They're a rum lot to deal with I can tell you, her brothers are accused of bushranging and are both wanted men.'

'I must take care of myself,' he said, laughing. 'I have done so in other lands, and I suppose yours is no exception.'

'This is a dashed queer country in some ways, and with deuced strange people in it, too, as you'll find by the time you've had your colonial experience,' says Bill Dawson; 'but there goes the saddling-bell!'

The course had twenty thousand people on it now if there was one. About a dozen horses stood stripped for the race, and the betting men were yelling out the odds, as we got close enough to the stand to hear them. We had a good look at the lot. Three or four good-looking ones among them, and one or two flyers that had got in light as usual.

Rainbow was nowhere about. Darkie was on the card, but no one seemed to know where he was or anything about him. We expected he'd start at twenty to one, but somehow it leaked out that he was entered by old Jacob Benton, and that acted as a damper on the layers of the odds. 'Old Jake's generally there or thereabouts. If he's a duffer, it's the first one he's brought to the post. Why don't the old varmint show up?'

This was what I heard about and round, and we began to get uneasy ourselves, for fear that something might have happened to him or the horse. About eight or nine to one was all we could get, and that we took over and over again.

As the horses came up the straight, one after the other, having their pipe-openers, you'd have thought no race had been run that week, to see the interest all the people took in it. My word, Australia is a horsey country, and no mistake. With the exception of Arabia, perhaps, as they tell us about, I can't think as there's a country on the face of the earth where the people's fonder of horses.

From the time they're able to walk, boys and girls, they're able to ride, and ride well. See the girls jump on barebacked, with nothing but a gunny-bag under 'em, and ride over logs and stones, through scrub and forest, down gullies, or along the side of a mountain.

And a horserace, don't they love it? Wouldn't they give their souls almost – and they do often enough – for a real flyer, a thoroughbred, able to run away from everything in a country race. The horse is a fatal animal to us natives, and many a man's ruin starts from a bit of horse-flesh not honestly come by.

As I said, everybody was looking at the horses – coming along with the rush of the thoroughbred when he's 'on his top' for condition, with his coat like satin, and his legs like iron, when there was a stir in the crowd, and old Jacob came along across the course leading a horse with a sheet on, just as easy-going as if he'd a day to spare. One of the stewards rode up to him, and asked him what he meant by being so late.

The old chap pulls out his watch. 'You'll stick to your advertised time, won't you? I've time to weigh, time to pull off this here sheet and my overcoat, time to mount, and a minute to spare. I never was late in my life, governor.'

Most of the riding mob was down with the racehorses, a distance or so from the stand, where they was to start, the course being over two miles. So the weighing yard and stand was pretty well empty, which was just what old Jacob expected.

The old man walks over to the scales and has himself weighed all regular, declaring a pound overweight for fear of accidents. He gets down as quiet and easy as possible to the starting point, and just in time to walk up steadily with the other horses, when down goes the starter's flag, and 'Off' was the word. Starlight and the Dawsons were down there waiting for him.

As they went away one of the ringmen says, 'Ten to one against Darkie. I lay Darkie.' 'Done,' says Starlight, 'will you do it in tens?' 'All right,' says the 'book'. 'I'll take you,' say both the Dawsons, and he entered their names.

They'd taken all they could get the night before at the hotel; and as no one knew anything about Darkie, and he had top weight, he hadn't many backers.

Mr Dawson drove pretty near the stand then, and they all stood up in the drag. I went back to Aileen and Bella. We were close by the winning post when they came past; they had to go another time round.

The Sydney horses were first and second, the diggers' favourite third; but old Rainbow, lying well up, was coming through the ruck hard held and looking full of running. They passed close by us. What a sight it is to see a dozen blood horses in top condition come past you like a flash of lightning!

How their hoofs thunder on the level turf! How the jockeys' silk jackets rustle in the wind they make! How muscle and sinew strain as they pretty near fly through the air! No wonder us young fellows, and the girls too, feel it's worth a year of their lives to go to a good race. Yes, and will to the world's end.

'O you darling Rainbow!' I heard Aileen say. 'Are you going to win this race and triumph over all these grand horses? What a sight it will be! I didn't think I could have cared for a race so much.'

It didn't seem hardly any time before they were halfway round again, and the struggle was on, in good downright earnest. One of the Sydney horses began to shake his tail. The other still kept the lead. Then the Turon favourite – a real game pebble of a little horse – began to show up.

'Hotspur, Hotspur! No. Bronzewing has it – Bronzewing. It's Bronzewing's race. Turon forever!' the crowd kept yelling.

'Oh! Look at Rainbow!' says Aileen.

Just then, at the turn, old Jacob sat down on him. The old horse challenged Bronzewing, passed him, and collared Hotspur.

'Darkie! Darkie!' shouts everybody. 'No! Hotspur – Darkie's coming – Darkie – Darkie! I tell yer Darkie.'

And as old Jacob made one last effort, and landed him a winner by a clear head, there was a roar went up from the whole crowd that might have been heard at Nulla Mountain.

Starlight jumps off the drag and leads the old horse into the weighing yard. The steward says 'Dismount'. No fear of old Jacob getting down before he heard that. He takes his saddle in his lap and gets into the scales.

'Weight,' says the clerk. Then the old fellow mounts and rides past the judge's box. 'I declare Mr Benton's horse Darkie to be the winner of the Turon Grand Handicap, Bronzewing second horse, Hotspur third,' says he.

Well, there was great cheering and hollering, though none knew exactly whose horse he was or anything about him; but an Australian crowd always likes to see the best horse win – and they like fair play – so Darkie was cheered over and over again, and old Jacob too.

Aileen stroked and petted him and patted his neck and rubbed his nose, and you'd have to think the old horse knew her, he seemed so gentle-like. Then the Commissioner came down and said Mrs Hautley, the police magistrate's wife, and some other ladies wanted to see the horse that had won the race. So he was taken over there and admired and stroked till old Jacob got quite crusty.

'It's an odd thing, Dawson,' says the Commissioner, 'nobody here knows this horse, where he was bred, or anything about him. Such a grand animal as he is, too! I wish Sir Ferdinand could have seen him; he's always raving about horses. How savage he'll be to have missed all the fun!'

'He's a horse you don't see every day,' says Bill Dawson. 'I'll give a couple of hundred for him right off.'

'Not for sale at present,' says old Jacob, looking like a cast-iron image. 'I'll send ye word when he is.'

'All right,' says Mr Dawson. 'What a shoulder, what legs, what loins he has! Ah! Well, he'll be weighted out now, and you will be glad to sell him soon.'

'Our heads won't ache then,' says Jacob, as he turns round and rides away.

'How their hoofs thunder on the level turf!'

'Very neat animal, shows form,' drawls Starlight. 'Worth three hundred in the shires for a hunter; if he can jump, perhaps more; but depends on his manners – must have manners in the hunting-field, Dawson, you know.'

'Manners or not,' says Bill Dawson, 'it's my opinion he could have won that race in a canter. I must find out more about him and buy him if I can.'

'I'll go you halves if you like,' says Starlight. 'I weally believe him to be a good animal.'

Just then up rides Warrigal. He looks at the old horse as if he had never seen him before, nor us neither. He rides close by the heads of Mr Dawson's team, and as he does so his hat falls off, by mistake, of course. He jumps off and picks it up, and rides slowly down towards the tent.

It was the signal to clear. Something was up.

I said goodbye to Aileen and Bella – a hard matter it was, too – and sloped off to where my horse was, and was out of sight of Turon in twenty minutes.

Starlight hails a cabby (he told me this afterwards) and gets him to drive him over to the inn where he was staying, telling the Dawsons he'd have the wine put in ice for the dinner, that he wanted to send off a letter to Sydney by the post, and he'd be back on the course in an hour in good time for the last race.

In about half an hour back comes the same cabman and puts a note into Bill Dawson's hand. He looks at it, stares, swears a bit, and then crumples it up and puts it into his pocket.

Just as it was getting dark, and the last race just run, back comes Sir Ferdinand and all the police. They'd ridden hard, as their horses showed, and Sir Ferdinand (they say) didn't look half as good-natured as he generally did.

'You've missed a great meeting,' says the Commissioner. 'Great pity you had to be off just when you did. But that's just like these infernal scoundrels of bushrangers. They always play up at the most inconvenient time. How did you get on with them?'

'Get on with them?' roars Sir Ferdinand, almost making a hole in his manners – he was that tired out and done he could hardly sit on his horse – 'Why, we've been sold as clean as a whistle. I believe some of the brutes have been here all the time.'

'That's impossible,' says the Commissioner. 'There's been no one here that the police are acquainted with; not that I suppose Jackson and Murphy know many of the cross boys.'

'No strange men nor horses, no disguises?' says Sir Ferdinand. Here he brings out a crumpled bit of paper, written on –

> If sur firdnand makes haist back heel be in time to see Starlite's Raneboe win the handy capp.
>
> Billy the Boy

'I firmly believe that young scoundrel, who will be hanged yet, strung us on after Moran ever so far down south, just to leave the coast clear for the Marstons, and then sent me this, too late to be of any use.'

'Quite likely, but the Marstons couldn't be here, let alone Starlight, unless – by Jove! But that's impossible. Impossible! Whew! Here, Jack Dawson, where's your Indian friend?'

'Gone back to the inn. Couldn't stand the course after the handicap. You're to dine with us, Commissioner; you too Sir Ferdinand, kept a place for you on the chance.'

'One moment, pardon me. Who's your friend?'

'Name Lascelles. Just from home – came by India. Splendid fellow! Backed Darkie for the handicap – we did too – won a pot of money.'

'What sort of a horse is this Darkie?'

'Very grand animal. Old fellow had him in a tent, about a mile down the creek; dark bay, star in forehead. Haven't seen such a horse for years. Like the old Emigrant lot.'

Sir Ferdinand beckoned to a senior constable.

'There's a tent down there near the creek; I think you said, Dawson. Bring up the racehorse you find there, and anyone in charge.

'And now I think I'll drive in with you, Dawson' (dismounting, and handing his horse to a trooper). 'I suppose a decent dinner will pick me up, though I feel just as much inclined to hang myself as do anything else at present. I should like to meet this travelled friend of yours; strangers are most agreeable.'

Sir Ferdinand was right in thinking it was hardly worthwhile going through the form of seeing whether we had waited for him. Lieutenant Lascelles, on leave from his regiment in India, had taken French leave. When inquiry was made at the hotel, where dinner had been ordered by Mr Dawson and covers laid for a dozen, he had just stepped out. No one seemed to know exactly where to find him. The hotel people thought he was with the Mr Dawsons, and they thought he was at the hotel.

When they surrounded the tent, and then rushed it, all that it contained was the body of old Jacob Benton, lying dead drunk on the floor. A horse-rug was over him, his racing saddle under his head, and his pockets stuffed with five-pound notes. He had won his race and got his money, so he was not bound in honour to keep sober a minute longer.

IN THE STABLE

A. B. ('Banjo') Paterson

What! You don't like him; well, maybe, we all have our fancies, of
    course:
Brumby to look at you reckon? Well, no; he's a thoroughbred
    horse;
Sired by a son of old Panic, look at his ears and his head,
Lop-eared and Roman-nosed, ain't he? Well, that's how the Panics
    are bred.
Gluttonous, ugly and lazy, rough as a tip-cart to ride,
Yet if you offered a sovereign apiece for the hairs on his hide
That wouldn't buy him, nor twice that; while I've a pound to the
    good,
This here old stager stays by me and lives like a thoroughbred
    should:
Hunt him away from his bedding, and sit yourself down by the
    wall,
Till you hear how the old fellow saved me from Gilbert,
    O'Mealley and Hall.

Gilbert and Hall and O'Meally, back in the bushranging days,
Made themselves kings of the district, ruled it in old-fashioned
    ways,
Robbing the coach and the escort, stealing our horses at night,
Calling sometimes at the homesteads and giving the women a
    fright:
Came to the station one morning, and why they did this no one
    knows,
Took a brood mare from the paddock, wanting some fun, I
    suppose,
Fastened a bucket beneath her, hung by a strap round her flank,
Then turned her loose in the timber back of the seven-mile tank.

Go! She went mad! She went tearing and screaming with fear
   through the trees,
While the curst bucket beneath her was banging her flanks and
   her knees.
Bucking and racing and screaming she ran to the back of the run,
Killed herself there in a gully; by God, but they paid for their fun!
Paid for it dear, for the black-boys found tracks, and the bucket,
   and all,
And I swore that I'd live to get even with Gilbert, O'Mealley and
   Hall.

Day after day then I chased them, 'course they had friends on the
   sly,
Friends who were willing to sell them to those who were willing to
   buy.
Early one morning we found them in camp at the Cockatoo Farm
One of us shot at O'Meally and wounded him under the arm:
Ran them for miles in the ranges, till Hall, with his horse fairly
   beat,
Took to the rocks and we lost him, the others made good their
   retreat.
It was war to the knife then, I tell you, and once, on the door of
   my shed,
They nailed up a notice that offered a hundred reward for my
   head!

Then we heard they were gone from the district; they stuck up a
   coach in the West,
And I rode by myself in the paddocks, taking a bit of a rest,
Riding this colt as a youngster, awkward, half broken and shy,
He wheeled round one day on a sudden; I looked, but I couldn't
   see why,
But I soon found out why, for before me, the hillside rose up like
   a wall,
And there on the top with their rifles were Gilbert, O'Mealley and
   Hall!

'Twas a good three-mile run to the homestead, bad going, with
    plenty of trees,
So I gathered the youngster together, and gripped at his ribs with
    my knees.
'Twas a mighty poor chance to escape them! It puts a man's nerve
    to the test
On a half broken colt to be hunted by the best mounted men in
    the West.
But the half broken colt was a racehorse! He lay down to work
    with a will,
Flashed through the scrub like a clean-skin, by heavens we flew
    down the hill!
Over a twenty-foot gully he swept with the spring of a deer
They fired as we jumped, but they missed me, a bullet sang close
    to my ear,
And the jump gained us ground, for they shirked it: but I saw as
    we raced through the gap
That the rails at the homestead were fastened, I was caught like a
    rat in a trap.
Fenced with barbed wire was the paddock, barbed wire that
    would cut like a knife,
How was a youngster to clear it that never had jumped in his life?

Bang went a rifle behind me, the colt gave a spring, he was hit;
Straight at the sliprails I rode him, I felt him take hold of
    the bit;
Never a foot to the right or the left did he swerve in his stride,
Awkward and frightened, but honest, the sort it's a pleasure to
    ride!
Straight at the rails, where they'd fastened barbed wire on the top
    of the post,
Rose like a stag and went over, with hardly a scratch at the most;
Into the homestead I darted, and snatched down my gun from the
    wall,
And I tell you I made them step lively, Gilbert, O'Mealley and
    Hall!

Yes! There's the mark of the bullet, he's got it inside of him yet
Mixed up somehow with his victuals, but bless you, he don't seem
  to fret!
Gluttonous, ugly, and lazy, eats any thing he can bite;
Now, let us shut up the stable, and bid the old fellow good night:
Ah! We can't breed 'em, the sort that were bred when we old 'uns
  were young ...
Yes, I was saying, these bushrangers, none of 'em lived to be hung,
Gilbert was shot by the troopers, Hall was betrayed by his friend,
Campbell disposed of O'Meally, bringing the lot to an end.

But you can talk about riding, I've ridden a lot in the past,
Wait till there's rifles behind you, you'll know what it means to go
  fast!
I've steeplechased, raced, and 'run horses', but I think the most
  dashing of all
Was the ride when the old fellow saved me from Gilbert,
  O'Mealley and Hall!

VICTOR SECOND

A. B. ('Banjo') Paterson

We were training two horses for the Buckatowndown races – an old grey warrior called Tricolor – better known to the station boys as The Trickler – and a mare for the hack race. Station horses don't get trained quite like Carbine; some days we had no time to give them gallops at all, so they had to gallop twice as far the next day to make up.

One day the boy we had looking after The Trickler fell in with a mob of sharps who told him we didn't know anything about training horses, and that what the horse really wanted was 'a twicer' – that is to say, a gallop twice round the course. So the boy gave him 'a twicer' on his own responsibility.

When we found out about it we gave the boy a twicer with the strap, and he left and took out a summons against us. But somehow or other we managed to get the old horse pretty fit, tried him against hacks of different descriptions, and persuaded ourselves that we had the biggest certainty ever known on a racecourse.

When the horses were galloping in the morning the kangaroo-dog, Victor, nearly always went down to the course to run round with them. It amused him, apparently, and didn't hurt anyone, so we used to let him race; in fact, we rather encouraged him, because it kept him in good trim to hunt kangaroo.

When we were starting for the meeting, someone said we had better tie up Victor or he would be getting stolen at the races. We called and whistled, but he had made himself scarce, so we started and forgot all about him.

Buckatowndown Races. Red-hot day, everything dusty, everybody drunk and blasphemous. All the betting at Buckatowndown was double-event – you had to win the money first, and fight the man for it afterwards.

The start for our race, the Town Plate, was delayed for a quarter of an hour because the starter flatly refused to leave a fight of which he was an interested spectator. Every horse, as he did his preliminary gallop, had a string of dogs after him, and the clerk of the course came full cry after the dogs with a whip.

By and by the horses strung across to the start at the far side of the course. They fiddled about for a bit; then down went the flag and they came sweeping along all bunched up together, one holding a nice position on the inside. All of a sudden we heard a wild chorus of imprecations – 'Look at that dog!' Victor had chipped in with the racehorses, and was running right in front of the field. It looked a guinea to a gooseberry that some of them would fall on him.

The owners danced and swore. What did we mean by bringing a something mongrel there to trip up and kill horses that were worth a paddockful of all the horses we had ever owned, or would ever breed or own, even if we lived to be a thousand. We were fairly in it and no mistake.

As the field came past the stand the first time we could hear the riders swearing at our dog, and a wild yell of execration arose from the public. He had got right among the ruck by this time, and was racing alongside his friend The Trickler, thoroughly enjoying himself. After passing the stand the pace became very merry; the dog stretched out all he knew; when they began to make it too hot for him, he cut off corners, and joined at odd intervals, and every time he made a fresh appearance the people in the stand lifted up their voices and 'swore cruel'.

The horses were all at the whip as they turned into the straight, and then The Trickler and the publican's mare singled out. We could hear the 'chop, chop!' of the whips as they came along together, but the mare could not suffer it as long as the old fellow, and she swerved off while he struggled home a winner by a length or so.

Just as they settled down to finish Victor dashed up on the inside, and passed the post at old Trickler's girths. The populace immediately went for him with stones, bottles, and other missiles, and he had to scratch gravel to save his life. But imagine the amazement of the other owners when the judge placed Trickler first, Victor second, and the publican's mare third!

The publican tried to argue it out with him. He said you couldn't place a kangaroo-dog second in a horserace.

The judge said it was *his* (hiccough) business what he placed, and that those who (hiccough) interfered with him would be sorry for it. Also he expressed a (garnished) opinion that the publican's mare was no rotten good, and that she was the right sort of mare for a poor man to own, because she would keep him poor.

Then the publican called the judge a cow. The judge was willing; a rip, tear, and chew fight ensued, which lasted some time. The judge won.

Fifteen protests were lodged against our win, but we didn't worry about that – we had laid the stewards a bit to nothing. Every second man we met wanted to run us a mile for one hundred pounds a side; and a drunken shearer, spoiling for a fight, said he had heard we were 'brimming over with bally science,' and had ridden forty miles to find out.

We didn't wait for the hack race. We folded our tents like the Arab and stole away. But it remains on the annals of Buckatowndown how a kangaroo-dog ran second for the Town Plate.

LUNCH FOR DIPSO DAN

Jim Haynes

Dipso Dan is a man who can strike anytime,
You rarely get any warning.
He's thrown out of the pub as the minister passes,
Late one Saturday morning.

'G'day there, Reverend,' says Dipso Dan,
'Got any good tips today?'
'Well, Dan,' says his Reverence, 'lunch might be
A good thing for you, I'd say.'

'Thanks for that, Reverend,' says Dipso Dan,
'I never forget what I'm told.'
And, to himself, he mutters, 'Never heard of Lunch,
It must be a two-year-old.'

Back into the pub goes Dipso Dan,
The drinking day is still young,
And the first thing he sees is a sign that says,
'Lunch is 12 to 1'.

'Look at the odds!' says Dipso Dan,
'That's gotta be worth a chance!'
But a firm hand grips his collar
And another the seat of his pants.

He's back on the street, but now he's obsessed
'That Lunch might be a goer.
I'll go down to the Royal and back it,' says Dan,
'Before the odds get any lower!'

So Dan staggers off to the other pub,
At the other end of the shops,
Halfway down there's the Chinese restaurant,
And that's exactly where Dan stops.

He stares at the sign in the window,
It says 'Lunch is 11 to 2'.
'They're backing the thing for a fortune!' says Dan.
'That minister musta knew!

'Fancy missin' out on twelves!
That's just the thing to spoil
Me afternoon. I'll hurry up
And I'll back it at the Royal.'

Dan staggers on and he's almost there
When he stops, with a strangled yell.
'Lunch 1 to 2' says the blackboard sign
At the door of the Royal Hotel.

'Bloody odds-on! I've missed it!' says Dan,
'Me chance of a fortune is wrecked!'
Then he slides down the wall of the Royal Hotel,
Booze and exercise take their effect.

He sleeps through the paddy-wagon ride,
But he wakes when they lock the cell.
He hears them walking away with the keys,
And he knows he'll have to yell.

'I wanna know about Lunch!' yells Dan,
'An' I gotta terrible thirst!'
'Bad luck about lunch,' the sergeant yells back,
''Cos I'm telling ya, sober up first!'

'Sober Up first, eh?' says Dipso Dan.
'Well, so much for the minister's hunch!'
He lies down on the bed, 'Sober Up first, eh?
Thank gawd I didn't back Lunch!'

PART FOUR

CUP DAY IS SUPREME

Nothing, with the possible exception of Anzac Day, comes anywhere near the Melbourne Cup in the Australian psyche. Those two events on the annual calendar are our own truly unique Australian celebrations.

The Cup was, in a sense, born out of rivalry between two racing clubs: the Victoria Turf Club and the Victoria Jockey Club. It was the brainchild of Captain Standish, Chief Commissioner of Police in Melbourne and Victoria Turf Club Chairman at the time.

Until 1854 Melbourne races were run annually in the autumn. Then the Victoria Turf Club decided to hold a spring meeting as well. The Cup was first run in November 1861 at Flemington, which had originally been called Melbourne Racecourse and was first used as a racecourse as far back as March 1840.

The new race attracted top inter-colonial horses, including the winner, Archer, from New South Wales. This established a great Cup tradition of interstate rivalry, or inter-colonial rivalry as it was back then.

One of the main reasons for inaugurating the Cup was to assert Melbourne's superiority over Sydney both as a city and as a sporting capital. For many years, from the time of the gold rushes, Melbourne was the most populous and richest city in Australia. Victorians were keen to establish Melbourne as the sporting capital, as well as the financial capital, of all the colonies.

So the Victoria Turf Club announced the running of a great new race. It was to be an egalitarian affair with the best horses carrying extra weight to make the race more equal. The trophy was a gold watch and the prize money, of £710, was the most ever put up for a race in the colonies.

The wonderful aura of myth, legend and history that surrounds the Cup developed right from the start.

The story of Archer's two victories in the first two Cups is the stuff of legend. He is supposed to have walked from his home near Nowra to Melbourne twice, but there is evidence to suggest that he made at least one of the journeys, if not both, by the more conventional means of coastal shipping.

His trainer, the legendary Etienne de Mestre, was to upset the local owners and bookmakers just as his horse upset the local champion and race favourite, Mormon.

Archer won the first Cup convincingly by six lengths from Mormon. Seventeen horses started and a dreadful fall resulted in two being killed. A crowd of some five thousand saw the race and de Mestre, who had prepared his horse for the race away from prying eyes at St Kilda, backed Archer from ten to one into six to one and made a killing.

The irony of a New South Wales horse winning a race organised to display Victorian superiority was reinforced when Archer started favourite and won again the following year, this time defeating Mormon by eight lengths in spite of carrying 10 stone 2 pounds.

A further irony, which modern race-goers may not realise, is that there was no prize at all for running second back then.

The story of how Archer missed running in a third Melbourne Cup is also part of the Cup legend. Although Archer was given the massive weight of 11 stone 4 pounds by the handicapper in 1863, de Mestre accepted by telegram on the due date. However, while that particular day was a normal working day in New South Wales, it was a holiday in the colony of Victoria and the telegram was not delivered until the following day, and the entry was not accepted. All the interstate entrants pulled out in protest and only seven local horses ran.

It is another delightful irony that the public holiday which enabled this act of unbridled inter-colonial perfidy to be perpetrated was Separation Day, the day that Victoria celebrated its official separation from New South Wales in 1851.

The original success of the new race, followed by the debacle of 1863, eventually led to the end of the rivalry between the two race clubs, which merged to become the Victoria Racing Club in 1864. The VRC has run the Cup at Flemington every spring without fail since that time, as its feature race for the year.

Like his famous horse, Etienne de Mestre was a larger-than-life character. The son of an American merchant who had been granted land at Shoalhaven, he had eleven children who, according to his descendant Jeanne de Mestre, 'all had to make their own way in life while he concentrated on his horses'.

He had been the most successful jockey of his time. He trained Archer to win the first two Cups and, with three further Melbourne Cup winners to his credit, he set a record that lasted for ninety-nine years, until Bart Cummings broke it in 1977.

Whether de Mestre owned or simply trained Archer is another piece of Cup history that is still being debated. What we do know is that Archer raced in de Mestre's colours, which were, rather ominously for the bookies of Melbourne in 1861, all black.

The Cup legends and stories that have grown and multiplied since those first few years have filled many volumes. The prose and verses which follow are a small fraction of the stories that make up the Cup legend.

'... Archer raced in Etienne de Mestre's colours ...
all black.'

Extract from WESTWARD HO!

Harry Morant ('The Breaker')

The night's a trifle chilly, and the stars are very bright,
A heavy dew is falling, but the tent-fly is rigged right;
You may rest your bones till morning, then, if you chance to wake,
Give me a call about the time that daylight starts to break.

We may not camp tomorrow, for we've many a mile to go,
'Ere we turn our horses' heads round to make tracks for down
  below.
There's many a water-course to cross, and many a black-soil plain,
And many a mile of mulga ridge 'ere we get back again.

That time five moons shall wax and wane we'll finish up the work,
Have the bullocks o'er the border and truck 'em down from Bourke,
And when they're sold at Homebush, and the agents settle up,
Sing hey! A spell in Sydney town ... and Melbourne for the 'Cup'.

CUP DAY IS SUPREME

Mark Twain

> There is a Moral Sense, and there is an Immoral Sense.
> The Moral Sense enables us to perceive morality and
> avoid it; the Immoral Sense enables us to perceive
> immorality and to enjoy it.
>
> *Pudd'nhead Wilson's New Calendar*

The things which interest us when we travel are, first, the people; next, the novelties; and finally, the history of the places and countries visited. Novelties are rare in cities which represent the most advanced civilisation of the modern day. When one is familiar with such cities in the other parts of the world he is in effect familiar with the cities of Australasia. There may be shades of difference, but these can easily be too fine for detection by the incompetent eye of the passing stranger.

Even in the famous so-called 'larrikin', for instance, the traveller will not be able to discover a new species, but only an old one met elsewhere, and variously called loafer, rough, tough, bummer, or blatherskite, according to his geographical distribution. The larrikin differs by a shade from those others, in that he is more sociable towards the stranger, more kindly disposed, more hospitable, more hearty, more friendly.

As I have suggested, novelties are rare in the great capitals of modern times. Even the wool exchange in Melbourne could not be told from the familiar stock exchange of other countries. Wool brokers are just like stockbrokers; they all bounce from their seats and put up their hands and yell in unison ... though no stranger can tell what they yell. Then the president calmly says, 'Sold to Smith and Co, threepence farthing ... next!' when probably nothing of the kind happened; for how should he know?

Melbourne spreads around over an immense area of ground. And what was the origin of this majestic city and its efflorescence of palatial town houses and country seats? Its first brick was laid and its first house built by a passing convict.

Australian history is almost always picturesque; indeed, it is so curious and strange, that it is itself the chiefest novelty the country has to offer, and so it pushes the other novelties into second and third place. It does not read like history, but like the most beautiful lies, and all of a fresh new sort, no mouldy old stale ones.

Australian history is full of surprises, and adventures, and incongruities, and contradictions, and incredibilities; but they are all true, they all happened.

Melbourne is the largest city of Australasia, and fills the post with honour and credit. It is a stately city architecturally as well as in magnitude. It has an elaborate cable-car system; it has museums, and colleges, and schools, and public gardens, and electricity, and gas, and libraries, and theatres, and mining centres, and wool

'... the mitred Metropolitan centre of the Horse Racing Cult.'
The Carriage Paddock and Lawn at Flemington 1889

centres, and centres of the arts and sciences, and boards of trade, and ships, and railroads, and a harbour.

Melbourne has social clubs, and journalistic clubs, and racing clubs, and a squatter club sumptuously housed and appointed, and as many churches and banks as can make a living. In a word, it is equipped with everything that goes to make the modern great city.

Yet, Melbourne has one specialty that must not be jumbled in with those other things. It is the mitred Metropolitan centre of the Horse Racing Cult. Its raceground is the Mecca of Australasia.

On the great annual day of sacrifice – the fifth of November, Guy Fawkes's Day, business is suspended over a stretch of land and sea as wide as from New York to San Francisco, and deeper than from the northern lakes to the Gulf of Mexico; and every man and woman, of high degree or low, who can afford the expense, put away all their other duties and come to the racetrack.

They begin to swarm in by ship and rail a fortnight before the day, and they swarm thicker and thicker day after day, until all the vehicles of transportation are taxed to their uttermost to meet the

'... all the vehicles of transportation are taxed to their uttermost to meet the demands of the occasion ...' The road to Flemington on Cup day 1890.

demands of the occasion, and all hotels and lodgings are bulging outward because of the pressure from within.

They come a hundred thousand strong, as all the best authorities say, and they pack the spacious grounds and grandstands and make a spectacle such as is never to be seen in Australasia or elsewhere.

It is the 'Melbourne Cup' that brings this multitude together.

Their clothes have been ordered long ago, at unlimited cost, and without bounds as to beauty and magnificence, and have been kept in concealment until now, for unto this day are they consecrate. (I am speaking of the ladies' clothes; but one might know that.)

And so the grandstands make a brilliant and wonderful spectacle, a delirium of colour, a vision of beauty. The champagne flows, everybody is vivacious, excited and happy.

'It is the 'Melbourne Cup' that brings this multitude together.'
View from the flat 1891

Everybody bets, and gloves and fortunes change hands right along, all the time. Day after day the races go on, and the fun and the excitement are kept at white heat; and when each day is done, the people dance all night so as to be fresh for the racing in the morning.

At the end of the great week the swarms secure lodgings and transportation for next year, then flock away to their remote homes and count their gains and losses, and order next year's Cup-clothes, and then lie down and sleep for two weeks, and get up sorry to reflect that a whole year must be put in somehow or other before they can be wholly happy again.

The Melbourne Cup is the Australasian National Day. It would be difficult to overstate its importance. It overshadows all other holidays and specialised days of whatever sort in the colonies.

Overshadows them? I might almost say it blots them out. Each special day gets attention, but not everybody's attention. Each holiday evokes interest, but not everybody's interest. Each of them rouses enthusiasm, but not everybody's enthusiasm. In each case a part of the attention, interest, and enthusiasm is a matter of habit and custom, and another part of it is official and perfunctory.

Cup Day, and Cup Day only, commands an attention, an interest, and an enthusiasm, which are universal and spontaneous, not perfunctory.

In America we have no annual supreme day, no day whose approach makes the whole nation glad.

We have the fourth of July, and Christmas, and Thanksgiving. None of them can claim primacy; none of them can arouse an enthusiasm which comes near to being universal. Eight grown Americans out of ten dread the coming of the fourth of July, with its pandemonium and its perils, and they rejoice when it is gone … if they are still alive.

The approach of Christmas brings harassment and dread to many excellent people. They have to buy a cart-load of presents, and they never know what to buy to hit the various tastes. People put in three weeks of hard and anxious work, and when Christmas morning comes they are so dissatisfied with the result, and so disappointed, that they want to sit down and cry. Then they give thanks that Christmas comes but once a year.

The observance of Thanksgiving Day, as a function, has become general of late. The thankfulness is not so general. This is natural. Two-thirds of the nation have always had hard luck and a hard time during the year, and this has a calming effect upon their enthusiasm for giving thanks.

We have a supreme day, a sweeping and tremendous and tumultuous day, a day which commands an absolute universality of interest and excitement; but it is not annual. It comes but once in four years when the President is elected; therefore it cannot count as a rival of the Melbourne Cup.

In Great Britain and Ireland they have two great days, Christmas and the Queen's birthday. But they are equally popular; there is no supremacy.

I think it must be conceded that the position of the Australasian Day is unique, solitary, unparalleled, and likely to hold that high place a long time.

Cup Day is supreme, it has no rival. I can call to mind no specialised annual day, in any country, which can be named by that large name ... Supreme! I can call to mind no specialised annual day, in any country, whose approach fires the whole land with a conflagration of conversation and preparation and anticipation and jubilation. No day save this one; but this one does it.

LISTEN, ELAINE!

C. J. Dennis

Listen, Elaine. Tho' I'm not mad on racing,
I like a little flutter now and then;
But I maintain you would not be disgracing
The family, or look like some old hen
If you just wore ... Now, just a minute, please ...
That pinkish frock ... No, wait! Let me explain.
That pinkish frock with spots ... You wouldn't freeze!
You've got your furs. Aw, listen, please, Elaine!

Now, look. We've twenty pounds. Don't let us quarrel.
Surely we can be sane and quite grown-up.
If you take most of that, what of the 'moral'
That Percy Podgrass gave us for the Cup?
Of course he's sure to win. What are vain dresses
Compared ... My dear! I did not call you vain!
Nor selfish either. Gosh! What married messes
Start over clothes, and ... Listen, please, Elaine.

We're partners, aren't we? Well, then, listen, darling.
We might discuss this calmly, don't you think?
Now! Please be sensible ... I am not snarling!
Rubbish! Of course, you do look nice in pink.
I always thought that spotted pink looked dandy,
And comfy, too. Supposing it should rain.
Nice sight you'd look in ... What's it called ... organdie ...
I was not wishing ... Listen, please! Elaine!

Women just dress to spite some other tabby.
Who *said* you were a cat? One moment, pet.
Of course, I wouldn't have my wife look shabby.
Take what you need. We'll make a smaller bet ...
Eight ... ten ... twelve quid! Whew! Not much left for betting.
Still, just a flutter and expenses ... What?
Listen, Elaine. What could I be forgetting?
Hat? Stockings? Shoes to match? ... Here ... Take the lot!

'Of course he's sure to win.'
Even Stevens goes onto the track to win the 1962 Cup and complete the Caulfield/Melbourne Cups double

CARBINE'S MELBOURNE CUP, 1890

Anon

The race is run, the Cup is won, the great event is o'er.
The grandest horse that strode a course has led them home once
    more.
I watched with pride your sweeping stride before you ranged in line,
For far and near a ringing cheer was echoed for Carbine.

The start was made, no time delayed before they got away,
Those horses great, some thirty-eight, all eager for the fray.
No better start could human heart to sportsmen ever show
As Watson did, each jockey bid get ready for to go.

With lightning speed, each gallant steed along the green track tore;
Each jockey knew what he must do to finish in the fore.
But Ramage knew his mount was true, though he had ten-five up,
For Musket's son great deeds had done before that Melbourne Cup.

No whip, nor spur, he needs to stir a horse to greater speed;
He knew as well as man can tell when he could take the lead.
So on he glides with even strides, though he is led by nine;
But Ramage knows before they close he'll try them with Carbine.

The bend is passed; the straight at last: he takes him to the fore.
The surging crowd with voices loud the stud's name loudly roar.
The jockey too, he full well knew the race was nearly o'er,
As on his mane he slacked the rein: no need to urge him more.

Brave horse and man who led the van on that November day!
Your records will be history still when ye have passed away.
For such a race, for weight and pace, has never been put up
As that deed done by Musket's son in the 1890 Cup.

'... on his mane he slacked the rein: no need to urge him more.'
Carbine wins the 1890 Cup

MEMORIES OF MELBOURNE

Nat Gould

To chronicle all I have seen on the turf in Australia would fill two or three volumes, so I shall merely give reminiscences and incidents likely to interest the reader.

1889 Melbourne Cup

Bravo* won the Melbourne Cup in 1889 and when I arrived in Melbourne that year one of the first men I met was the late Mr Chapman, a racing journalist who wrote as 'Augur' for the *Australasian*. He was a good fellow and he told me he had backed Bravo at the forlorn odds of a thousand to one.

It appears some rash bookmaker, more in a spirit of bravado than anything else, had offered to lay a thousand pounds to a

'*Bravo won the Melbourne Cup in 1889 ...*'

sovereign against Bravo and Mr Chapman had stood in with a friend and taken a quarter of the bet and won £250 for his five shillings.

I was more interested in the fate of a horse called Chicago. He was a good horse and a Caulfield Cup winner; but, somehow, I managed to back him in the wrong race.

Bravo had been reported as so lame that his starting was regarded as out of the question. A few days before the race Bravo came into the market again and was well backed. The bookmakers who had been taking liberties with him felt uneasy, and a lot of the money they had laid against him at long odds was hedged at a loss.

The Melbourne Stakes on the Saturday had produced a terrific race between Abercorn, Melos and Carbine, who passed the post in that order. Abercorn on that day was at his best and I never saw him run a better race. At this particular time he was even better than Carbine, but it must not be forgotten that the son of Musket had one of his fore-hoofs tightly bound up due to a cracked heel, and was not at his best.

'Bravo's win put a good stake in the pocket of his owner ...'
Betting Paddock at Flemington on Cup Day 1889

After his forward running in the Stakes on the Saturday, Melos was naturally a great favourite for the Cup, as he had a lot less weight to carry, yet Bravo's Cup win was not such a surprise as many people imagined, for the horse was well backed at twelve to one on the day of the race. He beat Carbine and Melos, who finished in that order.

Bravo's win put a good stake in the pocket of his owner, Mr W. T. Jones of Ballarat, a good racing man.

The next year's Cup was won by Carbine; but that event I will leave for the present, as a special chapter is devoted to that great horse.

1891 Melbourne Cup

In 1891, Malvolio beat Sir William and Strathmore to win the Cup. His sire was the 1884 Cup winner, Malua, and his dam was Madcap. Malvolio was bred, owned and trained by Mr James Redfearn and ridden to victory by his son.

Mr Redfearn is a trainer well up in his business and a jolly good fellow to boot and the victory of his horse was popular although, had Sir William got home, it would have pleased the Sydney people better.

Sir William was a handsome horse trained by Mr Edward Keys, and had the advantage of Jack Fielder in the saddle. The astute Teddy Keys fancied he had a good thing in Sir William and the result proved that he was not far out. Had Sir William got home I know one or two men who would have been several thousand pounds richer.

Strathmore won the Derby that year and of course was heavily backed for the Cup as the Derby winner almost invariably is. Strathmore was a remarkably good horse and had a bad run in the Cup, or I think he would have finished nearer. Some people go so far as to say he would have beaten Malvolio, but that I cannot agree with.

Mr Forrester always maintained that his horse Highborn finished third that year, although the judge gave third place to Strathmore. I thought so too and the black fellow certainly ran well enough with his weight of 9 stone 1 pound to show that he was a good horse at the distance, having finished second to Carbine the year before with 6 stone 8 pounds.

'In 1891, Malvolio beat Sir William and Strathmore to win the Cup.'

Mr McCulloch, the judge, told me next morning in Scott's Hotel that it was a case of neck-and-neck for third place in the race, but Strathmore just beat Highborn in the last stride. That last stride did Highborn's owner out of a thousand pounds for third money and also sundry place bets.

There was some trouble about paying over the stakes in the 1891 Cup. Mr Etienne de Mestre put in a claim for them on the grounds that he owned Madcap, the dam of Malvolio, and had merely lent her to Mr Redfearn. This Mr Redfearn denied and I think Mr de Mestre was ill-advised to make the claim he did. Malvolio's owner got the stakes, and rightly so.

Although Malvolio was a good horse, I never had much fancy for him after his Cup win and it must have taken a lot out of him. Three very sensational Cups followed this win of Malvolio's. As a rule there is always plenty of excitement over a Melbourne Cup.

On the return journey from Melbourne in 1891 we had a fire alarm on the train. Lord Jersey, the Governor, was in a special car behind ours and the attendant roused us and said to me, 'There's a fire, sir! You'd better get out!'

'No, you don't,' I replied, 'It's not time to turn out yet.'

The attendant has a knack of rousing you up early in order to make the beds in the car. I fancied his fire alarm was a happy inspiration on his part to get me out.

When I saw the train had stopped and people were hurrying out of the car I felt it was time to make a move. Then a sudden thought occurred to me: I felt I could earn undying fame as a staunch supporter of our great Empire, so I sang out, 'Save the Governor!'

An old Scotsman was in the berth over mine, and he growled out, 'Save the Governor be damned! Where's me boots?'

Evidently the gentleman from the north did not coincide with my views and just wanted to make tracks.

Happily no great harm was done, only one side of the car was burned, through some of the rods being overheated.

An amusing account of the incident appeared in the Melbourne paper *Bohemian*. Here is the extract, which I happened to come across:

> The true story of the fire on board the Sydney express, about a week ago, has not yet been told. No one has yet ventured to describe the scene in the interior of the car after the alarm was sounded.
>
> The alarm of 'Fire', when uttered in a shrill voice in the small hours of the morning, never fails to have the desired effect on the soundest sleeper, especially if the cry be uttered by a female. On this occasion it had the desired effect on every soul in the carriage.
>
> A lady who slept in a berth by the door heard it first and, running out into the passage that traverses the carriage in her *robe de nuit*, was confronted by the stalwart figure of Dibbs, the new Premier, who was vainly trying to find his way into the trousers of Nat Gould, the author of *The Double Event*.

Nat Gould is fat and short and Dibbs is a big fellow, and slim with an altitude of six feet three inches. When the alarm was given, Gould promptly seized hold of Dibbs's clothes and made straight for the open air. By the time Dibbs got his eyes open there was only one pair of trousers available and they were Gould's.

When he met the hysterical female in the curl papers, the New South Wales Premier had only got one leg into Gould's unmentionables, but he struggled manfully to cover the other leg with a newspaper.

Gould's plight was even worse. He had got his legs into the sleeves of Dibbs's shooting-jacket and, when he was discovered out on the line a few minutes later by the guard, he was carrying over his arm a set of ladies' overalls, which he had borne off triumphantly in his flight.

Such is the account given of this memorable episode.

1892 Victorian Derby

Camoola won the Derby in 1892 as hot favourite, but failed behind Glenloth in the Cup. He was trained by Mr Tom Payton, who also had another good colt that year in Autonomy.

Mr Payton mystified the horse watchers on the Flemington track in the early morning with the doings of Camoola and Autonomy. Both were entered in the Derby and naturally there was a desire to find out which colt would carry the stable confidence in that race. They were generally galloped together and one morning Autonomy would beat Camoola badly and two mornings later, Camoola would leave Autonomy far behind.

All this was most annoying to those people who imagine other people's business ought to be theirs. I fancy the trainer merely had the heavy saddle changed occasionally.

There is a story attached to this saddle. It is reported that, on one occasion, when the painters were doing up the saddle room at

Newmarket, one of the men asked a stable lad to remove an innocent-looking saddle from one of the saddle trees.

Without a thought the lad pulled it down by the stirrup-leather, in order to catch it. When it fell the saddle nearly broke the youngster's neck, for it weighed about four stone!

The day Camoola won the Derby, Autonomy landed a win in the Melbourne Stakes. Much diversity of opinion existed as to whether Camoola or Autonomy was the better colt. I preferred Autonomy for any distance up to a mile-and-a-half. From the way he won the Stakes I think he would have won the Derby easier than Camoola. He was a beautiful bay horse and Camoola was a chestnut, with lop ears and a particularly laboured style of galloping. Both, however, were rattling good horses.

1892 Melbourne Cup

What an awful Cup it was in 1892.

I have been at race-meetings in all sorts of weather in the old country and elsewhere, but I never recollect a more uncomfortable day than when Glenloth won the Cup. Torrents of rain came down and deluged everybody and turned the course into a quagmire on the far side.

All the fashionable world turned out as usual. Nothing short of an earthquake would prevent Melbourne people from going to the Cup, and even then, when the course was clear, they would sit on the ruins of the stands and watch the race!

The lawn became very slippery and it was amusing to see the numerous spills as some well-dressed swell measured his length in the mud and then got up to shake himself like a Newfoundland dog.

The rain poured down like a second deluge when the horses came out. The mud flew up in a shower in the preliminary canter and in the actual race it can easily be imagined what it was like. I was in the press box on the top of the grandstand and at the back of this, some distance away, is 'the hill', which was crowded with a wet, miserable mass of people.

Umbrellas were put up by some people on the top of the stand, but loud shouts from the people on the hill ordered them to be shut.

Many declined to close their umbrellas and a shower of mud in lumps came rattling down on them from the irate crowd on the hill. This had the desired effect.

On the flat there was a perfect forest of umbrellas and it was a strange sight as seen from our box. As for seeing the race, it was well nigh impossible and, when the horses flashed past the post there was a cry of 'What's won?'

When Glenloth's number went up it put the finishing touches on backers' misery. The horse was a rank outsider and fifty to one could have been had about him in places.

Glenloth was a good stamp of a horse, but the wet day was all in his favour. He might have won under any circumstances, but the heavy going assisted a horse of his build.

Mr Forrester had two horses in the race, Ronda and Penance. The former had done a good trial but was beaten in the Trial Stakes on the first day of the carnival, which did not make his Cup chance look rosy. Nasty remarks were made about his performance in this race after the Cup; but they were uncalled for as the stable lost a lot of money over him in the Trial Stakes.

Penance was well handicapped. He had run Carbine a great race as a two-year-old but had never run up to that form since. I think the set-to with Carbine knocked all the pluck out of him, and no wonder, for it was a terrible task to set a two-year-old to beat Carbine.

Ronda finished second and Penance third, so Mr Forrester's bad luck in this race still stuck to him. In three years he had his horses run second, fourth, and second and third: not a bad record.

An incident that happened to me over this race shows how unwise it is to put a man off backing a horse when he fancies it.

Before I left my hotel in the morning, one of the waiters asked me to put a pound on Glenloth for him. I laughed at him, and told him to keep his money in his pocket. He did, with the result that he was about fifty pounds worse off after Glenloth won, as he would have procured that amount to his pound.

I shall never forget the mournful look with which he regarded me after the event. I had serious thoughts about changing my table, in case a concoction of arsenic fell into my soup by mistake. Thinking to make things better, I advised him to back Trieste in the Oaks. He did, and she lost, though she ought to have won, which only made matters worse.

Moral: always keep your information to yourself, and then you will be the only sufferer.

1893 Caulfield Cup

The year following Glenloth's wet Cup I again found myself in Melbourne for the two big meetings at Caulfield and Flemington.

We generally went overland from Sydney to Melbourne and we had some fun when we got a merry party together in the Pullman car.

The journey by train from Sydney to Melbourne is about five hundred miles. The express leaves Sydney at 5.15 pm and reaches Melbourne next day at 11.30 am, the sleeping-cars are models of comfort and the journey is made as pleasant as possible for travellers.

When I first travelled this journey there was a vexatious delay at Albury, the border town between New South Wales and Victoria, where we had to change from the Sydney train into the Melbourne train. This was done because the gauge of the railway lines is different.

Eight or nine years ago they were very particular about examining baggage, as the duty was heavy on certain articles. It seems a monstrous thing that it should be necessary to search passengers' luggage merely because they pass out of one colony into another. It is an absurdity, and so most travellers thought it.

In 1893 the Caulfield Cup proved sensational. Tim Swiveller won and Chris Moore rode him. Sainfoin was second and Oxide third. An objection was laid against Tim Swiveller on the grounds of interference by the connections of Sainfoin.

The Caulfield stewards decided not to interfere with the judge's decision and the race was given to Tim Swiveller. The owner of Sainfoin then appealed to the VRC, as he had a perfect right to do.

Much to the surprise of the ring, and racing men generally, the VRC awarded the race to Sainfoin, disqualified Tim Swiveller and placed Oxide second. This was very hard luck for the Honourable George Davis, the owner of Tim Swiveller, and he was not the sort of man to let the affair rest, for he defended his case admirably.

It seems a remarkable thing that the verdict of such a body of stewards as at Caulfield, who saw the race officially, should be over-ruled by the VRC, who did not see the race officially.

That Tim Swiveller interfered with Sainfoin I have very little doubt, as I saw the race, and had a splendid view of the finish. The horse that suffered most, however, was Oxide. He got jammed between Tim Swiveller and Sainfoin and his rider, Cis Parker, had to pull up his head otherwise he would probably have been down.

I do not believe Chris Moore, the rider of Tim Swiveller, wilfully did anything wrong. His mount was a horse that used to hang a lot at the finish of a race, and this caused him to bore in.

A photograph taken of the finish of the race was, I believe, the main point upon which the VRC based their decision. It is said the photographic apparatus cannot lie, but I have seen photos of people that looked very unlike them, so there must be something wrong somewhere. I am not much of a believer in the photographic evidence in cases of this kind.

Sainfoin getting the stakes made a vast difference to the ring, and there was a lot of grumbling over the matter.

1893 Melbourne Cup

The 1893 Cup was won by another outsider, Tarcoola. Once again I had a bad time, as I backed Carnage for the double, the Derby and the Cup. Carnage won the Derby all right, but just failed in the Cup as he ran second after making nearly all the running.

It was an extraordinary performance on the part of a three-year-old, as early in the season as November, to make nearly the whole of the pace in a two-mile race, and then just get beaten. It was about as good a performance as I ever saw a three-year-old do in November.

Tarcoola was trained by Mr Joe Cripps, and ran in his name, and, as in the case of Malvolio, was ridden by the son of the trainer. Mr Greenaway was the owner of Tarcoola for some time and the horse lost him a heap of money. He told me it nearly made him throw up racing when he saw Tarcoola land such a stake as the Melbourne Cup after he had sold him.

It is curious how men sometimes miss a good win. One morning I was coming off the track with Mr Frank Wilkinson, a well-known pressman and handicapper, when he turned around and said, 'Stop a minute, Nat; here's Tarcoola going for a spin.'

'Hang Tarcoola,' I said, 'I'm in a hurry for breakfast.'

Frank had, however, got his watch on them, and I waited until the gallop was over.

'By Jove! That's a great go!' said Frank, looking at his watch. 'It's worth taking a few pounds about Tarcoola at one hundred to two or three.'

I said, 'We'll think about it. You can get a bit of money in the Club, and I'll go you halves.'

Unfortunately, Frank did not get the money and, a day or two after, Tarcoola did such a bad gallop I forgot all about him until I saw him beating my pet fancy, Carnage, in the Cup. I believe Frank wired the result of the good gallop to a friend in Sydney who won a thousand pounds on Tarcoola. Such is luck.

Tarcoola won cleverly from Carnage and Jeweller, with Loyalty well up close, and again the public were floored, as Tarcoola started at a very long price.

1894 VRC Derby

The Harvester, a colt owned by the trainer, Mr Sam Cook, who also bred him, won the Derby the following year. There was a lot of bumping at the finish of the race and an objection was laid against the winner. Bonnie Scotland, who ran third, had a bad run but I think the stewards were right in not disturbing the judge's verdict.

Chris Moore rode the winner and was naturally very anxious about the result. The stewards were considering the matter long after the last race had been run and it was a curious sight to see the bars lighted with candles and the racecourse suddenly enveloped in darkness.

I was on the lawn with Mr Forrester, Mr James Redfearn and Mr John O'Loughlin, a worthy lawyer of Sydney and a good sort who was very fond of a racehorse and owned a good one in Correze.

To kill time I did a short sprint on the lawn and offered to run Mr Forrester a hundred yards for a bottle of champagne. I fancy the spurt I gave induced Mr Forrester to think that I could run, and he forfeited. I can assure him that the spurt I gave took it all out of me and it was lucky for me that he did not toe the scratch line.

When it was known The Harvester had got the race, we four left the course in a wagonette and, after sundry adventures on the road, reached Scott's Hotel, where I believe we had a very fair night of it.

1894 Melbourne Cup

The last Cup I saw, before sailing for London, was in 1894. Again an outsider landed the race when Patron* won, and it was a most extraordinary victory, as I will endeavour to show.

Patron was a very good three-year-old and, naturally, he was backed early in the season for the Cup. On paper his chances looked as good as anything in the race. Some of the first double-event wagers booked were for Paris in the Caulfield Cup and Patron in the Melbourne Cup.

Before the date for the Cup arrived Patron went wrong, and his name gradually receded from the betting list until, shortly before the race, long odds could be had about his chances.

Paris, who won the Caulfied Cup in 1894, won his first Caulfield Cup in 1892. Cis Parker rode him on the first occasion and Jack Fielder on the second. Both were good races but his second win was a brilliant performance in such a big field with his heavy weight of 9 stone 4. Over a mile few horses could beat him and he was a thorough stayer as well. I never saw a horse that could equal him on the track and morning after morning he used to do the fastest gallop of any horse out. He was certainly one of the very best horses I saw in the colonies.

A well-known jockey, whose name I will not mention, had the double, Paris for the Caulfield Cup and Patron for the Melbourne Cup; but so confident was he, from information received, that Patron could not win, that he hedged the whole of his Patron money to two bookmakers.

Dawes, the jockey who rode Patron, had not much faith in his mount either and Mr Purchas, the owner, also laid off as much of his money as he could. I believe as late as the evening before the race it was not decided whether Patron would run or be scratched. This was certainly not encouraging to anyone who had backed the horse.

It was, however, decided to start the horse and let him take his chance, and, much to the surprise of everyone, he won the Cup after a good race with Devon and Nada. The latter was in Mr Wilson's stables and was backed for a heap of money. She had done a good trial at St Alban's and evidently ran up to it.

Devon was the unlucky horse of the season. He won the Toorak Handicap at Caulfield and thereby earned a penalty for the Caulfield Cup, or he would have won it for a certainty. As it was he crossed his legs at a critical part of the race and was beaten right on the post by Paris. Devon followed this up by running second in the Melbourne Cup and a few days after he ran second in the Williamstown Cup to Taranaki. It was very bad luck indeed to run three seconds in such important races.

The jockey alluded to previously, who had the Paris–Patron double, actually backed Devon in the Melbourne Cup with the money he drew back over Patron. If that's not the devil's own luck, I don't know how it could be beaten!

*Bravo and Patron were both sired by the only unbeaten Cup winner in history, Grand Flaneur, who won in 1880 and started nine times for nine wins.

THE NARK

C. J. Dennis

Wait till after Chewsday, wife.
'Taint far ahead to look,
A change is comin' in your life,
Or else I'm much mistook,
I'll buy you rugs an' furs an' things
An' di'monds by the ton.
We're 'ome at last when Chewsday's past
An' Melbun Cup is run.

Wait till after Chewsday, Bill.
You're silly if you frets;
I'll pay that quid; you know I will;
An' settle all me debts.
The tip's cert; the 'orse can spurt
An' last the distance too.
I'm 'ome all right by Chewsday night
When all me dreams come true.

I knows, I knows; too well I knows
I've said it all before;
But blokes 'as got to learn I s'pose;
I'll never switch no more.
Me mind's made up. This Melbun Cup
You'll 'ave no chance to scoff.
I mean to stick to my first pick
An' never git put off.

So wait till after Chewsdy, mate.
Till after Chewsday, wife.
A man can't be the fool of fate

For all 'is nach'ril life.
An' yet, an' yet, I can't forget
Past years, an' nags I backs.
In pichers grim I visions 'im,
That coot wot dogs me tracks –

Never the same bloke year by year,
'E waits there on the course
To pour 'is poison in my ear –
That 'ound wot knows a 'orse.
'E knows a man wot knows a man
Wot knows the stable well.
'E knows, 'e knows – Lord! Wot 'e knows
'Ud take a book to tell.

An' must I meet 'im once again –
My Jonah, still disguised?
An' must I 'ark to that dead nark
An' stand there, 'ipnertised?
Keep 'im away! Keep me, I pray,
From speakin', still bewitched,
The bitterest word a man 'er 'eard:
'I 'ad it, but I switched.'

A POST CUP TALE

C. J. Dennis

I 'ad the money in me 'and!
Fair dinkum! Right there, by the stand.
I tole me wife at breakfus' time,
Straight out: 'Trivalve,' I sez, 'is prime.
Trivalve,' I sez. An', all the week,
I swear there's no one 'eard me speak
Another 'orse's name. Why, look,
I 'ad the oil straight from a Book
On Sund'y at me cousin's place
When we was talkin' of the race.
'Trivalve,' 'e sez. ''Is chance is grand.'
I 'ad the money in me 'and!

Fair in me 'and I 'ad the dough!
An' then a man 'as got to go –
Wot? Tough? Look, if I 'adn't met
Jim Smith (I ain't forgave 'im yet)
'E takes an' grabs me by the coat.
'Trivalve?' 'e sez. 'That hairy goat!'
(I 'ad the money in me 'and
Just makin' for the bookie's stand)
'Trivalve?' 'e sez. 'Ar, turn it up!
'Ow could 'e win a flamin' Cup?'
Of course, I thort 'e muster knoo.
'Im livin' near a trainer, too.

Right 'ere, like that, fair in me fist
I 'ad the notes! An' then I missed –
Missed like a mug fair on the knock
Becos 'is maggin' done me block.

'That hairy goat?' 'e sez. 'E's crook!'
Fair knocked me back, 'e did. An' look,
I 'ad the money in me 'and!
Fair in me paw! An', un'erstand,
Sixes at least I coulder got –
Thirty to five, an' made a pot.
Today I mighter been reel rich –
Rollin' in dough! Instid o' which,
'Ere's me – Aw! Don't it beat the band?
I 'AD THE MONEY IN ME 'AND!
Put me clean off, that's wot 'e did ...
Say, could yeh lend us 'arf a quid?

'Trivalve,' I sez, 'is prime.' 1927 Cup Winner, Trivalve

AS UNLUCKY AS SHADOW KING

Jim Haynes

'As unlucky as Shadow King' was a common saying in Australia in the 1930s and 1940s. True, it was mostly a racetrack saying but, as Shadow King was six times a player in that most Australian of all events, the Melbourne Cup, it was a saying that all Australians understood.

Shadow King was a son of Comedy King, the first imported horse to win the Melbourne Cup. Comedy King had arrived in Australia as a foal. Mr Sol Green purchased his dam, Tragedy Queen, in Britain in 1906. She was in foal to the famous English Derby winner, Persimmon, and the resulting foal was Comedy King, who dominated Australian racing in 1910 and defeated another great horse, Trafalgar, in the Melbourne Cup of that year. Indeed, he defeated Trafalgar on eight occasions.

Comedy King also proved to be an outstanding sire. Two of his sons won the Cup – Artilleryman (1919) and King Ingoda (1922) – and he was grandsire on the dam side to Comic Court, who won in 1950. Artilleryman was reputed to be the best looking horse ever seen on an Australian racetrack and many feel he could have been the greatest racehorse of his era. He won the Cup as a three-year-old but was tragically dead from illness before the season ended.

Shadow King's dam, Beryllia, was by the Irish stallion Land of Song from the English mare, Berylium, so he was truly of migrant stock, yet the racing public loved him as the archetypal Aussie battler.

It has been much discussed that our premier race is a handicap rather than a true test of quality. A brief study of the race's history will show that it is exactly that element that has made the Cup the great Australian event that it is.

We want to see if our champions can overcome the odds and win with the weight, and we love our champions whether they win or lose the Cup. Wakeful, Kingston Town, Gunsynd and Phar Lap in 1931 were cheered from the course, gallant in defeat.

We want to know if the three-year-olds can run above their experience with the smaller weights. We also want to see if that dour battling old stayer we have watched over the years can run a brave race against the odds.

Americans, it is said, love winners, and the British love quality and breeding. Australians appreciate these things too; but, perhaps because of certain elements in our history and heritage, we are different: we believe everyone should be given a 'fair go' and our greatest sporting event is a handicap race.

If the Melbourne Cup is a celebration of the Australian's love of 'giving everyone a go', then Shadow King truly represents the 'everyone' we are talking about.

Shadow King was a 'trier'; he always 'had a go'. Trained by popular battling trainer Elwood Fisher, the dark-bay gelding ran in his first Melbourne Cup as a four-year-old in 1929. Nightmarch won the Cup that year, from Paquito and the three-year-old Phar Lap, who was even-money favourite.

Most experts think that Phar Lap lost the 1929 Cup by pulling all through the early stages so badly that his jockey that day, the fifty-year-old Bobby Lewis, had little choice but to let him have his head and stride away at the six-furlong post. This enabled Nightmarch to run him down in the straight. Shadow King followed them, in a respectable sixth place.

The following year Phar Lap, ridden by Jim Pike, won the Cup easily, carrying a record weight for a four-year-old and at the prohibitive odds of eleven to eight on. It was the only time in history that the bookies sent a horse out at odds-on in the Cup.

The appropriately named Second Wind was three lengths away in second place and Shadow King was there, earning one thousand pounds for his owner, Mr Schillaber, by finishing three-quarters of a length away in third place.

The following year Phar Lap was asked to carry the record weight of 10 stone 10 pounds, which proved to be too much even for that great horse. White Nose, with the featherweight of 6 stone

12 pounds, finished two lengths ahead of a gallant Shadow King, who carried 8 stone 7 pounds. Phar Lap finished eighth. Prize money had been reduced due to the Depression and Shadow King took home just a little more than he had for finishing third the year before, £1250.

There was no Phar Lap in 1932. Instead of the 'Red Terror' there was the showy golden chestnut with the silver mane and tail, Peter Pan. With the standard three-year-old's weight of 7 stone 6 pounds, Peter Pan started favourite and defeated Yarramba, a five-year-old who carried the even lighter weight of 7 stone 3 pounds, in a close finish. Two lengths behind them came Shadow King, now officially 'aged' and carrying 8 stone 12 pounds. Third prize money was £750.

Now we come to the highlight of Shadow King's Cup career, the Cup he really should have won.

In 1933 Shadow King was eight years old. Only one eight-year-old had ever won the Cup up to that time, the mighty little grey Toryboy, in 1865. (The New Zealander, Catalogue, would become the only other eight-year-old to win the Cup, in 1938.)

The two best horses in Australia at the time were Peter Pan and Hall Mark. Peter Pan had come back from his Cup win in 1932 to win the AJC St Leger, Cumberland Plate and AJC Plate but he was out for the spring with a severe bout of muscular rheumatism.

Hall Mark had won the premier two-year-old races in Victoria in 1932 and also the Fairfield Handicap, Sires Produce and Champagne Stakes in Sydney. As a three-year-old he won the AJC and VRC Derbies and he would race on to win a Doncaster in 1935.

Hall Mark was surely a champion but he was under an injury cloud with a leg infection on Cup Day 1933. Finally, at 1.30 pm Hall Mark was passed fit to run by the VRC vet and he took his place at the start carrying 7 stone 8 pounds. Shadow King carried 8 stone 9 pounds.

It was one of the closest finishes in Cup history. Hall Mark raced on the pace in sixth position throughout and made a run to take the lead at the furlong post. Shadow King raced back in the field, struck dreadful trouble on the turn and was almost flattened. His jockey,

Scobie Breasley, managed to get him balanced again and he made a long run in the straight from well back and just failed to catch Hall Mark, who won by a head. Topical and Gaine Carrington dead-heated for third a further head behind Shadow King, who again earned £1250 for running second.

Two weeks later Shadow King won the Williamstown Cup, at his fifth attempt, at the good odds of twelve to one. Despite the fact that few had backed him, he was cheered into the winners' enclosure.

Peter Pan returned to win his second Cup in 1934 but, for the first time in six years, Shadow King was not fit enough to take his place in the Cup field.

When the Cup came around in 1935 Peter Pan was favoured early but he disappointed in the Melbourne Stakes on the Saturday before the Cup. Marabou, who had been placed in the Caulfield Cup and the Melbourne Stakes, started favourite on the day.

That is to say Marabou started the 'money' favourite. There was no doubt who was 'favourite' with the crowd, despite being quoted at one hundred to one in the betting-ring.

In a wonderful gesture the VRC allowed Shadow King, ten years old and carrying saddlecloth number 7, to lead the field onto the track for the Melbourne Cup of 1935, and how the crowd of 110,739 cheered!

Marabou won carrying 7 stone 11 pounds. Shadow King, ridden again by the great Scobie Breasley, flew home to run fourth and create a Melbourne Cup record that will never be beaten: six starts for two seconds, two thirds, a fourth and a sixth.

In those six Melbourne Cups Shadow King competed against three of the greatest horses to ever draw breath in Australia in Hall Mark, Peter Pan and Phar Lap. He was never the 'money' favourite. He started at ten to one in 1929, ran third at fifty to one in 1930, second at twenty-five to one in 1931, third at twenty-five to one in 1932, second at thirty-three to one in 1933 and fourth at one hundred to one in 1935! But there was no horse the punters would rather have seen win, whether they lost their money or not.

Apart from his 1933 Williamstown Cup win, Shadow King was a good enough stayer to also win the Hotham Handicap in 1929,

The Coongy Handicap and Moonee Valley Gold Cup in 1930 and the Herbert Power Handicap in 1931.

After all that, he didn't get to retire to a lucerne paddock somewhere. As a gelding with good temperament he was still a useful horse and he was re-trained after he quit racing and became a police horse.

One advantage of being a trooper's horse was that Shadow King was called upon to do ceremonial police duty at the Melbourne Cup each year and he attended every Cup until he passed away in 1945. He was buried beneath a little headstone at the Bundoora Police Depot.

Back in the 1930s and 1940s 'as unlucky as Shadow King' was a common saying. It is forgotten today, along with most of the horses that have won the Melbourne Cup.

Every November the media remind us about some of the great names in Cup history. There are trivia contests on radio and the same famous names are usually referred to.

Among the names remembered by average Aussies, when they are reminded, are Phar Lap, Peter Pan and maybe Carbine, along with a few of the winners of recent years.

Oh ... and there's another horse everyone seems to remember too, whenever the Cup comes around, which seems odd, because he never won the Cup ... his name was Shadow King.

THE BARBER'S STORY

C. J. Dennis

Phar Lap won the Cup of 1930 at the shortest price ever, eleven to eight on. It was a small Cup field of only fifteen, with the Depression and Phar Lap's dominance of racing keeping many owners from starting their horses. The rest of the field were all at sixteen to one or better, except Tregilla.

Many punters backed Tregilla, with 7 stone 9 pounds, to beat Phar Lap, who carried the huge weight of 9 stone 12 pounds, fifteen pounds over weight-for-age. Tregilla was a talented Sydney four-year-old who finished second to Phar Lap at weight-for-age in the W. S. Cox Plate and the Melbourne Stakes in the lead-up to the Cup. He had won the Australian Derby earlier that year at Randwick.

Phar Lap won easily by three lengths slowing down. Tregilla started at five to one and ran seventh. This verse by C. J. Dennis appeared in the *Melbourne Herald* the following day.

'Mornin',' I sez to 'im. Gloomy, 'e seemed to be.
Glum an' unsociable, comes in the shop.
'Mornin',' I sez to 'im, 'e don't say anythin'.
'You're next,' I sez; and 'e sits with a flop.

'Great Cup?' I sez to 'im. Shakin' the wrappin's out.
He don't say nothin'; but jist give a grunt.
'Great win?' I sez to 'im, smilin', encouragin'.
'Wonderful way that 'e come to the front.'

He don't reply to me. Sits sorta glarin' like.
'Phar Lap,' I sez to 'im. 'Wonder 'orse, what?
Have a win yestidy?' Still 'e don't answer me.
'Phar Lap,' I sez, 'he made hacks of the lot.'

'Champeen,' I sez to 'im. 'Wonderful popular …
This 'ere Tregilla, 'e never showed up …
Phar Lap,' I sez to 'im, 'must be a wonder 'orse.
But that Tregilla run bad in the Cup.'

'What?' 'e come back at me, lookin' peculiar,
Red in the face, so I thought 'e would choke.
'Cab-horse!' 'e sez to me, nasty an' venomous,
Real disagreeable sort of a bloke.

'Tregilla!?' 'e sez to me, glarin' real murderous.
'Tregilla!!?' 'e barks at me. 'That 'airy goat!'
Surly, 'e seemed to me, man couldn't talk to 'im …
'Hair-cut?' I sez to 'im. 'No!' 'e sez … 'Throat!'

IRISH LAD

J. C. Bendrodt

Outside the bunk-house where Andy Macguire and his mates slept, dawn crept up to the horizon and over it, spilling a world of gentle radiance on a sleeping world. Old Andy tossed restlessly, and muttered as his subconscious mind drew patterns in his slumbering brain. Psychic, the neighbours called him, this queer old man who sometimes told of future happenings and who, strangely enough, was often right. When at last he woke, shouting loudly, 'Spam has won the Melbourne Cup!' the other men in the room woke, too, and looked with interest at him.

Jim Devine said, 'What did you say?'

Andy said, 'I saw Spam win the Melbourne Cup.'

Then Jim, who spent his life studying and backing horses, asked sharply, 'But who is Spam?'

'I couldn't tell you,' the old man said, 'but I saw him win it. A chestnut horse with four white legs and a great white blaze, and I heard them shout his name. I saw him win it as plain as day, and they called him Spam.'

'But there is no such horse in this country,' Jim Devine said sharply, and the others relaxed as they heard him say it. If Jim didn't know such a horse, then he couldn't exist within the far-flung confines of Australia, because Jim would know, and the others knew that he would know. Old Andy shook his head.

'It's no good, Jim. I tell you I saw him as plain as day. Four white legs and a great white blaze, and his name was Spam. I say I saw it!'

Now here was something not one of them could disregard. The old man had been right about so many things. There was the time he had said the Murrumbidgee Bridge would go out within a week, and they laughed at him, because the drought was on, and in the cruel sun sheep and lambs just stood and then fell down and died in multitudes. Rain was a thing they had not seen for eighteen weary months. And yet on the third day, the brazen sun was gone, and from a leaden sky a deluge dropped. Millions of tons of rain, and on the seventh day the bridge went out on a roaring tumult of river water.

There was the time old Andy had awakened and said he'd dreamed that Murray King would win the Sydney Cup, when Murray King was two hundred pounds to one. And folk had laughed and openly derided him, and said he couldn't win if the starter let him go the day before; but Murray King had won, and that was a miracle they never did forget. Two hundred pounds to one! How could they? He had prophesied so many things, awakening from his early morning dreams that had come true, until nowadays when old Andy woke up and shouted something, word of what he said went through the countryside, and folk just shrugged and said, 'He's psychic,' but paid attention and pondered carefully.

So on this occasion they got their racebooks and their papers, these folk to whom the Sport of Kings is near religion, and they studied them, and looked for 'Spam', but they didn't find a horse with such a name, and Jim said with almost real conviction, 'I tell you, lads, there's no such horse, even if Andy saw him in a dozen dreams.'

But in the long hot day, as they went about the station's business, these men remembered old Andy's cry about a horse called Spam, and wondered. And so in the quiet evening, when they sat at supper, and the Missus brought them the evening paper that the mail plane had dropped, they studied its racing pages carefully; but they couldn't find a horse with a name like Spam, and at last they put it down on the hardwood table, and the light from the kerosene lantern fell on the red-etched stop-press news, and Jim Devine said suddenly, in a voice of low awed wonder, 'Struth, mates, will you look at that!' They gathered round and they read laboriously where his thick strong finger pointed. Four little lines in bright-red ink:

'London, Wednesday. The Irish Champion Spam left Liverpool today, consigned to an unknown person in Australia. No other particulars are available. Spam is Ireland's greatest racehorse.'

And as they read, each of them fell silent, and then they looked at Andy and at one another, and said in soft awed tones, 'Struth!' But that isn't all they did, as I shall tell you. There are so many kinds of tales that a man can write, so many kinds of folk will read and pass judgement on. But most of those that deal with swift, high drama are written by scribes who dreamed these things, or tell a yarn that someone else had lived through. But if you want to read this tale then be sure you can believe it. I think it is an interesting story. And it's true. I saw that stop-press item, too, and swore gently, and now I suppose I'd better tell you why.

It hardly matters who you are who read this tale, you'll have heard of the Melbourne Cup – a famous race in the world-wide Sport of Kings, a race of legend, a glamour contest over two terrific miles, with a hundred thousand roaring race-goers looking on, and countless millions betting on it from a distance and listening in, and a treasure like that of Ali Baba's Cave changing hands on the result. Yes, a glamour race indeed, and many men have thought their lives well lived if some mighty horse of theirs has brought the golden trophy home to rest upon their sideboard.

Well, I had tried to win it with a horse I loved, and failed, and folk had laughed at him and made a joke of him, and I'd sworn to find a horse to go back and have revenge. And so, with secretaries and cable forms and telephones and lettergrams, I quietly searched the world for a horse to win a Melbourne Cup. A mighty quest, certainly. But I have friends who live with horses in many lands, and they searched and talked with me on telephones at a pound a minute in midnight hours. And then a great red horse, with four white legs and a big white blaze, won the Irish Leger in a canter, and the Cesarewitch, a long two miles on the terrific Curragh Course, with a weight on his back that no three-year-old had mastered, and with his ears pricked and Wing sitting up on him like a hussar enjoying his morning canter in old Hyde Park, and he belonged to a man I knew with half a million pounds in blooded horses.

And so that night a voice came softly from over ten thousand miles away, a friend's easy English accent with a touch of the Irish brogue in it, talking softly, yes, but with a vein of excitement running like a streak of gold in every word, 'Sure, Jim, here's your horse. I've found him, and his owner will let you have him. Sure he will, and he'll win that Cup for you by about as far as a hefty man can throw a stone, if you have got the time to get him used to your tough Australian heat.'

And my voice answered, and he must have heard the thrill in it, 'Just send him out, Major, but quietly. I'll get him ready. I'll have five months.'

His voice was sharp as he said quickly, 'Only five months, Jim? That's hardly time enough.'

I said, 'It's time enough. Just send him out, but quietly, with no fuss and fanfare.' And that was that!

They shipped him out from Liverpool with an old-time English jockey to care for him, and they did it quietly because when the Irish folk asked, 'And who is going to get our champion?' no one answered.

The folk in Ireland didn't even know. And you who read this tale will say, 'But why did you go about this thing with all this secrecy? What sensible reason have you got to give for that?'

There were many reasons, but above them all was the memory of people laughing at my good brown horse who had done his best that last November day when he was beaten in the Cup, and I was angry. I'd make them laugh at my new horse, and when they had had their funny say, I'd take the next Cup with him in an 'easy morning' canter. A little boy's revenge? Well, maybe so, but there it was.

But you cannot take a horse as great as Spam was and ship him overseas without the news-hawks noting it in the country where they know him. Or so it seemed, because here in the stop-press was the story of his departure in that day's cables, in bright-red ink. And so I swore gently and hoped no one else would notice it. And no one did particularly as far as I could see, because there was no talk about him. That in itself was a truly weird thing in a nation made up of people who worship champion horses. But old Andy dreamed and woke up shouting, and a bunch of station-hands a thousand miles away from where I read that paper found a little note in bright-red ink, and they had learnt to have a great respect for Andy and for the things he dreamed about.

I know that the tale of an old man who woke and shouted news of things he'd seen in dreams is hard to credit. But you can take my word this happened just as I have told the yarn to you. Before the episode had finished I had cause to wish that old Andy had chosen some other day to dream.

Spam seemed such a long, long time coming. They'd put him on the *Nestor*, an old Blue Funnel liner with the honour of a thousand voyages thick upon her, and she pottered her ancient tired way down through the latitudes for ten long weary weeks – anxious weeks, because time was short. Already June was just round the corner, and then November a bare five months away, and the Melbourne Cup is run early in November. It wasn't long to acclimatise a foreign horse. It wasn't long enough! But I would try.

And so one winter morning an old ship rolled in heavy seas beyond the Heads, and I climbed a ladder from a little launch to her broad, stained deck, and Jim Clark, Spam's attendant, said, 'Good morning, sir, and here he is.'

I said swiftly, 'Have the papers questioned you about him?'

'Yes, sir, but I've told them nothing. Just a horse, I've said, of whom I know very little. Won some race or other in Ireland, I told them, and they have taken no further interest.' And we looked at one another and grinned. Won some race or other in Ireland, Clark had told them!

I'll say he had – four of them on end and the last two among Ireland's greatest classics! So there he was at last, this horse I'd searched the world for. A great red chap with a broad white blaze, shut in a little softwood box on the well-deck aft. I opened its door, and sized him up in one quick survey.

I put my hand up just at the base of his ears and rubbed gently with my fingers, and he put his head down and studied me with eyes that were a deep mahogany with the look of eagles in them, and I whispered softly, because I know a racehorse when I see one, 'We'll teach 'em to laugh, boy, you and I! I'll say we will!' But he just studied me, benign and gentle, and then he put his nose down to my pocket where he smelled the sugar, and we were friends.

It was incredible. This is a country where a famous racehorse is always headline news, yet no one showed the slightest interest in Spam. Some papers mentioned casually that he had arrived, and that was all.

In the stable my lads said, 'And what is this one, boss?'

I said, 'Some friends have sent him out to me, so I suppose we'll acclimatise him and try him out. Arch, you take care of him.'

And old Arch lifted his silver head from his scrutiny of the red horse and answered quietly, 'Sure, boss, I'll take care of him.' Then he looked at me and I saw his blue eyes crinkle at the corners, though his face was still, and I knew I hadn't fooled *him*, but the rest of them went back to the horses they looked after and just forgot him, except that when he appeared on the tracks they answered questions as I knew they would.

'The boss will turn him out, I guess, when he has been in work awhile, and let him acclimatise before he tries him.'

So that story grew and was accepted. But when they asked old Arch, he looked at them and answered, 'He's just a horse to me. I wouldn't know.' But what he *did* know was that he was Randwick's greatest liar, because old Arch knows a great horse just by instinct. And Clark said nothing and I said nothing and people just forgot him.

We entered him in the Melbourne Cup, and in a little while the bagmen's charts came out with the prices on them, and he was at a thousand pounds to five. A thousand pounds to five about a horse as great as Spam was! It seemed impossible. But there it was. Truly we must have kept our secret well.

A thousand pounds to five about a famous foreign racehorse, who had won two staying classics in a canter, was just fantastic. I took the charts out and showed them to old Arch in a quiet corner. He studied them, but I saw that he looked for the price against one horse only, and when he found it, his blue eyes gleamed, and he smiled, and then his face was still again. And then he asked me, 'Well, what now, boss?'

I said, 'You've got two thousand pounds to nothing if you can keep your mouth shut.'

'It's been shut from the start, boss,' he answered briefly, 'when there wasn't any thousand pounds to five. It would still be shut if the money wasn't there. You needn't worry.' And I knew that a modern Torquemada would get nothing out of him.

You train a horse in the early stages with work that's not spectacular. Work that to the casual eye discloses nothing. Just walk and trot and canter. But as time wore on we knew we'd have to gallop him, this mighty one whom no one cared about or wondered at.

There was the rub. The clever men who spend their lives with horses don't bother much to watch a horse in pace work unless they own him, or unless they know a great deal more about him than these folk knew of Spam. But let him gallop and then you'd see their keen eyes focus. You'd see their lined faces grow quiet and contemplative, and then they'd put their glasses down and turn away. They would go on talking casually about anything except the horse they had just been watching, but you'd wonder in the morning where the bagmen had put their thousand pounds to five.

Spam was a mighty galloper. A stride so long, so effortless, so strangely like a great machine, was something a thousand horsemen wouldn't miss if they saw him once, and they'd be watching if he galloped. I could depend on that.

And so I took him away from Randwick to quiet tracks where news-hawks and trainers were conspicuous by their absence, and there we gave him fast work that grew longer and then grew longer still. But we were lucky. No one noticed him.

I had men in Melbourne in the sporting clubs where the bagmen play and work, men who watched the market carefully, though they didn't know which horse they had to back for me. Yes, I had two horses in the Cup, though I knew from the start that one would never run in it, but if you would catch these wily birds who bet in tens of thousands, the details matter, the seemingly inconsequentia! nothings.

Spam would go for a spell in a great green paddock. He would be out there when the Melbourne Cup was run. That was the story, though I hadn't told it. Remember that! But Sun King, my other entry. *He* might run. Folk knew I thought a lot of him.

The idea is held that a man may back a horse for a lot of money months before the Melbourne Cup is run. Don't believe it. You can take your doubles, but the straight-out chance is strictly limited. Doubles disclose the hand of owners, because when you take a double Australia knows of it from that evening's papers, and the bookies know, and the price comes down and that is that! So I took no doubles with Spam, though I threw a pound or two away on my Sun King.

You can put a little money on a Cup horse months before the race is run if that amuses you. A little, a fiver or tenner here and there, but even these little bets will bring a long shot's quotation tumbling down. I'd have to wait until the real market was available before I struck. I knew of one bet of fifteen thousand to a hundred I could get, but if I took it my horse's price would topple like an avalanche, and fifteen thousand was chicken-feed to the coup that I was after.

So I waited. And then I knew someone was backing him, because on the weekly charts his price began to shrink until, in a bare two weeks, Spam's quotation was cut in half.

And still no one took any interest in the horse. I was certain no one talked. No one saw him gallop. No one cared. Yet someone backed him and went on backing him, that I knew. But who? And then I learnt by chance who the gamblers were. From a thousand miles away a woman wrote to me and told me the tale I have told you. Of old Andy and his psychic reputation, and of how he had awakened shouting, 'Spam has won the Melbourne Cup!' and of how her drovers and her station-hands were sending little bits of money down to back him with any bookmaker that they knew, and of how other drovers and bushmen heard the tale from her men, and they joined in and sent their money, too.

So that was it! That night I talked to my men in Melbourne and gave an open order. 'Back Spam in little bits and quietly for all that the books would care to bet, and go on betting.' And so from that time on, they did this thing, and because his price was still like a respectable cricket score, the fortune I could win grew rapidly.

You race a horse before the Melbourne Cup, no matter how great a horse he may be. No horse could ever win it without a run or runs beforehand, though some have tried it. And we raced Spam at first at seven furlongs, where a staying horse like him would run a distant last, and Spam did – almost a furlong last, and there was a little titter from the papers.

It should have pleased me. But it didn't please me! Then we ran him over a good nine furlongs at weight-for-age, and he was last again, and the laughter grew. And still I did not like it. Pride in a horse? Well, it's a queer thing in some men – perhaps it's a queer thing in me. Then we ran him in the King's Cup, and he managed to beat one horse home, and then the funny fellows really laid the whip on. And I was angry.

I threw to the four winds of heaven all secrecy, all caution. I told them just how good my red horse really was. And still they laughed. Psychologically, I still think that's an interesting thing. But there were some who didn't laugh. I noticed that his price has stabilised. In the bagmen's wary brains an alarm bell had sounded, just a tiny bell perhaps, but it was enough. No scientific prodigy measuring variations to a millionth of an inch is more sensitive than these wily men are. No prowling jungle beast can freeze immobile when danger threatens more rapidly. They had him at nominal sixty-six to one, but they would not bet a single silver piece. They would wait and see. And so would I, because I was worried.

The King's Cup had been a race where the horses ran a mile and four furlongs. You'd expect a staying racehorse from the land he came from to run last at seven furlongs, or even nine. They are not like our staying horses who'll win at sprinters' distances when fresh and 'new'. But we had thought he'd win the King's Cup or go very close to it, and he'd been many lengths away and second last. And after the race, old Arch had shaken his head and said he couldn't understand it.

So I pondered on this problem and at last I had the answer. Sydney gets some fierce summer heat on days in early springtime, and King's Cup Day had been very hot and still. I remembered that Spam had been nervous and excitable, that he had dripped with perspiration long before he raced, that he'd been very hard to handle. All unusual things for him. And I remembered that towards four o'clock when the race was over, a cold wind commenced to blow and that he had grown quiet and contented almost instantly.

So that was it. He couldn't take the fierce Australian sunshine, this horse from his cold green rain-swept Irish isle. He was not acclimatised. There had not been time. I told old Arch, and he said at once, 'Yes, that's the answer, no doubt of it. Well, we'd better take him south at once, boss. It will be cold enough down there. You can bet on that – and wet, maybe, it nearly always is. We'd better go.'

A long, long journey, six hundred miles over hills and grasslands, but a journey that had a lot of laughs until we came to the border. Then the others grew silent because I was quiet, and I grew silent because we were coming close to a city in which Fortune had never favoured me.

One hundred and ninety miles away lay Melbourne. So many times I'd tried for success in that cold grey town with its tree-lined roads and its lovely parks and its charming people and its atrocious climate. So many times, in so many ways. On the stage, in the rinks, on the racetracks and radio, in the dance-halls, and always I'd come travelling back with a whipping to make me glad to see the last of it. Yes, so many times, but *this* time would be different.

This time I had the edge on a town that had always beaten me. This time I'd win. But when at last we left the blue skies of New South Wales behind us, and trundled down the long flat road with the spires of Melbourne thrusting through the dismal dripping clouds and I shrugged the thick sheepskin jacket I had taken with me over the thin silk shirt I had worn until then, my heart was like a stone and just as heavy.

Tom said, 'He'll love this weather, boss, remember that. This cold and rain is made to order. It's just what we wanted.' And the laughter came back and the confidence, and we joked our way through the rest of that dreary day. 'Just what we wanted.' Of course it was. It was all we wanted.

I've never liked the early mornings on cold drear winter days, but I liked them then. And so did Spam.

We raced him first at Moonee Valley. A saucer track with a short sharp straight and a mile and five for a cup of gold, a chill wet day and a bright-green track, and Spam went out with Bill Cook up, at a hundred pounds to one. And again they laughed! I remember it so well. Some news-hawks came before the race and questioned me and a puzzled bookie came and asked me questions, too. But he didn't laugh. He was a serious man of business, I assure you. I answered him because he was one of those who had laid thousands of pounds at cricket score odds against my horse in the Melbourne Cup, two weeks and a day or so away. He didn't know, of course, that I was the one he had laid the wagers to. There wasn't any way that he could have worked that out, because no one could have possibly connected the men who had made the bets with me.

I told him with a sort of grim determination, with the news-hawks standing by, exactly how good my red horse really was, of his mighty deeds abroad, of everything, with complete and utter confidence and pride. And the news-hawks laughed when I'd finished my eulogy with the flat uncompromising statement, 'And if it's anywhere near a cool and wet spring day, he'll win the Melbourne Cup as far as a hefty man can throw a stone.'

The *Globe* man smiled and asked, 'What kind of a stone, Jim?'

But the bookmaker shook his head in a puzzled way and didn't laugh. 'There is something queer here. I just don't understand. No one gives this horse a dog's chance, yet someone's backing him, and Jim's no fool, however you may laugh.' He shook his head again and walked away.

Then, as we led Spam down to the saddling paddock, a bystander said sourly, 'The Irish champion running at last, eh? Well, they'll run clean over *him*.' And an old chap, with keen blue eyes that dropped a little at the corners, answered quietly, 'Someone told me that he won the Cesarewitch with 8 stone 10 as a three-year-old, on the tough old Curragh Course, in mud up to his fetlocks, and if he did that he's not a horse to laugh at in any company.'

I remember that quick gratitude made me answer, 'You're quite right, mister, he won the Cesarewitch in a common canter and the Irish Leger, too, with the Derby and the Oaks winner far behind him. You go and back him for the Melbourne Cup.'

And the old man said, 'Why, thank you, son, I believe I will,' and walked away to where the books were shouting.

And then they were racing in the Moonee Valley Cup, and Spam was cantering past the judge's box the first time round and running last. How far the leaders were in front of him as they went out of the straight that first time, I couldn't tell you, but it was a long, long way, and he was only cantering with his ears pricked and his mahogany eyes taking in the strange surroundings, and Bill Cook sitting up and riding easily because last was where he expected this mighty staying horse to be on this tricky little track.

It was just exercise for both of them, or so Bill thought. But when they had come seven furlongs from home, I saw Cook do something that brought jaw muscles taut, and I think the hands that held my race glasses must have trembled. Because I know Bill Cook. Many are the winners this little chap has ridden for me. You can't fool him with horses. And at the seven furlongs where the red horse cantered last, still far behind the leaders, a thought had struck the horseman on his back, though how he knows these things is quite beyond me. But, as he told me afterwards, it was at this point that he realised the chestnut horse could win. I watched him sit down with that perfect balance that racing folk admire so often, and Spam just flew! He came round the turn wide out, a fatal thing to do at Moonee Valley where the straight is short. Then he cut in and a horse knocked him sideways and he recovered and a roar went up as they watched his great white blaze flash up on the rails, a bit too late but very close.

Three mighty strides beyond the post he was in front, and Tom and the boys were running swiftly to the back of the stand where the bagmen were who hadn't seen the race, and they piled my money on Spam for the Melbourne Cup at sixty-six to one in the bare few minutes before the betting lads woke up! On Tuesday morning the horse was second favourite at eight to one, thousands to five to eight to one, a things that rarely happens, but there it was.

Papers hadn't talked of Spam before the Moonee Valley Cup, but that smashing run had awakened them. No doubt of that. We didn't move or speak, sometimes it seemed we couldn't think, unless our names flamed in newsprint along with Spam's name, what he did or

'It was just exercise for both of them …' Billy Cook rides trackwork

didn't do, where he lived, how he looked, what he ate – any tiny detail was torrid news.

He flashed up along the rail in the Moonee Valley Cup, and overnight the horse was famous, and so I basked complacently in the glamour that surrounded him, while those who'd laughed just hurried now to praise my Irish horse. This was the way I'd planned the thing, and here it was, and just around the corner was a fortune. But it's completely true that I seldom thought of that. Snuggled away in my leather wallet were little slips of paper that men would pay more money for on presentation than I had ever hoped to own, but I never looked at them.

Even today I'm doubtful of the total, though I know it was enough for any man. I dreamed of my red horse taking a race I'd sworn to win a year ago. I thought of men who laughed, or men who sneered, but that didn't seem to matter now. Pride in a chestnut horse and his coming triumph – truly that was the thing that lived both night and day with me. And the wind was cold and the rain came down.

As I look back on it, those long ten days before the Cup was run seem an eternity. I had ceased to worry about my favourite and so had Cook and Tom and Arch and all the boys, and countless hosts of other people. We watched the weather. But it stayed cool or cold, or both and wet, as we had expected. It is practically always cool or cold or wet in Melbourne at this time of the year. In the dim light of early morning, I wore my sheepskin jacket or my mackintosh, and mostly needed both, and I kept on saying flatly, 'If the weather's right in Melbourne, he'll win the Cup,' and my forecast must have been printed in a hundred papers a multitude of times. And no one laughed. They had a fairly solid notion that this time I was right.

You guard a Melbourne Cup horse when he is favourite for the race. We hadn't bothered while folk had laughed at him. No need to. But now that his name flamed in headlines nationwide, we knew that danger followed on his footsteps every hour of every day and night before the Cup was run.

Fortunes were at stake on him and on other horses, and cold grim men who would stop at nothing would plan to 'finish' him. But I knew their foul ways. Australia has its wicked, hopeless hoodlums, just as any other country has, but here I sometimes think these rats are worse. They had tried to kill with bullets from a sneaking hidden gun, or to send a favourite writhing down in agony with dope before today, so now we guarded him.

I used to travel to his stable and walk softly up the driveway about twelve o'clock at night to see that all was well with him, and when I put my guard on I tested him. But I need not have worried. I hadn't taken ten steps up that driveway when a low voice whose owner I couldn't see said, 'Hold it, mister,' and immediately the beam from a hand-torch lighted up my face, and I saw the steady gun in my watchman's other hand.

The torch went out and blackness came, and his voice said, 'OK, boss,' and I said, 'How's everything?'

'Quiet, boss,' he said, and nothing else. He didn't even say good night. I can see him now, this night guard whom the Melbourne hoodlums knew, sitting on a pile of cornsacks ten feet from Spam's locked door, with his heavy-lidded eyes so nearly closed you could imagine that he slept until someone moved, or something made a tiny sound. But when *he* moved you didn't hear him, and you hardly saw him go, but if your ears were quick you could hear the click a hammer made where his thumb moved in his right-hand pocket. He was the kind of man who wouldn't trust an automatic. And if he raised his voice in one strong call, there were a dozen men who slept not twenty yards away who would have tumbled out and fought for Spam.

You take no risks with cold-eyed gamblers when you train a favourite for the famous Melbourne Cup. No, that isn't the kind of thing a wise man cares to do. And in the daytime we guarded him just as carefully. He never moved a yard without men who examined every living thing that moved within a hundred yards of him.

We had entered Spam on Saturday in the McKinnon Stakes at weight-for-age at Flemington, an easy mile and a quarter run before the Tuesday of the Cup. A foolish thing to do. Oh, sure! I knew it then and I know it now. He didn't need the run. The horse was fit. We should have let it go at that.

I'd watched the weather, but I had never quite understood just what heat could do to the Spam. He had fretted in the King's Cup, but not like this. And then I knew that I'd take another whipping to add to those that had gone before if the sun bathed this town in fierce heat on Tuesday afternoon.

It was as if someone had torn aside a curtain to show a view that I didn't care to look at, and I think the picture threw me off balance, because I ran him. Well, Spam came third, a good performance for a horse for whom a mile and a quarter was too short to win at. And the racing world was satisfied and no expert left him out of calculations for the Cup. But fear had come to live with me. The old, old dreary notion that this town would beat me this time as it always had before. But Sunday was cold again and dull, with a little misty rain, and so was Monday.

I'll always remember that Monday night before Spam went out to run for a fortune I had forgotten. In my hotel folk flocked round me to wish him well, and the headlines of a continent and the radios blared his name.

You've got to see this thing to believe it happens. You've got to see a nation stop and scarcely breathe while the Melbourne Cup is run. The taxis with their meters ticking over parked along the city streets with the drivers and their fares with intent faces leaning forward. You've got to see the patients and the nurses and the doctors in the hospitals, and the people in the restaurants, stop and listen.

You have to realise that in a million nearly silent homes and in the dance-halls and the theatres in far-flung outback stations, in the parliaments of the people, the nation stops and listens carefully, scarcely breathing lest they miss a vital word of its description.

You've got to know the records broken in the yearly race of papers to be the first upon the streets with the story of the Cup. You've got to see a nation stop. Yes, you've got to see it to believe it, but it does.

I was never one to chat about a horse's chances, because it always gets you nowhere, so I escaped from the Cup Eve fever to the quiet of my room, away from folk who wanted to talk of Spam with me. But at two o'clock in the morning I came downstairs and the Irish liftman took me outside and pointed at the sky.

'He'll be liking a bit of that, I think, sir,' he said, and I looked at the waterlogged clouds so close above my head that it seemed to me that I could reach up and thrust a fist into their moisture-laden depths.

'It'll rain, sir,' the Irishman said. 'There'll be a deluge before an hour has passed. I haven't seen such a sky in years, not even in this town, and my folks at home have written me that Spam's a mighty mud-lark.'

And I said, 'Pat, it really doesn't matter whether it is wet or not, though if it rains he is indeed a certainty. But if you're a good Irishman, just pray that it is cool or cold. That's all, Pat.' I remember that he looked at me for a long half-minute, and then he nodded.

'So it's the heat that you're afraid of, sir. So that's it. Well, never worry, sir, why it's as cold as an iceberg now, and it will be colder in the morning.'

But I'd been whipped so many times in Melbourne, and 2 am is a deadly hour for optimism. I shivered in the cold night wind and said, 'Yes, Pat, it's cold as an iceberg – now!' Then I turned and climbed the stairs to bed, but I didn't sleep. I opened the window, and the thick black clouds seemed to press closer to earth than ever, so I lay on my bed and listened but I didn't hear it rain.

I listened for what seemed an endless time, and then I know I slept because I remember waking up. In a split second I was at the open window, and I saw that a soft blue sky stretched across the rooftops. I could not see a cloud and the sun was coming up.

We took him to the racecourse early, long before another horse arrived. We thought that in the early quiet at Flemington, before anyone else was there, he would 'settle down'. We brought some food and all of the special dainties we knew he loved to eat. We thought they'd serve to keep him quiet. We brought so many things we thought might help.

We would have taken him there a long five hours later, but we knew we could never keep him quiet with a hundred thousand folk round him on a day like this was. But if we took him early, when all was still and peaceful, perhaps we could get him to be contented in his stall. There was no shade for him in any other place, and last Saturday we had to walk him because he would not stand, and no man on earth could make him stand on a day like this if crowds upset him.

It was a bitter choice. If he wouldn't stand in the quiet of the morning, if the things we'd brought to tempt him failed, if every trick was useless, we'd have to walk him five long moral hours in the shadeless heat. No, don't tell me you'd have made him stand or hobbled him or tied him up or anything. No man on earth, no dozen men would make Spam stand if this blazing heat just drove him crazy. *I'm* telling *you*!

We led him to his stall, a stall we'd tried to change to one behind a hedge where it was quieter; not one where this one was, where milling crowds would press around and worry him. A quiet stall was what we wanted, but a counter-jumper in the Race Club's city office had refused to help us – a little racing potentate.

Perhaps he was right! Spam was the Irish champion a million folk had put their money on, the glamour horse of the world-famed Melbourne Cup. I suppose they wanted him to be where folk could see him. I bear no ill-will, but it made it tough for us.

Well, he wouldn't stand. We could see from the start that it was useless. It would have been better if we'd faced the crowds an hour before the race. But it was too late now, we couldn't take him home and bring him back. It was hot and still with the thermometer in the early eighties at 10 am. So we took him out and walked him as slowly and as quietly as we could. We then led him back when an hour had gone and tried again with tricks and tempting food and titbits.

The thermometer was in the middle eighties. He wouldn't stand. So we took him out again and walked him. And then tens of thousands of race-goers converged on Flemington. You could hear the roar of the trains and the trams and the motors bringing them from all directions.

A hundred thousand people. An avalanche of human beings. And Spam heard them where he walked in the blazing heat on the shadeless lawns at Flemington, and we only had to look at him to know that he'd have to go on walking now. And eventually it was noon, and the thermometer was at ninety, and there was no wind. No tiny breath of wind at all. No minute stirring in the atmosphere to shift that sullen burden of remorseless heat. Spam's chestnut coat was nearly black as the brazen sun grew hotter, and we watched his Melbourne Cup chance drip from his glistening flanks into the hot green grass.

We watched a treasure like that they kept in Ali Baba's Cave go west, as the leaden hours dragged by. We knew a million folk had backed him, and they wouldn't know of this. That in the ring away there in the distance the crowds would gather round and bet on Spam, a horse whose chance was hopeless, and we couldn't say a word to warn them.

There was nothing we could do. Then we got a hose and bathed him in water that was like tepid tea. Then we took him back and walked him and the thermometer was at ninety-four degrees of windless jungle heat. And that was in the shade! But there was no shade here where Spam walked and fretted, and God knows what that cursed heat was in the sun. And then the bookmakers' runners came and looked at him and fled swiftly back to their masters and whispered urgently. And Tom came back and told me that he was drifting in the market. That the red horse had gone out to sixteen pounds to one.

After a little while, I walked with old Arch at the horse's head, and I saw that, under the sweat that dripped off the old man, his face was grey, that his eyes were like caverns and the whites were bloodshot, and I said, 'Arch, we should scratch Spam.'

He said, 'You can't, boss, folks have backed him. You've got to let him run.'

Yes, there was the inexorable fact we couldn't overcome. Those little slips of paper in my wallet, that golden cup, the honour and the glory! These didn't matter now. I would give them all and more to be able to send my red horse home, away from this malignant sun that tortured him. But I couldn't; it was impossible. The old man gave the answer. A million folk had backed him. They had to have their chance to win, though it was hopeless. You simply couldn't let them down. I looked at Arch for a long time, and at the suffering horse, and then I said, 'I know. I've got to.'

I took a cigarette from a golden case and scratched a match and lit it, and held the cigarette quite still, and watched the smoke curl skyward in lazy spirals. It was like an inverted corkscrew boring its way into infinity with no tremor or variation whatsoever. Even the faintest breath of wind would have made it waver, but there was no wind. Almost it seemed to me that there wasn't even air to breathe.

The jungle in the Congo is like that for hours before the storms break, bringing rain to save its creatures from insanity. But this was not the Congo. This was Melbourne. You didn't expect this sullen, malignant weather here. I looked about me and saw that men who had travelled far to see the Cup were stretched flat out with their hats above their eyes, exhausted. I looked up in the middle distance to the towering grandstands where flags drooped flat against their poles, and found no movement. And then I prayed.

It was one o'clock, the race two hours away. And when I'd prayed I lifted my face up to the sky and almost immediately I felt a little stirring in the sullen heavy air. I looked up swiftly to the flagpoles and I saw their bunting stir, and in another minute the flags were snapping in the wind.

I sprang up shouting. 'Arch! Tom! A breeze! It's getting cooler!' And it was, and Spam knew it. It was wonderful to see the difference a little bit of wind could make. They tell me that the temperature dropped twenty degrees in twenty minutes. The sweat dried off him, and his head came up, and then he dropped his head and grazed contentedly.

Then for a little while there was excitement among old Arch and Tom and Clark and me. Here was a prayer the gods had answered. There was still time. We'd let him graze a bit, then freshen him with water and a little ice. We'd do it yet, and I threw my head up and laughed, and then I froze as still as any statue and stood with my face still lifted to the sky. The wind was gone, and I knew it was getting hotter. In a bare ten minutes the savage heat was back, but worse than ever. It caused the grass beyond the course to light, and great waves of stinking smoke rolled down, and the sun was a blood-red ball in a yellow sky.

There was the low thunder a field of racing horses makes, but I couldn't see them come at me, and then, when they were no more than one hundred yards away, they appeared vague and unreal through the yellow murk, the jockeys shouting and the whips flailing, and then they were going away from me and the hot gloom swallowed them as if someone had shut a furnace door.

I could hear the multitudes in the great stands roaring in the middle distance, but I couldn't see them. All I could see was Spam standing with his head up and his ears pricked, searching with his bloodshot eyes for the field he couldn't find through the blistering gloom, and I could see the sweat drop off him faster than ever into the grass. So *this* was hell!

We saddled him eventually and we led him down a long rope-bordered laneway, and the good folk whispered, 'Here comes Spam,' and gaped at him and wished him luck, and with the saddle on he knew his ordeal was nearly over. He walked with his head held proudly like the gentleman he was. But when I legged Bill Cook up, he leaned down and asked me swiftly with amazement in his eyes, this lad who also said that Spam would win the Melbourne Cup:

'Boss, where's the horse gone?'

And I looked up at him and smiled and said, 'You'll find a lot of him where it dripped back there on the paddock grass. He's walked for five solid hours, Bill, and his chance is hopeless.'

I suppose, though I smiled when I said it, that he saw the misery in my eyes, because he laughed and said, 'Don't you believe it, boss; he'll win, don't ever doubt it. He's just a certainty.'

I watched him go down the flower-lined alleyway that leads to the main course at Flemington, and thousands crowded closer to look at him, and then I saw him stagger. I saw Bill Cook shift his weight in the saddle and lean forward and look down anxiously. So the big horse was as done as that! To be forced to run an exhausted horse in this tough two-mile race! To a man who loves a thoroughbred, perhaps that was the bitterest thing of all.

Spam cantered nearly last past the stand the first time and made the turn wide out, and along the back made very little ground up. But four furlongs from home, when most of them began to have enough, I thought he might challenge even then. A big red horse who'd gone out to race and staggered as he walked! He made a run that took him into a winning position at the turn, and then Magnificent, who had won two Derbies but may never win again, hit him hard. Even that wasn't the end of Spam. He fought it out to the bitter end, but he couldn't win.

I never heard the cheers and the tumult that a hundred thousand joyous folk can make. I never saw the Governor-General give the Cup. I only knew that some intolerable burden had been lifted from my shoulders. That the long ordeal was over. And as I waited for him to come back with Cook walking him very slowly, my friend Guy Raymond came and said, 'Hard luck, Jim. The heat affected him.'

And I answered, 'Thank you, Guy,' and smiled and added, 'yes, just a little.'

'Well, never mind, Jim, you'll have another go some other time.'

I think my eyes must have been like stones when I looked at him, and the smile couldn't have travelled beyond my cheekbones, and I didn't answer. Some other time! It was as if someone had suggested that, having escaped from hell, that I'd return.

Then Spam came up, and Cook got off him and looked about him, and then he whispered, 'He was staggering, boss, when I took him out to race. He didn't have a dog's chance, but he wouldn't quit.'

I said, 'Yes. I know, Bill, many thanks,' and led my horse away, walking with my head up through the laneway of kindly people who made remarks to comfort me, and I smiled at them and lied to them and said, 'Some other time.'

There is a great tree at Guy Raymond's stables, where we quartered Spam, and a little table under it where Mrs Boyden brought us tea. It was five o'clock, and along the horizon great black clouds gathered, and the wind was cool.

Then it was night and old Arch and I sat outside Spam's stable and smoked our cigarettes. It was a quiet night and very still. We had given Spam his supper and made him comfortable, but we knew he wouldn't eat. We knew he'd stand in the dark with his head almost between his knees, and rest. As we did. The past twenty weeks had been a long, long time, and those last five hours before the Melbourne Cup was run had been a grimy eternity.

I could hear the night wind whistle in the dry tops of the spear grass round the stable's corner, and I could see old Arch's snow-white hair show faintly in the dark. Then I wondered what this old man was thinking. I'd promised him two thousand pounds if our red horse won the Melbourne Cup – a handy nest egg for a horseman growing old. He wouldn't have so many other chances to win a sum of money as great as that. And he had it so nearly in his square old fingers, and now the chance was gone. He would be thinking of that, though he wouldn't complain. But I was sorry that I was wrong, because that wasn't what old Arch was thinking about at all.

I heard a rustle in the dark of the stable behind us, the noise a horse makes in the straw when he prepares to go to sleep. There was a little thud as he laid down, and then there was a long deep sigh and then silence.

Old Arch said gently, 'What will you do with him now, boss? Will you go on racing him?'

'Why do you ask, Arch?' I said.

'Well, boss,' the old man answered, 'he's pretty tired, and I thought you might rest him now.' So that was what old Arch was thinking of, not of two thousand useful pounds.

So I said, 'I'll rest him, Arch,' and he didn't answer, but I knew, though it was dark, that he relaxed.

In a little while Arch got up and brought my sheepskin jacket from the feed house and said, 'Put it on, boss, it's getting cold.'

'Yes, it's cold now. A bit too cold, Arch.'

'Yes, boss, a little bit.'

And then all I heard was the wind again in the spear grass tops round the corner. Then, after a time, he said, 'Take a look, boss,' and I looked up and saw that the stars were gone, that the heavy waterlogged clouds seemed to rest just above the stable door. As I looked upward, a great drop of water hit me just between the eyes.

And then it rained – day after day.

Spam finished twelfth behind Russia in a field of thirty-five in the 1947 Cup. Magnificent, who bumped him badly before the turn, finished thirty-third. Forty-five years later another Irish Leger winner, Vintage Crop, won the Cup.

CUP COUPLETS

C. J. Dennis

Out of great wisdom, long stored up,
I would write me a rhyme of the Melbourne Cup.
With words of wisdom then let us begin;
For many shall wager, but few shall win.
And first a warning: Go slow this trip,
For there's many a slip 'twixt the Cup and the tip.
And the Sport of Kings, tho' it capture the town,
Is never for one with but half a crown.
And this oft is the rule when the lucky man sups:
He is in on the Cup and he's on in his cups.
So this is the motto to hold and to hug:
There is but one Cup; but there's many a mug.
So, out or in, if you still can grin,
Here's a glorious day to you, lose or win!

MYSTERIES IN THE MIST

Les Carlyon

It's like no training track in the world. At 6.25 am, the lake in the infield looks like the opening shot from a horror movie. Mists swirl out of it, languid and curling, as if, down in the grey depths, a witch's cauldron is boiling. Roll opening titles. The sun is a fiery ball exploding behind the gums on the hill. Magpies warble and sea birds bicker. A fox trots up the hill. Very casual, he is, pausing to look back over his shoulder.

A lone horse, stringy like a greyhound, trots over wisps of frost on the course proper. He's Double Trigger, from Yorkshire, the Melbourne Cup favourite, and he's pretty casual too. Jim Woodcock, his rider, stands in the irons and leans forward, resting his hands on the wither. The chestnut is on a loose rein and happy. Why not? Right now, he and a fox own the place.

That's right: we're not at Flemington. We know what's happening over there at this time. Hundreds of horses in the stripping sheds. Scraping hoofs and clanking tie chains. Maybe fifty horses out on the track, and not many of them trotting on a loose rein either. Too many dramas there. On the crossing where the horses come onto the track, Russian roulette is played just about every morning. A bug-eyed colt props halfway across, drops his hocks, wrings his tail, uncertain whether to buck, rear, or demand counselling. A galloper going at racing-speed bears down on him. Riders shout and onlookers shake their heads. One day ...

No, we're at Sandown, the racetrack on Melbourne's south-eastern fringe, and it doesn't go like that here. For three weeks or so every year, this is a trainer's dream. Beautiful grass, and only two or three imported horses galloping on it. Lest there be a suggestion of favouritism, it has to be so: Sandown is the only place foreign horses can be trained while in quarantine. For three years now, ever since the VRC turned the Melbourne Cup into World Series Staying, it has been like this. And the spring rituals have changed.

It is no longer enough to hang around Flemington, waiting to see if Bart Cummings is smiling or frowning, or to drive to Ballarat to peer at some New Zealand stayer in a paddock and wonder if, somewhere under all those rugs, there exists a horse. Now we have to go to Sandown, to stare at horses we have never seen race, and to try to line up their track work with the local race form.

Except Sandown isn't like anywhere else. No slather and whack here. No clockers. No shouted orders. No crossing. No hurry. Double Trigger walks onto the track just before 6.25 and leaves at 7.50. He does nine laps, 17,019 metres, give or take. He walks a lap, trots one, canters one, walks again, trots again, gallops on the sixth lap, walks the seventh, gallops strongly on the eighth, walks the last.

He has silver in his mane and tail, a splash of a blaze, an eye that is sometimes less than trusting, and likes to nip. He's tall enough but not robust-looking, more like a gelding from New Zealand's south isle than a European stallion. He's 470 kilograms of muscle and bone, and he can't afford to lose one kilogram.

Still, the faster he works, the better he looks. He's just won staying's triple crown: the Ascot Gold Cup, the Goodwood and Doncaster Cups. He came race-fit. All he has to do is hold his condition and keep his head right.

The same with Ireland's Vintage Crop, the 1993 Melbourne Cup winner and seventh last year after covering more ground than Livingstone and Stanley combined. He comes out to work when Double Trigger is on his sixth lap. Double Trigger is flashy but Vintage Crop, his face loaded with character, is the real presence. He wants to work, leaning on the bit and breaking into a canter as soon as he comes onto the track. He does four laps, a mere 7500 metres, and never lets go.

There's a big gallop in this horse waiting to get out, but you won't see it until Tuesday. As Dave Phillips, his track rider, said a few days earlier: 'We'll keep his long hard gallop for the Melbourne Cup.'

It's the last day of quarantine. The two horses walk back behind the hessian and barbed wire that screens their enclave. At the gate, there are plastic buckets filled with chemical solutions, gumboots and overalls, and a notice that threatens intruders with a fifty thousand dollar fine and ten years' jail. It's another world in there. North country and Irish accents; pellets and hayage (a cross between hay and silage) brought from home so that the horses stay on their usual feed; quarter sheets, bib martingales and other items of English tack seldom seen here. Outside, Woodcock and Phillips are bemused by the media frenzy and the rough democracy of the Australian turf. Inside, they can be themselves. A galah screeches overhead as Vintage Crop rolls in white sand. We peer over the hessian ... and wonder some more.

Here is the mystery of the modern Melbourne Cup. How do you line up these imports and their rituals with the locals? How do you line up Double Trigger doing nine laps at Sandown with Doriemus galloping two thousand metres at Flemington and running home the last three?

How do you line up race form? European staying tests often seem like essays in good manners: small fields hacking along without bumping or finessing for the first two thousand metres or so before sprinting home. How do you relate this to our Cup? Twenty-four runners and a roistering crowd, nervous tension, jockeys riding tight, horses pulling and reefing, non-stayers getting in the way of stayers, unrelenting pace, a raw and reckless thing. Or, as Mark Johnston, Double Trigger's trainer, said on Wednesday, a cavalry charge over 3200 metres.

One way of looking at it is to say the imports' owners have taken twenty to one about themselves. The trip will cost them sixty-five thousand dollars apiece; first prize in the Cup is $1.3 million. 'They pay it all,' says Les Benton, the VRC's racing manager, who is at Sandown today to look over the horses. 'All we provide is the facility.'

Born in Cambridge, England, just fifteen miles north of the fabled gallops at Newmarket, Benton came to Australia as a fifteen-year-old. He wanted to work for a sports body. On his fifth day here, he landed a job as an office boy at the VRC. Now, at forty-eight, his place in our sporting history is assured: he's the man who reinvented the Melbourne Cup by turning it into an international contest. He knows, as so many in racing do not, how to create interest.

With the blessing of David Bourke, the VRC Chairman, Benton sold the Cup to the world. 'I think any major sporting event has to be international,' he says. 'Look at the golf, look at the Grand Prix. The Melbourne Cup should be international too. I'd like to see foreign horses in more of our spring races – sprinters in the Moir, milers in the Nissan. But to bring that about, we need to build a permanent quarantine facility.'

'The Melbourne Cup should be international too.' Ireland's Vintage Crop returns to scale after the 1993 Cup

In 1992, Benton fought for his dream as others tried to trample it. They told him he'd never attract the horses. And if he did, they wouldn't acclimatise. And if they did acclimatise, they'd be too bloody slow anyway.

Benton didn't flinch; he's a believer. But when, in 1993, the dream was about to be realised, on the very night Drum Taps and Vintage Crop flew in, Benton had an attack of nerves. What had he done?

'It was all very strange. I can remember Vintage Crop and Drum Taps arriving here. It was like something out of a Dick Francis thriller. The float arrived at midnight. For the next two weeks I was tentative. I wondered how the horses would adapt. They'd left England going into winter and we were going into summer. After two weeks, the quarantine was up and Drum Taps went to Flemington to work over two thousand metres.

'Oh, he galloped beautifully – really well. And that day I thought: these horses *have* acclimatised – one of them could win the Cup.'

One did. And the Cup would never be the same. Which is why, before the last fox slinks off, we go to Sandown to stare at horses from a gentler world. And to wonder if they are up to the rough heroics of Flemington on the first Tuesday in November.

THE PONDERING PUNTER

C. J. Dennis

From now until Tuesday thousands of racing enthusiasts will spend a great deal of spare, and other, time in brain-racking attempts to sort out candidates and pick winners of the Melbourne Cup.

I've been watching them for weeks;
And if anybody speaks
Of a likely candidate, I test the truth
Of every tip and claim.
I am well up in the game,
And I follow form and figures like a sleuth.

I am fairly saturated
In the hopes and fears debated
By the seers and scribes who write the sporting notes.
I've the favourite's every feat;
Times, weight, distance ... all complete.
And a black list, too ... of all the hairy goats!

Now then, this one has a chance,
Certain winner at first glance,
But, his weight! Well, that one carries ten pounds less.
But the scribes, with strange insistence,
Say he cannot do the distance.
Well then, this one? Odds too short! Oh, what a mess.

Ah! And what about this other?
He has breeding, he's full brother
To ... but someone told me was over-trained.
Hang it all! I was forgetting ...
Here's the nag for my tote betting ...
Good long odds ... but wait ... I've heard his fetlock's strained.

What about this fast outsider?
Um! He's got a rotten rider.
Well this? If he could beat that he might win.
Or this! Or that might win it.
But ... if ... isn't it the limit?
Give it up! ... Has anybody got a pin?

'Now then, this one has a chance.' Evening Peal, jockey George Podmore and the strapper celebrate winning the 1956 Cup

PART FIVE

JUMPS RACING IS DIFFERENT

Jumps racing has always been more popular in the cooler southern states of Australia. The winter weather there is more reminiscent of the cold climate in Britain, where jumping is a winter activity.

The first Australian steeplechase was run in Sydney in 1832. It was conducted over almost seven miles, from the Botany Road Bridge, adjacent to the 'old Randwick' track, to South Head Road via Coogee. I assume spectators had a choice of watching either the start or the finish, or riding along to observe.

Originally steeplechases were cross-country events and hurdles were conducted on normal racetracks. Tasmania's first hurdle race was held at Oatlands in 1833 and Victoria's first jumping race, a hurdle event at Batman's Hill, where Spencer Street Station now stands, occurred in 1839.

By 1841 Victoria's first steeplechase had been conducted near Flemington racecourse and, by the 1850s, jumps racing was well established in all colonies.

'Originally steeplechases were cross-country events ...'

'... there are few sports as exciting and exhilarating.' In the straight at Aintree

Tasmania and Victoria led the way in the development of jumping as a sport. Provincial cities such as Warrnambool, Coleraine and Ballarat developed winter carnivals during the nineteenth century and, on 1 January 1866, the VRC Grand National Steeplechase over three miles was run for the first time on a programme that featured the Derby and the Intercolonial Champion Stakes over three miles.

In 1868 the poet Adam Lindsay Gordon, whose famous steeplechasing poem, 'How We Beat the Favourite', appears in another section of this book, rode three steeplechase winners in one day at Flemington.

In South Australia hurdle racing developed in the 1840s and Oakbank's first race-meeting was held in 1877.

The heyday of jumps racing in Australia was probably the latter half of the nineteenth century. All comers were able to compete back then and, as late as 1927, an amateur rider, Mr J. Grice, was able to win the Grand National Steeple.

While enthusiasm for the sport continued to grow in the south, with new races being added to the calendar, like the A. V. Hiskens Steeple in 1936, other states were responding to changing public sentiment.

Reaction against the injuries and huge weights being carried (the entire field fell in the 1934 Grand Annual and, in 1935, Greensea won a Rosehill Hurdle carrying 13 stone 12 pounds) eventually led to steeplechasing, then hurdling, being phased out in New South Wales, Queensland and Western Australia.

Perth's last hurdle was run in 1941 and a horse named Anpapejo went down in history as the winner of the last hurdle race at Randwick, in 1942.

In recent times the new-style brush jumps, and innovations such as the Australian jockeys versus Irish jockeys series, have led to a revival of sorts. Annual hurdle races were even run again in Sydney for a few years from 1986.

You either love jumps racing or you don't; there's no in-between. I think there are few sports as exciting and exhilarating. Many horses love to jump and are bred for it. Reducing fences to mere trip obstacles as a knee-jerk reaction to uninformed minority groups will only allow faster times and cause more accidents. I hope that we can continue to tolerate regional differences in this country so that great events like those at Oakbank and Warrnambool can continue to challenge horses and riders and thrill spectators for many years to come.

THE OLD TIMER'S STEEPLECHASE

A. B. ('Banjo') Paterson

The sheep were shorn and the wool went down
At the time of our local racing:
And I'd earned a spell – I was burned and brown –
So I rolled my swag for a trip to town
And a look at the steeplechasing.

'Twas rough and ready – an uncleared course
As rough as the pioneers found it;
With barbed-wire fences, topped with gorse,
And a water-jump that would drown a horse,
And the steeple three times round it.

There was never a fence the tracks to guard,
Some straggling posts defined 'em:
And the day was hot, and the drinking hard,
Till none of the stewards could see a yard
Before nor yet behind 'em!

But the bell was rung and the nags were out,
Excepting an old outsider
Whose trainer started an awful rout,
For his boy had gone on a drinking bout
And left him without a rider.

'Is there not one man in the crowd,' he cried,
'In the whole of the crowd so clever,
Is there not one man that will take a ride
On the old white horse from the northern side
That was bred on the Mooki River?'

'Twas an old white horse that they called The Cow,
And a cow would look well beside him;
But I was pluckier then than now
(And I wanted excitement anyhow),
So at last I agreed to ride him.

And the trainer said, 'Well, he's dreadful slow,
And he hasn't a chance whatever;
But I'm stony broke, so it's time to show
A trick or two that the trainers know
Who train by the Mooki River.

'The first time round at the further side,
With the trees and the scrub about you,
Just pull behind them and run out wide
And then dodge into the scrub and hide,
And let them go round without you.

'At the third time round, for the final spin
With the pace, and the dust to blind 'em,
They'll never notice if you chip in
For the last half-mile – you'll be sure to win,
And they'll think you raced behind 'em.

'At the water-jump you may have to swim –
He hasn't a hope to clear it –
Unless he skims like the swallows skim
At full speed over, but not for him!
He'll never go next or near it.

'But don't you worry – just plunge across,
For he swims like a well-trained setter.
Then hide away in the scrub and gorse
The rest will be far ahead of course –
The further ahead the better.

'You must rush the jumps in the last half-round
For fear that he might refuse 'em;
He'll try to baulk with you, I'll be bound,
Take whip and spurs on the mean old hound,
And don't be afraid to use 'em.

'At the final round, when the field are slow
And you are quite fresh to meet 'em,
Sit down, and hustle him all you know
With the whip and spurs, and he'll have to go –
Remember, you've GOT to beat 'em!'

The flag went down and we seemed to fly,
And we made the timbers shiver
Of the first big fence, as the stand flashed by,
And I caught the ring of the trainer's cry:
'Go on! For the Mooki River!'

I jammed him in with a well-packed crush,
And recklessly – out for slaughter –
Like a living wave over fence and brush
We swept and swung with a flying rush,
Till we came to the dreaded water.

Ha, ha! I laugh at it now to think
Of the way I contrived to work it.
Shut in among them, before you'd wink,
He found himself on the water's brink,
With never a chance to shirk it!

The thought of the horror he felt beguiles
The heart of this grizzled rover!
He gave a snort you could hear for miles,
And a spring would have cleared the Channel Isles
And carried me safely over!

Then we neared the scrub, and I pulled him back
In the shade where the gum-leaves quiver:
And I waited there in the shadows black
While the rest of the horses, round the track,
Went on like a rushing river!

At the second round, as the field swept by,
I saw that the pace was telling;
But on they thundered, and by-and-by
As they passed the stand I could hear the cry
Of the folk in the distance, yelling!

Then the last time round! And the hoofbeats rang!
And I said, 'Well, it's now or never!'
And out on the heels of the throng I sprang,
And the spurs bit deep and the whipcord sang
As I rode! For the Mooki River!

We raced for home in a cloud of dust
And the curses rose in chorus.
'Twas flog, and hustle, and jump you must!
And The Cow ran well – but to my disgust
There was one got home before us.

'Twas a big black horse, that I had not seen
In the part of the race I'd ridden;
And his coat was cool and his rider clean,
And I thought that perhaps I had not been
The only one that had hidden.

And the trainer came with a visage blue
With rage, when the race concluded:
Said he, 'I thought you'd have pulled us through,
But the man on the black horse planted too,
And nearer to home than you did!'

Alas to think that those times so gay
Have vanished and passed for ever!
You don't believe in the yarn you say?
Why, man! 'Twas a matter of every day
When we raced on the Mooki River!

DEATH IN THE AFTERNOON

Les Carlyon

Jumps racing is different. The Grand National had been robbed of its star, Sharp As, then its best supporting act, Derrydonnell. In the cold and the rain at Flemington, we stared at the bit players remaining, looking for a greatness we had assumed, until now, not to be there. Who, among these old warriors, could gallop for two laps and six minutes?

Tacloban looked the way a national horse should. He carried his head low and his hip bones stuck out to prove he had galloped hundreds of kilometres to harden up for this one day. But Andallah, the baby of the field at five, was the eye-catcher. Even in the grey light, his brown coat shone. And when Billy Londregan was legged up, the horse wanted to jig, to get on with it.

Here was the one doubt: national horses should never look too fresh. Long steeples are seldom about brilliance; they are always about cleverness. Jump racing is different. It is not so much about who is right but who is left.

John Craddock, a thirty-nine year old stock agent and trainer from Arthurs Creek on Melbourne's northern fringe, casually led Trei Gnaree around by the bit ring. He patted the old bay with the long back but looked at Andallah. Craddock had seen the horse who could beat him. With his hunting clip, Trei Gnaree looked right enough: big, strong, seasoned. Few fancied him, though. He had a problem you could not see. It was in his head. The racebook said Trei Gnaree had been 'pulled up' two starts back in a steeple in the Valley. The truth was Trei Gnaree had pulled himself up.

When the gates opened, the leggy Andallah jumped to the lead, ears pricked, no problems in *his* head. He stayed there for nearly two laps, going lightly for Londregan, who sat high, bridging his reins on the wither, and riding as if he knew he was on a good one. Andallah stayed there while the attrition, fall after fall, went on behind. He stayed there for around 4500 metres, for twenty-six of the twenty-eight jumps. Coming to the second last, in front of the cypresses just before the home turn, Andallah was about a length ahead of Bar the Shouting and Trei Gnaree. Andallah's ears were stilled pricked. He was still going sweetly.

Because of the angle, one cannot be sure what happened. Probably Andallah took off too soon. Certainly his forelegs struck the top of the jump. Andallah described a single awful somersault. His hindquarters hung in the air. He finished lying on his near side, his offside legs in the air and convulsing as if an electric current were charging through them, convulsing the way animals' legs do when the link between the brain and the extremities is lost. Andallah's head was facing the wrong way, back towards the fence that had killed him. The jumps are different. They do not forgive.

Brian Constable on Trei Gnaree glanced back at death, then ahead at life. Trei Gnaree, the horse they said wasn't putting in, the horse they said couldn't stay five thousand metres, fairly surged into the last jump, shook off Bar the Shouting, and strolled in by twelve lengths. John Craddock then gave his horse the finest reward an old chaser can hope for. He retired him.

The jumps are different, all right. They are an old sporting print come to life, a throwback to the world of Adam Lindsay Gordon and Tommy Corrigan, both of whom had to die to obtain idolatry. They are about a different sort of horse, too. Slow horses by flat standards, and older. Sound, tough horses with maybe not much blood, big and small, coarse and refined, united only by one quality – courage.

The rich sprints for two-year-olds are the new world. They are like rock videos: frantic and bug-eyed and reeking of money. You learn the colours, and all you see is a technicolour stampede. Sneeze on Slipper Day and you miss 'the incident'. The jumps are like epic novels: long, crowded with subplots and sidetracks, hard on their heroes. They do not flash by but grind on, not one chapter but many.

Eleven set out in the Grand National. Pal O'Mine fell at the third, sliding along spectacularly on his side. Then there were ten, Andallah gliding along in front, Trei Gnaree fifteen lengths back. Just after entering the straight at the end of the first lap, McMurphy bungled the thirteenth and tumbled over and over. Then there were nine.

At the last of the five jumps in the straight, Andallah stood off and took a breathtaking leap; it might be only his third start over the big fences, but he was starting to look special. Vim was inspired. He was a couple of lengths off the main bunch and decided to fly just like Andallah. He stood right off the jump – and planted his front legs right in it. Then there were eight, and Trei Gnaree was cruising up to second.

In this last lap, Oakleigh Jack was finally coming to terms with his limitations. A chestnut with a big blaze, Oakleigh Jack is the very horse who makes jumping different. A seven-year-old, bred in the beige rather than the purple, he had been to the races thirty-one times and had never run a place, earned not a cent. Still if everything fell …

At the second on the river side, old Oakleigh landed awkwardly and suddenly looked tired. He seemed to run half-heartedly to the next jump, blundered through, then fell down quietly. He is a modest horse with a lot to be modest about, and he had the grace not to make a spectacle of himself. Then there were seven. Trei Gnaree had dropped back to fourth. Maybe they were right; maybe he couldn't stay.

'He's my horse.' Trei Gnaree on his way to winning the 1990 Grand National Steeple at Flemington

Coming to the final turn, Trei Gnaree had come with another surge. He, Andallah and Bar the Shouting, last year's winner, could all win. A tight finish was possible. The other two were more seasoned but Andallah was going the easiest. Until he fell. And then there were six, and the plot changed again.

Instead of a tight finish, it was a procession. Commission Red ran past Tacloban near the line for third. King Dollar was half a furlong back imitating Cliff Young. Somewhere behind him was Waldara, last but not dishonoured. He was still on his feet – sort of.

Jumps races are different. After the major flat races, the ritual is for the trainer to go for a drink in the committee bar, as though he, rather than the horse, had done all the work. After Saturday's presentation, Craddock went to head off with Trei Gnaree. He was called back. Didn't he want a drink?

'No,' he said. 'No, I'm going with the horse. He's my horse.'

THE GROG-AN'-GRUMBLE STEEPLECHASE

Henry Lawson

'Twixt the coastline and the border lay the town of Grog-an'-
    Grumble
In the days before the bushman was a dull 'n' heartless drudge,
An' they say the local meeting was a drunken rough-and-tumble,
Which was ended pretty often by an inquest on the judge.
An' 'tis said the city talent very often caught a tartar
In the Grog-an'-Grumble sportsman, 'n' returned with broken heads,
For the fortune, life, and safety of the Grog-an'-Grumble starter
Mostly hung upon the finish of the local thoroughbreds.

Pat McDurmer was the owner of a horse they called the Screamer,
Which he called 'the quickest shtepper 'twixt the Darling and the
    sea,'
And I think it's very doubtful if the stomach-troubled dreamer
Ever saw a more outrageous piece of equine scenery;
For his points were most decided, from his end to his beginning,
He had eyes of different colour, and his legs they wasn't mates.
Pat McDurmer said he always came 'within a flip of winnin','
An' his sire had come from England, 'n' his dam was from the
    States.

Friends would argue with McDurmer, and they said he was in error
To put up his horse the Screamer, for he'd lose in any case,
And they said a city racer by the name of Holy Terror
Was regarded as the winner of the coming steeplechase;
But he said he had the knowledge to come in when it was
    raining,
And irrevelantly mentioned that he knew the time of day,
So he rose in their opinion. It was noticed that the training
Of the Screamer was conducted in a dark, mysterious way.

Well, the day arrived in glory; 'twas a day of jubilation
With careless-hearted bushmen for a hundred miles around,
An' the rum 'n' beer 'n' whisky came in wagons from the station,
An' the Holy Terror talent were the first upon the ground.
Judge McArd – with whose opinion it was scarcely safe to wrestle –
Took his dangerous position on the bark-and-sapling stand:
He was what the local Stiggins used to speak of as a 'vessel
Of wrath,' and he'd a bludgeon that he carried in his hand.

'Off ye go!' the starter shouted, as down fell a stupid jockey –
Off they started in disorder – left the jockey where he lay –
And they fell and rolled and galloped down the crooked course
    and rocky,
Till the pumping of the Screamer could be heard a mile away.
But he kept his legs and galloped; he was used to rugged courses,
And he lumbered down the gully till the ridge began to quake:
And he ploughed along the siding, raising earth till other horses
An' their riders, too, were blinded by the dust-cloud in his wake.

From the ruck he'd struggled slowly – they were much surprised
    to find him
Close abeam the Holy Terror as along the flat they tore –
Even higher still and denser rose the cloud of dust behind him,
While in more divided splinters flew the shattered rails before.
'Terror!' 'Dead heat!' they were shouting – 'Terror!' but the
    Screamer hung out
Nose-to-nose with Holy Terror as across the creek they swung,
An' McDurmer shouted loudly, 'Put yer tongue out! Put yer
    tongue out!'
An' the Screamer put his tongue out ... and he won by half a tongue.

STEEPLECHASING

A. B. ('Banjo') Paterson

Of all the ways in which men get a living there is none so hard and so precarious as that of steeplechase riding in Australia. It is bad enough in England, where steeplechases only take place in winter, when the ground is soft, where the horses are properly schooled before being raced, and where most of the obstacles will yield a little if struck and give the horse a chance to blunder over safely.

In Australia the men have to go at racing-speed, on very hard ground, over the most rigid and uncompromising obstacles, ironbark rails clamped into solid posts with bands of iron. No wonder they are always coming to grief, and are always in and out of hospital in splints and bandages. Sometimes one reads that a horse has fallen and the rider has 'escaped with a severe shaking'.

That 'shaking', gentle reader, would lay you or me up for weeks, with a doctor to look after us and a crowd of sympathetic friends calling to know how our poor back was. But the steeplechase rider has to be out and about again, 'riding exercise' every morning, and 'schooling' all sorts of cantankerous brutes over the fences. These men take their lives in their hands and look at grim death between their horses' ears every time they race or 'school'.

The death record among Australian cross-country jockeys and horses is very great; it is a curious instance of how custom sanctifies all things, that such horse-and-man slaughter is accepted in such a callous way. If any theatre gave a show at which men and horses were habitually crippled or killed in full sight of the audience, the manager would be put on his trial for manslaughter.

Our racetracks use up their yearly average of horses and men without attracting remark. One would suppose that the risk being so great the profits were enormous; but they are not. In 'the game' as played on our racecourses there is just a bare living for a good capable horseman while he lasts, with the certainty of an ugly smash if he keeps at it long enough.

And they don't need to keep at it very long. After a few good 'shakings' they begin to take a nip or two to put heart into them before they go out, and after a while they have to increase the dose. At last they cannot ride at all without a regular cargo of alcohol on board, and are either 'half muzzy' or shaky accordingly as they have taken too much or too little.

Then the game becomes suicidal; it is an axiom that as soon as a man begins to funk he begins to fall. The reason is that a rider who has lost his nerve is afraid of his horse making a mistake, and takes a pull, or urges him onward, just at the crucial moment when the horse is rattling up to his fence and judging his distance. That little, nervous pull at his head or that little touch of the spur, takes his attention from the fence, with the result that he makes his spring a foot too far off or a foot too close in, and ... smash!

The loafers who hang about the big fences rush up to see if the jockey is killed or stunned; if he is, they dispose of any jewellery he may have about him; they have been known almost to tear a finger off in their endeavours to secure a ring. The ambulance clatters up at a canter, the poor rider is pushed in out of sight, and the ladies in the stand say how unlucky they are, that brute of a horse falling after they backed him.

A wolfish-eyed man in the Leger stand shouts to a wolfish-eyed pal, 'Bill, I believe that jock was killed when the chestnut fell,' and Bill replies, 'Yes, damn him, I had five bob on him.' And the rider, gasping like a crushed chicken, is carried into the casualty room and laid on a little stretcher, while outside the window the bookmakers are roaring 'Four to one bar one,' and the racing is going on merrily as ever.

TOMMY CORRIGAN

A. B. ('Banjo') Paterson

Tommy Corrigan died of his injuries several hours after falling while riding a horse called *Waiter* in the Caulfield Grand National Steeple on 11 August 1894. He had a remarkable record of 235 wins from 794 rides including the 1881 Grand National Hurdle, the 1881, 1885 and 1886 Grand National Steeple, the 1882 and 1889 Caulfield Grand National Steeple and the 1875, 1876, 1879 and 1882 Grand Annual Steeple.

You talk of riders on the flat, of nerve and pluck and pace,
Not one in fifty has the nerve to ride a steeplechase.
It's right enough, while horses pull and take their fences strong,
To rush a flier to the front and bring the field along;
But what about the last half-mile, with horses blown and beat,
When every jump means all you know to keep him on his feet.

When any slip means sudden death, with wife and child to keep,
It needs some nerve to draw the whip and flog him at the leap,
But Corrigan would ride them out, by danger undismayed,
He never flinched at fence or wall, he never was afraid;
With easy seat and nerve of steel, light hand and smiling face,
He held the rushing horses back, and made the sluggards race.

He gave the shirkers extra heart, he steadied down the rash,
He rode great clumsy boring brutes, and chanced a fatal smash;
He got the rushing Wymlet home that never jumped at all,
But clambered over every fence and clouted every wall.
You should have heard the cheers, my boys, that shook the
   members' stand
Whenever Tommy Corrigan weighed out to ride Lone Hand.

'The gallant Tommy
Corrigan ...'

They were, indeed, a glorious pair, the great upstanding horse,
The gamest jockey on his back that ever faced a course.
Though weight was big and pace was hot and fences stiff and tall,
'You follow Tommy Corrigan' was passed to one and all.
And every man on Ballarat raised all he could command
To put on Tommy Corrigan when riding old Lone Hand.

But now we'll keep his memory green while horsemen come and go;
We may not see his like again where silks and satins glow.
We'll drink to him in silence, boys, he's followed down the track
Where many a good man went before, but never one came back.
And, let us hope, in that far land where the shades of brave men
    reign,
The gallant Tommy Corrigan will ride Lone Hand again.

CRISP

Jim Haynes

Ask racing men and historians in Australia to name the top ten Aussie horses of all time and I doubt that any lists would include the name Crisp. Ask any British racing fans to name an Aussie champion racehorse, before Choisir took Ascot by storm in 2003, and Crisp would be the only Australian name they'd be likely to know.

Crisp was a great Aussie battler who did what Aussies love doing – taking on the Poms at their own game. Australians take perverse delight in 'beating the Poms' at any sport originally devised in Britain. We have done it often at cricket, rugby and tennis, but we don't do it often in the Sport of Kings.

The great chestnut sprinter Choisir proved it could be done on the flat in 2003. He took on the English and he won their races, but he didn't win their hearts the way a horse called Crisp did back in 1973.

Crisp and Choisir probably had the biggest impact on the British racing scene of any Australian horses since Carbine sired an English Derby winner over a hundred years ago. But it took thirty-two years for Choisir to come along and have anywhere near the same impact on racing in the Old Dart that Crisp had.

It's generally considered by racing pundits in Britain that Crisp was the best chaser to never win the Grand National. It's also generally thought that he deserved to win the great race in 1973.

Crisp was a first generation Australian. He was foaled here in 1963 although he was by the English stallion Rose Argent from an English mare named Wheat Germ. His return to the 'Old Country' in 1972 was, therefore, the sort of journey made by many first generation Aussies around that time.

Crisp was a big raw-boned gelding who raced over jumps in Australia with great success, winning the Cup Steeple in 1969 and the A. V. Hiskens Steeple at Moonee Valley in 1969 and 1970. On the second occasion he carried seventy-three kilograms.

Crisp was obviously something special. He was a naturally talented jumper and could carry weight easily. So, with opportunities for really gifted jumps horses so limited in Australia, it was decided to sell him to interests in Britain in 1971.

The original intention was to run Crisp in races up to two miles. It was thought that he would not 'get the journey' over the much longer English classic steeplechase distances of three and four miles.

On arrival in Britain he was entered in a two-mile handicap at Wincanton. Back then the National Hunt rules stated that any horse not having had three starts in the UK could not be properly handicapped and should be given top weight.

Crisp was given top weight of 12 stone 7 pounds in his first race. He swept to the lead after a mile and ran away from the field to win easily. He was then entered in the two-mile Champion Chase, an international event of considerable stature, which he won impressively. Crisp was always able to carry weight and run time. He broke race records both in Australia and Britain.

Crisp was trained in England by ex-jumps jockey Fred Winter who, although he had been champion jockey four times, winning two Cheltenham Gold Cups, two Grand Nationals and riding a record 121 winners in the season 1952–53, was about as close to being a 'battler' as an English trainer can be.

When Winter retired in 1964 he had no intention of applying for a training licence. In fact he had applied for a job as a starter but the Jockey Club turned him down. So he set up the Uplands Stables in Lambourn and, in 1965, just three years after riding Kilmore to victory in the Grand National, he trained Jay Trump to win the event. The following year he did it again when fifty to one shot Anglo beat forty-six starters.

Fred Winter was to go remarkably close to an Aintree hat trick in 1973 when Crisp produced one of the best jumping displays ever seen over the big fences, only to be caught in the final stride by a horse carrying twenty-four pounds less weight.

In spite of Crisp being a two-miler rather than a Grand National type, it was decided to have a crack at the world's most famous jumping race and connections entered Crisp for the Grand National of 1973.

Crisp was given top weight of twelve stone and Fred Winter's riding plan for jockey Richard Pitman was not to hold him up at all, as he always liked to bowl along in his races, but to let him settle in front and try to slow the pace.

Crisp, however, had his own idea of how the race should be run; perhaps he didn't know he had four-and-a-half miles to cover that day.

When the tape lifted he set off at a merry pace, jumping fence after fence as if he was out hunting. He took Becher's Brook in his stride the first time around and made ground consistently, jumping the enormous fences like an old pro. At the end of the first circuit he was twenty lengths in front.

At Becher's on the second circuit he was twenty-five lengths in front and still racing alone, but another horse had broken from the following pack and started to make up some ground on him. That horse was to go down in history as the greatest Grand National horse of all time. His name was Red Rum.

Crisp seemed safe; he appeared to be too far in front for anything to catch him if he just stayed on his feet. But, at the second last jump Crisp ran out of steam and began to falter.

As he approached the last he began to roll sideways but his instinct took him over safely and he began the long five-hundred-yard run in with his strength visibly failing.

Richard Pitman said later, 'It happened after the second last ... just the way I had feared. It all fell apart ... suddenly his legs were going sideways instead of forwards, grabbing instead of reaching. Those big lop ears went floppy. All of a sudden, his strength was gone. And on the firm ground I could hear hoofbeats, like thunder.'

With Red Rum coming up fast behind, Richard Pitman made what he later considered to be a dreadful error: the jockey gave Crisp a slap with the whip. Crisp was so tired that he shied when hit, staggered sideways away from the whip and lost all momentum. Pitman was forced to stop riding to get him round the Elbow.

Red Rum was finishing fast and, although Crisp was out on his feet, Pitman recalled, 'I could feel him tighten as he sensed the other horse approach. He was absolutely bottomed, but that racing instinct was in-built. Only he had nothing left to fight with.'

In the end the weight was too much, and two strides before the finish Red Rum, carrying twenty-four pounds less, passed Crisp and went on to immortality by winning the first of a record three Grand Nationals. In the process he broke the record and ran the fastest time in the history of the race.

Red Rum won the race again in 1974 and 1977 and ran second in 1975 and 1976. He became the hero of Aintree and is buried there, near the winning post.

Crisp never ran in the Grand National again but he did run against Red Rum the following year, at level weights at Haydock Park, and defeated him convincingly.

After retiring from racing at the end of 1974, Crisp lived out his life as a hunter in the countryside around County Durham and North Yorkshire.

It is rare in sport for a second place-getter to be remembered as well as the winner, but Crisp is revered in the annals of British

'... *two strides before the finish Red Rum, carrying 24lbs less, passed Crisp ...*' *Redrum, on the outside, defeats Crisp in the 1973 Grand National at Aintree*

racing and many, including commentator and television personality John Francome, list him as their favourite horse of all time.

When he died he was buried beneath a flowering cherry tree in the North English countryside. Richard Pitman, who still blames himself for Crisp losing the Grand National in 1973, was asked to write his obituary for *Horse & Hound* magazine. He ended the obituary by saying that every year, at Grand National time, the cherry blossoms would float down like tears onto Crisp's grave.

THE AMATEUR RIDER

A. B. ('Banjo') Paterson

HIM going to ride for us! Him – *with the pants and the eyeglass
    and all.*
Amateur! Don't he just look it – it's twenty to one on a fall.
*Boss must be gone off his head to be sending our steeplechase
    crack*
Out over fences like these with an object like that on his back.

*Ride! Don't tell me he can ride. With his pants just as loose as
    balloons,*
How can he sit on his horse? And his spurs like a pair of harpoons;
*Ought to be under the Dog Act, he ought, and be kept off the
    course.*
Fall! Why, he'd fall off a cart, let alone off a steeplechase horse.

*   *   *

Yessir! the 'orse is all ready – I wish you'd have rode him before;
*Nothing like knowing your 'orse, sir, and this chap's a terror
    to bore;*
Battleaxe always could pull, and he rushes his fences like fun –
*Stands off his jump twenty feet, and then springs like a shot
    from a gun.*

*Oh, he can jump 'em all right, sir, you make no mistake,
    'e's a toff;*
*Clouts 'em in earnest, too, sometimes, you mind that he don't
    clout you off –*
Don't seem to mind how he hits 'em, his shins is as hard as a nail,
*Sometimes you'll see the fence shake and the splinters fly up
    from the rail.*

All you can do is to hold him and just let him jump as he likes,
Give him his head at the fences, and hang on like death if he
 strikes;
Don't let him run himself out – you can lie third or fourth in
 the race –
Until you clear the stone wall, and from that you can put on
 the pace.

Fell at that wall once, he did, and it gave him a regular spread,
Ever since that time he flies it – he'll stop if you pull at his head,
Just let him race – you can trust him – he'll take first-class care he
 don't fall,
And I think that's the lot – but remember, he must have his head
 at the wall.

Well, he's down safe as far as the start, and he seems to sit on
 pretty neat,
Only his baggified breeches would ruinate anyone's seat –
They're away – here they come – the first fence, and he's head
 over heels for a crown!
Good for the new chum, he's over, and two of the others are
 down!

Now for the treble, my hearty – by Jove, he can ride, after all;
Whoop, that's your sort – let him fly them! He hasn't much fear of
 a fall.
Who in the world would have thought it? And aren't they just
 going a pace?
Little Recruit in the lead there will make it a stoutly run race.

Lord! But they're racing in earnest – and down goes Recruit on
 his head,
Rolling clean over his boy – it's a miracle if he ain't dead.
Battleaxe, Battleaxe, yet! By the Lord, he's got most of 'em beat –
Ho! did you see how he struck, and the swell never moved in his
 seat?

Second time round, and, by Jingo! He's holding his lead of 'em
  well;
Hark to him clouting the timber! It don't seem to trouble the
  swell.
Now for the wall – let him rush it. A thirty-foot leap, I declare –
Never a shift in his seat, and he's racing for home like a hare.

What's that that's chasing him – Rataplan – regular demon to
  stay!
Sit down and ride for your life now! Oh, good, that's the style –
  come away!
Rataplan's certain to beat you, unless you can give him the slip;
Sit down and rub in the whalebone now – give him the spurs and
  the whip!

*   *   *   **

Battleaxe, Battleaxe, yet – and it's Battleaxe wins for a crown;
Look at him rushing the fences, he wants to bring t'other chap
  down.
Rataplan never will catch him if only he keeps on his pins;
Now! The last fence! And he's over it! Battleaxe, Battleaxe wins!

Well, sir, you rode him just perfect – I knew from the first you
  could ride.
Some of the chaps said you couldn't, an' I says just like this a' one
  side:
Mark me, I says, that's a tradesman – the saddle is where he was
  bred.
Weight! You're all right, sir, and thank you; and them was the
  words that I said.

CONCERNING A STEEPLECHASE RIDER

A. B. ('Banjo') Paterson

He was a small, wiry, hard-featured fellow, the son of a stockman on a big cattle-station, and began life as a horse-breaker; he was naturally a horseman, able and willing to ride anything that could carry him. He left the station to go with cattle on the road, and having picked up a horse that showed pace, amused himself by jumping over fences. Then he went to Wagga, entered the horse in a steeplechase, rode him himself, won handsomely, sold the horse at a good price to a Sydney buyer, and went down to ride it in his Sydney races.

In Sydney he did very well; he got a name as a fearless and clever rider, and was offered several mounts on fine animals. So he pitched his camp in Sydney, and became a fully enrolled member of the worst profession in the world. I had known him in the old days on the road, and when I met him on the course one day I inquired how he liked the new life.

'Well, it's a livin',' he said, 'but it's no great shakes. They don't give steeplechase riders a chance in Sydney. There's very few races, and the big sweepstakes keep horses out of the game.'

'Do you get a fair share of the riding?' I asked.

'Oh, yes, I get as much as anybody. But there's a lot of 'em got a notion I won't take hold of a horse when I'm told (that is, pull him to prevent him winning). Some of these days I'll take hold of a horse when they don't expect it.'

I smiled as I thought there was probably a sorry day in store for some backer when the jockey 'took hold' unexpectedly.

'Do you have to pull horses, then, to get employment?'

'Oh, well, it's this way,' he said, rather apologetically, 'if an owner is badly treated by the handicapper, and is just giving his horse a run to get weight off, then it's right enough to catch hold a bit. But when a horse is favourite and the public are backing him it isn't right to take hold of him then. I would not do it.'

This was his whole code of morals, not to pull a favourite; and he felt himself very superior to the scoundrel who would pull favourites or outsiders indiscriminately.

'What do you get for riding?' I asked him.

'Well,' he said, looking about uneasily, 'we're supposed to get a fiver for a losing mount and ten pounds if we win, but a lot of the steeplechase owners are what I call "battlers", men who have no money and get along by owing everybody. They promise us all sorts of money if we win, but they don't pay if we lose. I only got two pounds for that last steeplechase.'

'Two pounds!' I made a rapid calculation. He had ridden over eighteen fences for two pounds, had chanced his life eighteen times at less than half a crown a time.

'Good Heavens!' I said. 'That's a poor game. Wouldn't you be better back on the station?'

'Oh, I don't know, sometimes we get laid a bit to nothing, and do well out of a race. And then, you know, a steeplechase rider is somebody, not like an ordinary fellow that is just working.'

I realised that I was an 'ordinary fellow who was just working', and felt small accordingly.

'I'm just off to weigh now,' he said. 'I'm riding Contractor, and he'll run well, but he always seems to fall at those logs. Still, I ought to have luck today. I met a hearse as I was coming out. I'll get him over the fences, somehow.'

'Do you think it lucky, then, to meet a hearse?'

'Oh, yes,' he said, 'if you *meet* it. You mustn't overtake it, that's unlucky. So is a cross-eyed man unlucky. Cross-eyed men ought to be kept off racecourses.'

He reappeared clad in his racing rig, and we set off to see the horse saddled. We found the owner in a great state of excitement. It seemed he had no money, absolutely none whatever, but had borrowed enough to pay the sweepstakes, and stood to make something if the horse won and lose nothing if he lost, as he had nothing to lose.

My friend insisted on being paid two pounds before he would mount, and the owner nearly had a fit in his efforts to persuade him to ride on credit. At last a backer of the horse agreed to pay two pounds ten shillings, win or lose, and the rider was to get twenty-five pounds out of the prize if he won.

So up he got; and as he and the others walked the big muscular horses round the ring, nodding gaily to friends in the crowd, I thought of the gladiators going out to fight in the arena with the cry of 'Hail, Caesar, those about to die salute thee!'

The story of the race is soon told. My friend went to the front at the start and led nearly all the way, and 'Contractor!' was on everyone's lips as the big horse sailed along in front of his field. He came at the log fence full of running, and it looked certain that he would get over. But at the last stride he seemed to falter, then plunged right into the fence, striking it with his chest, and, turning right over, landed on his unfortunate rider.

A crowd clustered round and hid horse and rider from view, and I ran down to the casualty room to meet him when the ambulance came in. The limp form was carefully taken out and laid on a stretcher while a doctor examined the crushed ribs, the broken arm, and all the havoc that the horse's huge weight had wrought.

There was no hope from the first. My poor friend, who had so often faced Death for two pounds, lay very still awhile. Then he began to talk, wandering in his mind, 'Where are the cattle?' his mind evidently going back to the old days on the road. Then, quickly, 'Look out there, give me room!' and again, 'Five-and-twenty pounds, Mary, and a sure thing if he don't fall at the logs.'

Mary was sobbing beside the bed, cursing the fence and the money that had brought him to grief. At last, in a tone of satisfaction, he said, quite clear and loud: 'I know how it was ... *there couldn't have been any dead man in that hearse!*'

And so, having solved the mystery to his own satisfaction, he drifted away into unconsciousness, and woke somewhere on the other side of the big fence that we can neither see through nor over, but all have to face sooner or later.

RIO GRANDE

A. B. ('Banjo') Paterson

Now this was what Macpherson told
While waiting in the stand;
A reckless rider, over-bold,
The only man with hands to hold
The rushing Rio Grande.

He said, 'This day I bid goodbye
To bit and bridle rein,
To ditches deep and fences high,
For I have dreamed a dream, and I
Shall never ride again.

'I dreamed last night I rode this race
That I today must ride,
And cantering down to take my place
I saw full many an old friend's face
Come stealing to my side.

'Dead men on horses long since dead,
They clustered on the track;
The champions of the days long fled,
They moved around with noiseless tread –
Bay, chestnut, brown, and black.

'And one man on a big grey steed
Rode up and waved his hand;
Said he, "We help a friend in need,
And we have come to give a lead
To you and Rio Grande.

'"For you must give the field the slip;
So never draw the rein,
But keep him moving with the whip,
And, if he falter, set your lip
And rouse him up again.

'"But when you reach the big stone wall
Put down your bridle-hand
And let him sail – he cannot fall,
But don't you interfere at all;
You trust old Rio Grande."

'We started, and in front we showed,
The big horse running free:
Right fearlessly and game he strode,
And by my side those dead men rode
Whom no one else could see.

'As silently as flies a bird,
They rode on either hand;
At every fence I plainly heard
The phantom leader give the word,
"Make room for Rio Grande!"

'I spurred him on to get the lead,
I chanced full many a fall;
But swifter still each phantom steed
Kept with me, and at racing-speed
We reached the big stone wall.

'And there the phantoms on each side
Drew in and blocked his leap;
"Make room! Make room!" I loudly cried,
But right in front they seemed to ride –
I cursed them in my sleep.

'He never flinched, he faced it game,
He struck it with his chest,
And every stone burst out in flame –
And Rio Grande and I became
Phantoms among the rest.

'And then I woke, and for a space
All nerveless did I seem;
For I have ridden many a race
But never one at such a pace
As in that fearful dream.

'And I am sure as man can be
That out upon the track
Those phantoms that men cannot see
Are waiting now to ride with me;
And I shall not come back.

'For I must ride the dead men's race,
And follow their command;
'Twere worse than death, the foul disgrace
If I should fear to take my place
Today on Rio Grande.'

He mounted, and a jest he threw,
With never sign of gloom;
But all who heard the story knew
That Jack Macpherson, brave and true,
Was going to his doom.

They started, and the big black steed
Came flashing past the stand;
All single-handed in the lead
He strode along at racing-speed,
The mighty Rio Grande.

But on his ribs the whalebone stung –
A madness, sure, it seemed –
And soon it rose on every tongue
That Jack Macpherson rode among
The creatures he had dreamed.

He looked to left, and looked to right,
As though men rode beside;
And Rio Grande, with foam-flecks white,
Raced at his jumps in headlong flight
And cleared them in his stride.

But when they reached the big stone wall,
Down went the bridle-hand,
And loud we heard Macpherson call
'Make room, or half the field will fall!
Make room for Rio Grande!'

'He's down! He's down!' And horse and man
Lay quiet side by side!
No need the pallid face to scan,
We knew with Rio Grande he ran
The race the dead men ride.